God, Creation, and Salvation

God, Creation, and Salvation

Studies in Reformed Theology

Oliver D. Crisp

t&tclark

LONDON · NEW YORK · OXFORD · NEW DELHI · SYDNEY

T&T CLARK
Bloomsbury Publishing Plc
50 Bedford Square, London, WC1B 3DP, UK
1385 Broadway, New York, NY 10018, USA

BLOOMSBURY, T&T CLARK and the T&T Clark logo are trademarks of Bloomsbury Publishing Plc

First published in Great Britain 2020

Cover design: Terry Woodley
Cover image: *Blue Sky* © Oliver D. Crisp, acrylic on board, 2019. Used with permission.

A catalogue record for this book is available from the British Library.

Library of Congress Cataloging-in-Publication Data
Names: Crisp, Oliver, author.
Title: God, creation, and salvation: studies in reformed theology / by Oliver D. Crisp.
Description: 1 [edition]. | New York: T&T Clark, 2020. | Includes bibliographical
references and index.
Identifiers: LCCN 2019020061 (print) | ISBN 9780567689535 (pbk.) |
ISBN 9780567689542 (hardback (hpod))
Subjects: LCSH: Reformed Church–Doctrines.
Classification: LCC BX9422.3 .C745 2020 (print) | LCC BX9422.3 (ebook) |
DDC 230/.42–dc23
LC record available at https://lccn.loc.gov/2019020061
LC ebook record available at https://lccn.loc.gov/2019981404

ISBN: HB: 978-0-5676-8954-2
PB: 978-0-5676-8953-5
ePDF: 978-0-5676-8955-9
eBook: 978-0-5676-8956-6

Typeset by Deanta Global Publishing Services, Chennai, India
Printed and bound in Great Britain

To find out more about our authors and books visit www.bloomsbury.com
and sign up for our newsletters.

To my friends and colleagues at Fuller Theological Seminary: gratias vobis ago.

CONTENTS

ACKNOWLEDGMENTS

Many people have helped make this volume possible. My wife, Claire, has been a great encourager, and I am grateful for her help with this work. Thanks too to Liberty, Elliot, and Mathilda, who make our house into a home. I am indebted to the members of the Fuller Seminary Analytic Theology Writing Salon (now a diaspora) who read a number of chapters in draft between 2015 and 2018. They are Rev. Dr. James Arcadi, Jesse Gentile, Steven Nemes, Rev. Martine Oldhoff, Dr. J. T. Turner, Dr. Jordan Wessling, and Christopher Woznicki. Steven Nemes did double duty in this regard, because he then gave me written comments on the whole manuscript as my research assistant in addition to being part of the Writing Salon—and very helpful comments they were! Professor Eddy van der Borght gave me feedback on an earlier draft of Chapter 4. A conversation with Professor Michael Rea about whether Christ had a fallen human nature was the inspiration for Chapter 7. Dr. S. Mark Hamilton provided helpful responses on an earlier iteration of Chapter 8. Dr. Kyle Strobel, Professor Christian Miller, and Dr. Angela McKay Knobel gave me comments on a previous version of Chapter 9. To all these friends and colleagues I offer my thanks.

I am also grateful to institutions that sponsored some of the research and writing of various chapters contained in this volume, and to various publishers for permission to reprint material here. Chapter 2 was originally given as a lecture to the students and faculty of Providence College, Rhode Island, as part of their Humanities Forum series in March 2017. My thanks to Dr. Raymon Hain as Director of the Forum, and especially to Dr. Holly Taylor Coolman, for the invitation and the hospitality I received on my visit to Providence. Chapter 5 was first read to a seminar of theology graduate students at Wheaton College. I also benefited from comments on the chapter from Professor Thomas H. McCall. Chapter 8 was originally composed as a contribution to a *Feschrift* for Rev. Professor Alister E. McGrath, and is reprinted here with permission. Chapter 9 was originally written with support from the John Templeton Foundation as part of the Character Project run through Wake Forest University under the direction of Professor Christian Miller (see: http://www.thecharacterproject.com), as a contribution to a symposium on moral character and Christian ethics in the journal *Studies in Christian Ethics*. It is also reprinted here with permission. Although many of the chapters contained in this volume have been written as occasional studies, they have all been revised for the present publication.

Life is full of changes, some of which are significant. I write these lines at the University of Notre Dame as the Frederick J. Crosson Research Fellow in the Center for Philosophy of Religion prior to moving across the globe from my home in Los Angeles to the Chair of Analytic Theology, the University of St. Andrews, Scotland. For me, it is a significant change in circumstances. Oddly, the last time I was the Crosson Fellow at Notre Dame fifteen years ago, I took up the fellowship upon leaving St. Andrews. *Exitus et reditus.*

Over the past eight years I have enjoyed the fellowship and camaraderie of the scholarly community of Fuller Theological Seminary in Pasadena, California, where I have been professor of systematic theology. This book is dedicated to my friends and colleagues there as a token of my esteem and an expression of my gratitude for what they have meant to me over the years. It seemed fitting to dedicate it to them, given that the work contained between the covers of this volume was composed during my tenure there.

PREFACE

Teach me how to seek you, and show yourself to me when
I seek. For I cannot seek you unless you teach me how, and
I cannot find you unless you show yourself to me. Let me
seek you in desiring you; let me desire you in seeking you.
Let me find you in loving you; let me love you in finding you.
ANSELM OF CANTERBURY (*PROSLOGION 1*[1])

The studies in this book represent different ways in which, over the
course of the last five years, I have been engaged in the task Anselm
of Canterbury so aptly described as "faith seeking understanding."
Anselm is, in many ways, a model for the sort of theology pursued
here, although the topics considered are many and various, and not
all of them are recognizably Anselmian in nature. Still, it might be
said that a certain *aspirational Anselmianism* can be found in the
pages that follow. By that I mean an aspiration to approach given
theological topics in a similar spirit, with similar sensibilities as
Anselm, and with the same concern for a kind of analytic pellucidity
as well as a sensitivity to the history, complexity, and texture of
theology.

This may seem strange to some. For the chapters of this volume
are all studies in Reformed theology. Can such Protestant thought
reflect an aspirational Anselmianism? I say, emphatically, yes. It is no
more odd to think of a Reformed thinker as one deeply indebted to
Anselm—as even a kind of *Protestant Anselmian*—than it is to think

---

[1]From *Anselm: Basic Works*, trans. Thomas Williams (Indianapolis, IN: Hackett,
2007), 81.

that there may be Protestant thinkers who are deeply influenced by pre-Reformation thinkers, such as Augustine or Thomas Aquinas. Augustinians are widely understood to include Protestants among their number, and Protestant Thomism is, in fact, an increasingly popular designation.[2] Protestant Anselmians (to coin a phrase) come in various flavors, not all of which are Reformed. But there is no reason why a Reformed theologian cannot look to Anselm as a model. In fact, there are good reasons for doing so. Anselm has many views that resonate deeply with Reformed intuitions.[3]

Well then, how does such aspirational Anselmianism manifest itself in this volume? The chapters that follow are arranged according to the way in which they would appear in a traditional dogmatics, in three divisions. The first division deals with issues concerning the task of theology, which is really another way of saying essays that fall under that division are more methodological in nature. This begins with a chapter on four contemporary challenges to systematic theology as a discipline. This seems important given the times in which we live, both in confessional contexts (in, say, North America) and in non-confessional institutions like research universities. Though these contexts are very different, and may produce rather different theology as a consequence, they are both places where the raison d'être of systematic theology is at stake in some important respects.

The second chapter is more concerned with the reception—retrieval, recovery, *use*—of the theology of John Calvin, as one of the great sources of Reformed theology. Although Calvin is only one of the fountainheads of Reformed thought, he is probably the best known, and the most influential. So how we use Calvin today, and what characteristic doctrines he has bequeathed his successors is a matter that Reformed theologians should care about, even if they do not agree with everything Calvin wrote or said. This chapter addresses just this issue, by focusing on four central

---

[2]See, for example, Manfred Svensson and David VanDrunen, eds. *Aquinas among the Protestants* (Oxford: Wiley-Blackwell, 2018).

[3]Many, but not all. He has a rather idiosyncratic libertarian account of human free will, for instance. However, it seems to me that in one important respect Anselm's views on free will are closer to Reformed theology than some other theological libertarians. But that is a discussion for another day.

themes in Calvin's work. These are not the only important themes
in Calvin's thought. Nevertheless, they are signature doctrines to
which Calvin made a particular contribution, namely, the doctrine
of the knowledge of God, union with Christ, election, and his
teaching on the Eucharist.

The second division comprises studies on God and his external
work in creation. The three chapters of this section focus on nodal
issues that are at the center of serious debate in contemporary
theology. Thus, Chapter 3 considers Jonathan Edwards's understanding of the relationship between the doctrine of creation and
the doctrine of divine ideas. The doctrine of the divine ideas has
a long history in theology going back at least to Augustine. The
idea is that if God is absolutely sovereign over all he has created,
as well as being metaphysically prior to, and independent of, his
creatures, then there can be no realm of abstract objects or objects
like platonic forms that are co-eternal with God. Instead, what we
think of as abstract objects must, in fact, be divine ideas—residing
within God's mind. Jonathan Edwards has interesting views on this
topic because he was an idealist. He thought that there are only
minds and their ideas. So how he makes sense of the claim that we
are the instantiation of divine ideas, and that there are no abstract
objects independent of the sovereign God, presents an interesting
theological conundrum. You might think of it as a limit case of a
doctrine of the absolute sovereignty, aseity, and ultimacy of God.

Chapter 4 deals with the lesser known nineteenth-century
Southern Presbyterian thinker John Girardeau. His views on
theological anthropology, and human free will in particular, are
of interest because he seems to advocate an account much closer
to some forms of libertarianism than is usually thought typical
in textbook treatments of Reformed theology, though Girardeau
insists that his position is, in fact, rooted in the thought of Calvin.
This chapter considers his account of human free will in relation
to salvation, with some potentially surprising results for Reformed
theology.

Chapter 5 focuses on the thought of the great Swiss Reformer,
Huldrych Zwingli. Although he is often in the shadow of Calvin
and Luther, Zwingli had some important theological contributions
to make, though they have sometimes been forgotten or set to one
side. In this chapter, I set out to reassess his doctrine of original
sin. Often, Zwingli's position on this topic has been regarded as

aberrant, not fully or completely Reformed, a kind of hangover from his catholic past. However, I argue that Zwingli's moderate doctrine of original sin has much to commend it, and has more theological support in early Protestant thought than is sometimes understood. Rather than being an embarrassment best forgotten, I think that Zwingli's doctrine of sin may have real lasting value, and not just for the Reformed theological community. It may also be of use in ecumenical theology as well.[4]

This brings us to the third, and the largest, division in the book, which focuses on Christ and salvation. Chapter 6 has to do with the Word's assumption of human flesh in the incarnation. In a recent article on this subject, J. T. Turner has taken issue with my previous work on this topic, and in this chapter I reply to two arguments he articulates. These are that in becoming incarnate, the Word could not have assumed any old human nature but only his particular human nature (i.e., the human nature of Christ), and that human natures are not configured in such a way that they could in principle be assumed by divine persons. In response, I argue that both of these claims are mistaken: human natures are configured so that they can in principle be assumed by a divine person, and the Word could have assumed some human nature other than the one he did, in fact, assume. Along the way I also show how these are claims that have far-reaching implications for what we say about the nature and scope of the incarnation in the divine plan for human salvation.

Chapter 7 considers the vexed issue of the vicarious humanity of Christ. This is another topic of considerable interest in recent systematic theology, particularly theology that looks to the work of Karl Barth and Thomas F. Torrance. In previous work in this area I have defended the view that Christ does not have a fallen human nature, but a sinless one. However, in light of recent work in this area I here offer a slightly different view, which (I hope) satisfies much the same concerns as motivate those who claim Christ had a fallen

---

[4] I have set out a Zwingli-inspired constructive account of original sin in Oliver D. Crisp, *Analyzing Doctrine: Toward a Systematic Theology* (Waco, TX: Baylor University Press, 2019). Interested readers may also like to consult an earlier essay that sets this Zwinglian view into a larger theological framework in Oliver D. Crisp, "Sin," in *Christian Dogmatics: Reformed Theology for the Church Catholic*, eds. Michale Allen and Scott R. Swain (Grand Rapids, MI: Baker Academic, 2016), ch. 9.

human nature, yet on a rather different model of the incarnation. On this view, which I call the vicarious humanity account in honor of Torrance, Christ assumes a fallen human nature that he sanctifies in the very act of assumption, cleansing it of any taint or stain of sin or fallenness. Although this is not my own view, it is one option for the theologian sympathetic to Torrance's line of thought.

Chapters 8 and 9 both have an Edwardsian flavor, though in the case of Chapter 8, the Edwardsian ingredient is really the point of departure for consideration of an important issue in atonement theology more generally speaking. The issue is this: If Christ's work of reconciliation in atonement is substitutionary in nature, and involves him taking a representational role standing in the place of sinners and taking upon himself the guilt of sinful human beings, then *how* in uniting himself to those guilty of sin does he remain without guilt for sin? This is an important theological consideration for those with an investment in such views of the atonement because it is difficult to see how someone guilty for sin can themselves offer up an atonement for sin. To return to our aspirational Anselmianism once more, it would appear (as Anselm says in *Cur deus homo*) that the God-man must be without sin in order to be able to offer up some reconciling work that may satisfy God. No one who is already guilty of sin can perform such a task because that person would already owe all they are as recompense for sin. So, is there some way out of what, in this chapter, I call the Edwardsian Quandary about Christ's acquired guilt in atonement? This chapter offers a positive response to this question.

Chapter 9 completes the final division of the book, focusing on the Christian life, lived in light of the salvation procured by Christ. Jonathan Edwards is well known for his virtue theory set forth most comprehensively in his dissertation *The Nature of True Virtue*.[5] There he gives the framework for the Christian life in which moral character plays a fundamental part. In this chapter I engage Edwards as a resource for Reformed theological ethics, in conversation with several other recent treatments of his work. To my mind Edwards represents an important and under-recognized

---

[5] Jonathan Edwards, "The Nature of True Virtue," in *The Works of Jonathan Edwards, vol. 8: Ethical Writings*, ed. Paul Ramsey (New Haven, CT: Yale University Press, 1989).

resource for Reformed moral theology where virtue and character play a central and defining role.

* * * *

There is no final statement of theology this side of the grave, no truly *complete* dogmatics. Theology is always *in via*—written along the way. This is especially true of the outputs of historic theologians, the vast majority of whom were not professors locked away in ivory towers, but pastors and teachers working in the midst of ecclesiastical struggles, and attempting to write their way through theological difficulties. These studies are no different in that respect. In fact, they are consciously written as soundings in theology—studies that are situated within the faith, so to speak, and in search of greater understanding of the doctrinal deposit of that faith. They are, in one sense, a sequel to previous works where I have attempted to do something similar.[6] However, in the studies contained within this volume readers will detect something of a shift in focus. Retrieval of ideas and arguments from the tradition are still important themes in this work, but theological construction is more emphasized in these chapters than in the two books *Retrieving Doctrine* and *Revisioning Christology*. This too reflects the influence of Anselm, who is surely an exemplar of a constructive theologian who is also deeply engaged with the Great Tradition of Christian thought.[7]

---

[6]See Oliver D. Crisp, *Retrieving Doctrine: Essays in Reformed Theology* (Downers Grove, IL: IVP Academic, 2011); and Oliver D. Crisp, *Revisioning Christology: Theology in the Reformed Tradition* (Aldershot: Ashgate, 2011).

[7]It might be thought that Anselm is not engaged with the tradition given that he almost never refers to earlier theologians in his work, or even to Scripture. But this is to confuse a stylistic decision to write direct, clear theology unencumbered by technical apparatus, with a deep formation in the Great Tradition (especially Augustine) that is evident below the surface, so to speak, in Anselm's work. For discussion of this, see Sandra Visser and Thomas Williams, *Anselm*. Great Medieval Thinkers (Oxford: Oxford University Press, 2009), especially ch. 1.

PART ONE

The Task of Theology

1

Challenges for
Systematic Theology

Strictly speaking, this chapter is not an essay in systematic theology. It is more of a reflection on some of the pressing challenges facing those practicing systematic theology today—an exploration in meta-theology, if you will. Just as an essay about the perils of writing a novel is not itself a novel, so theological reflection of the sort contained in this chapter is not itself theology (at least, so it seems to me). Nevertheless, I trust that it may be of some use to working theologians and those with an interest in theology, much as a book review in the *Los Angeles Review of Books* may be of some use to the bibliophile.

But before beginning my rumination, I should register a caveat. The sort of systematic theology I have in view in what follows is theologically realist in nature. By that I mean it is an approach to the theological task that conceives of the object of theological scrutiny (i.e., God, or the divine) as a mind-independent personal entity who is the creator of all things in heaven and earth. There are systematic theologians who repudiate this, usually for one of two possible reasons. The first reason involves denying that God is a mind-independent entity. For such theologians, God is a kind of fictional being generated by human religious reflection and projection. Ludwig Feuerbach is the classic example of a thinker who holds this sort of view, and he has a number of modern theological disciples.[1] A second possible reason involves denying

---

[1]See Ludwig Feuerbach, *The Essence of Christianity*, trans. George Eliot (New York: Prometheus Books, 1989 [1841]).

that God is a personal being. There are a variety of reasons why the theologian might espouse this view. But one important historic reason for doing so is attachment to a strong notion of divine transcendence coupled with skepticism about what can be known of the divine nature.

Fascinating though such theological contributions are, I shall have nothing to say about them here. My interest is in theologically realist systematic theology that thinks of God as a personal entity of a sort—even if, as I think, he is a very different sort of entity from anything created.[2] In order not to burden the text that follows with the cumbersome term "theologically realist systematic theology" I shall simply stipulate that from here on in that when I refer to "systematic theology" it is the theologically realist sort of systematic theology that is in question.

With this made tolerably clear, we may proceed to the question in hand. In my view, the contemporary systematic theologian faces various intellectual challenges that require some reflection in order for her to know how best to proceed with her task. This is the case despite the fact that there are very encouraging indications of the present health and vitality of systematic theology after a period in which its future was sometimes thought to be less than certain, at least in some quarters in the Anglophone world. I think that these signs of renewed health give us grounds for cautious optimism. There are several major multivolume works of systematic theology currently being undertaken by theologians like Sarah Coakley and Katherine Sonderegger;[3] there are significant recent and complete systematic contributions to theology from scholars like Thomas Finger, Paul Hinlicky, Robert Jenson, Veli-Matti Kärkkäinen,

---

[2]Language of "entity" might be thought to imply that God is one being among many beings, which, for many historic theologians, would be a serious mistake. For, on this classical view, God is not in a genus, and is not one being among many but entirely distinct from his creatures. As I hope is clear, I am sympathetic to this historic worry. Those concerned by the use of the term in this context may think of it as a placeholder.

[3]See Sarah Coakley, *God, Sexuality, and the Self: An Essay 'On the Trinity'* (Cambridge: Cambridge University Press, 2013); and Katherine Sonderegger, *Systematic Theology: The Doctrine of God, Vol. 1* (Minneapolis, MN: Fortress Press, 2015).

Kathryn Tanner, Anthony Thistleton, and Brian Gerrish;[4] and there have been several recent attempts to set forth systems of theology that were never finished, two notable examples being the projected works of the English theologians Colin Gunton and John Webster. I am also aware of other works of systematic theology that are currently in preparation or underway (e.g., the multivolume work that Kevin Vanhoozer intends to write, and the prospective work of my colleague at the University of St. Andrews, Christoph Schwoebel). Yet, despite these encouraging signs of a renewed interest in writing systematic theology, there remain significant obstacles before any contemporary practitioner of this branch of divinity.

In this chapter I will set out what I take to be four of the most serious challenges to the writing of systematic theology today. These comprise worries about the explanatory ambition of systematic theology; about the conceptual content of systematic theology; about the currently fractured state of the field; and concerns about the integrity of systematic theology. Having enumerated and explained them, I will then respond to these worries, providing reasons for thinking that none of these challenges preclude the ongoing task of systematic theology provided the task in view is rightly calibrated so that it has appropriate goals, and is pursued with appropriate sensibilities and intellectual virtues, such as "fallibilism" and "intellectual humility" (terms that I shall explain in due course).

---

[4]See Thomas Finger, *A Contemporary Anabaptist Theology: Biblical, Historical, Constructive* (Downers Grove, IL: IVP Academic, 2004); Paul R. Hinlicky, *Beloved Community: Critical Dogmatics after Christendom* (Grand Rapids, MI: Eerdmans, 2015); Robert W. Jenson, *Systematic Theology*, 2 vols. (New York: Oxford University Press, 1995, 1999); Veli-Matti Kärkkäinen, *A Constructive Christian Theology for the Pluralist World*, 5 Vols. (Grand Rapids, MI: Eerdmans, 2013–2017); Kathryn Tanner, *Jesus, Humanity, and the Trinity: A Brief Systematic Theology* (Minneapolis, MN: Fortress, Press, 2001); Anthony C. Thistleton, *Systematic Theology* (Grand Rapids, MI: Eerdmans, 2015); and B. A. Gerrish, *Christian Faith: Dogmatics in Outline* (Louisville, KT: Westminster John Knox, 2015).

Challenges to the systematic-theological task

The fundamental problem for contemporary systematic theology is that the systematic theologian has the unenviable task of trying to say something practically impossible about something truly ineffable. That is a daunting prospect. What she has to say is practically impossible because in this day and age it really is practically impossible for anyone to write a *systematic* theology. This problem has to do with what we might call *the explanatory ambition of systematic theology*. It is difficult to write a systematic account of anything, especially anything of significance that has generated a convoluted and complex historic literature. (Consider the ambitions of the recent spate of systematic analytic metaphysics, which is an interesting analog to systematic theology in this regard.[5]) Yet the systematic theologian has traditionally been tasked with giving a systematic account of Christian doctrine. (At least, that is one fairly traditional way of conceiving the task of systematic theology.[6]) Put more formally, it seems to me that much contemporary systematic theology is understood in terms of what I have elsewhere called the SHARED TASK of theology. This can be expressed as follows:

SHARED TASK: Commitment to an intellectual undertaking that involves (though it may not comprise) explicating the conceptual content of the Christian tradition (with the expectation that this is normally done from a position within that tradition, as an adherent of that tradition), using particular religious texts that are part of the Christian tradition, including sacred scripture,

---

[5]Examples include D. M. Armstrong, *A World of States of Affairs* (Cambridge: Cambridge University Press, 1997); David Lewis, *On the Plurality of Worlds* (Malden, MA: Blackwell Publishing, 1986); E. J. Lowe, *The Four-Category Ontology: A Metaphysical Foundation for Natural Science* (New York: Oxford University Press, 2006); Theodore Sider, *Writing the Book of the World* (Oxford: Oxford University Press, 2011); Peter Unger, *All the Power in the World* (New York: Oxford, 2006); and Peter van Inwagen, *Existence: Essays in Ontology* (Cambridge: Cambridge University Press, 2014).

[6]I have tried to indicate some of the very different ways in which systematic theology is currently envisaged in Oliver D. Crisp, "Analytic Theology as Systematic Theology," *Open Theology* 3 (2017): 156–66.

as well as human reason, reflection, and praxis (particularly religious practices) as sources for theological judgments.

I think this or something very like it is a way of understanding the systematic-theological task today that is widely (if tacitly) agreed upon, though I won't defend that claim here.[7] The problem is not merely that Christian doctrine is a complex web of different ideas and concepts, rooted in a long and diverse intellectual-religious tradition claiming numerous and different sorts of difficult textual material including but not limited to scripture, in multiple languages. It also includes the fact that the literature on the topic is now so vast that not even the most impressive and encyclopedic mind can encompass and assess every individual contribution to the field of systematic theology. Add to that the further difficulty that systematic theologians face in articulating their views on Christian doctrine in a world that is itself much more religiously pluralist and complex than in previous generations, a world where the pace of such change is exponential, and we have a task that is truly *practically* impossible for any one mere human being. The very idea that one might find an axial point from which to "write the book of the world," theologically speaking, is now almost universally considered to be a chimera. For some, the very explanatory ambition expressed in SHARED TASK is indicative of the fact that systematic theology is a hangover from a premodern mind-set from which such large-scale conceptual world-building was conceivable (at least in principle) even if it was seldom if ever achieved.

However, this is just the beginning of the systematic theologian's problems. For not only must she say something practically impossible (the problem of explanatory ambition); she must say something practically impossible about something truly ineffable—a problem about *the conceptual content of systematic theology*. In the case of systematic theology, it is the object of study that is said to be ineffable—literally beyond the reach of human words. Such high-octane apophaticism is deeply rooted in the Christian tradition. God is said to be both incomprehensible in his essence and ineffable in his being. An example from the ancient liturgy of St. John Chrysostom used by many Orthodox Christians down through the centuries

---

[7] See "Analytic Theology as Systematic Theology" for such a defense.

will make the point (and indicate how deeply such thinking has penetrated Christian spirituality). After the recitation of the Nicene faith in the midst of the liturgy, the priest says this:

> It is meet and right to hymn thee, to bless thee, to praise thee, to give thanks unto thee, and to worship thee in every place of thy dominion: for thou art God ineffable, inconceivable, invisible, incomprehensible, ever existing and eternally the same, thou and thine Only-begotten Son and thy Holy Spirit.[8]

Similar sentiments are in evidence in other patristic writings, in later medieval school theology, and in post-Reformation Protestant school theology. And it is a matter that is still on the lips of philosophical theologians today. Take the well-known example of Jean-Luc Marion. He worries that any attempt to grasp something of the divine nature, conceptually speaking, must lead to idolatry because God is not graspable by means of theological predication:

> Even if we were to comprehend God as such (by naming him in terms of his essence), we would at once be knowing not God as such, but less than God, because we could easily conceive an other still greater than the one we comprehend. For the one we comprehend would always remain less than and below the one we do not comprehend. Incomprehensibility therefore belongs to the formal definition of God, since comprehending him would put him on the same level as a finite mind—ours—, would submit him to a finite conception, and would at the same time clear the way for the higher possibility of an infinite conception, beyond the comprehensible.[9]

But if God is truly incomprehensible, then God is such that we cannot understand his essence or what he is. Similarly, if he is truly

---

[8]Cited by Jonathan D. Jacobs in "The Ineffable, Inconceivable, and Incomprehensible God: Fundamentality and Apophatic Theology," in *Oxford Studies in Philosophy of Religion 6*, ed. Jonathan L. Kvanvig (Oxford: Oxford University Press, 2015), 158. As Jacobs points out, there are a great host of historic Christian thinkers who would affirm these things.

[9]Jean-Luc Marion, "In the Name: How to Avoid Speaking of 'Negative Theology'," in *God, The Gift, and Postmodernism*, eds. John D. Caputo and Michael Scanlon (Bloomington: Indiana University Press, 1999), 36–37.

ineffable, then we cannot express in words what he is either. That makes systematic reflection on such an entity extremely challenging, to say the least. For whatever is incomprehensible is literally beyond our ken, and whatever is ineffable is literally beyond expression. Such conceptual challenges appear to stymie systematic theology at the outset.[10]

To these two challenges about the explanatory ambition and conceptual content of systematic theology, we may add a third, which we might call the "Balkanized" nature of modern systematic theology. By this I mean that a map of the field of theology as it exists today would reveal many different and (often) mutually hostile fiefdoms, each of which is vying for some larger segment of the religious landscape. This is a problem concerning *the currently fractured state of the field*. There are many different methods of doing theology, many different schools of thought associated with the theological task. The proliferation of differences in how one thinks about the theological task and how one prosecutes it has become so much a part of the modern theological scene that one is inescapably required to specify the sort of systematic theology being attempted.

Hence, there is no such thing as systematic theology *simpliciter*. Perhaps there never was such a thing except in the imaginary worlds of textbook surveys; but, in any case, it is well and truly extinct now. Instead, there are tradition-specific varieties of theology, confessional and constructive theologies, dogmatic and systematic theologies, "contextual" and "minority" theologies,[11] modern and postmodern theologies, and so on. This is systematic theology as "boutique theology," to coin a phrase—theology

---

[10]Although, not according to Jacobs. For another interesting treatment of similar themes applied to spiritual theology, see Sameer Yadav, "Mystical Experience and the Apophatic Attitude," *Journal of Analytic Theology* 4 (2016): 18–43. Marion thinks that divine incomprehensibility means that all predication with respect to God fails, so that we should resort to praise rather than predication. For a very helpful discussion of this material, see Kevin Hector, *Theology Without Metaphysics: God, Language and the Spirit of Recognition*. Current Issues in Theology, No. 8 (Cambridge: Cambridge University Press, 2011), ch. 1. For a rather different approach to these problems using the work of William Alston and John Hick, see Sebastian Gäb, "The Paradox of Ineffability," *International Journal of Philosophy and Theology* 78.3 (2017): 289–300.

[11]I place "contextual" and "minority" in parentheses because these are disputed terms.

catering to a particular, and often select or discerning, clientele. An example: suppose Jones, an American Protestant Christian, aligns herself with the Wesleyan tradition. What sort of Wesleyan is she? United Methodist, Holiness, Free Evangelical? What sort of Wesleyan theology does she find attractive—classical, revisionist, liberal, postmodern, Open Theist? What sort of theological purview shapes her theological vision—that of Dead White European males, of Majority World theologies, Liberation theology, Feminist, Womanist, Mujerista, Black theology? Even if her work represents none of these things, it must be written in a way that is cognizant of them, and of the challenges they present to her way of going about the theological task in the context of North America today.

Some of the distinctions just mentioned might be thought to fall outside the purview of systematic theology, strictly speaking. Sometimes constructive theology is regarded as something different from systematic theology, and as certainly different from confessional theology. But that need not be the case. One can do theological construction from within a given tradition as a contribution to that tradition rather than in opposition to it. Or take the dialectic between dogmatic and systematic theology. Are they the same thing? Not necessarily, though the distinction is a fuzzy one in much contemporary Protestant Christian doctrine.[12] However, if dogmatic theology is the examination of the dogmatic deposit of the faith (as understood by a given tradition), then this may function as a subfield within systematic theology. It is, on this way of thinking, a kind of systematic approach to Christian doctrine that privileges particular doctrines that have a dogmatic shape provided by confessions and creeds, in which case dogmatic theology is a species of systematic theology after all.

This leads to consideration of a fourth challenge for the systematic theologian, which has to do with *the integrity of systematic theology* as a discipline within the larger subject area of Christian theology or divinity. To what extent must systematic theology pay attention to its own history and the sources of authority that inform it? To

---

[12]For recent discussion of this point, see Oliver D. Crisp and Fred Sanders, eds. *The Task of Dogmatics: Explorations in Theological Method* (Grand Rapids, MI: Zondervan Academic, 2017), especially the introduction and the essays by Scott Swain and Sameer Yadav.

what extent is it a constructive discipline, one that makes new discoveries or that advances a new agenda in conversation with other, related disciplines like literary theory, or philosophy, or the natural and social sciences? Does systematic theology have its own integrity as a discipline, its own "substance," so to speak, or does it depend in important respects on being conceptually funded by other, related disciplines like philosophy, sociology, anthropology, and so on? *Should* systematic theology be dogmatic theology— that is, theology done in a confessional mode, taking seriously the dogmatic deposit of a given tradition as a constraint on what the theologian says about a given topic? Or should the theologian be free from such constraint in order to take forward a constructive theological project that makes better sense in the contemporary world? To what extent should systematic theology be done in the service of the academy or the church? These are all live issues for those seeking to practice systematic theology today, and there are no uncontested answers to these questions.

To sum up: the state in which contemporary systematic theology finds itself is, as the Americans say, *complicated*. This is due to a number of different factors. Several of the most important of these have to do with the explanatory ambition of systematic theology, its conceptual content, the current Balkanized state of the field, and the integrity of systematic theology as an intellectual discipline. There are other challenges that may be enumerated, but these seem to be some of the most pressing.[13] For this reason, it behooves us to spend some time responding to them.

---

[13]A further serious challenge, particularly for systematic theology in state-funded research universities, is whether there is a place for a confessional approach to theology in a de facto secular intellectual environment. This is a serious problem, but it is a problem about the relationship of systematic theology to the wider intellectual community of research universities, not a challenge that concerns the nature or integrity of systematic theology itself. As has already been indicated, in this chapter our task is limited to questions pertaining to the nature of systematic theology itself, not to issues about how systematic theology relates to other disciplines, or whether it should have a place in the modern research university at all. For helpful discussion of the place of theology in the modern research university (and some of the history behind this), see Mike Higton, *A Theology of Higher Education* (Oxford: Oxford University Press, 2012). For a rather different view, see Gavin D'Costa, *Theology in the Public Square: Church, Academy and Nation* (Oxford: Blackwell, 2005). Also of interest are the essays collected in Gavin Oliver D. Crisp, D'Costa, Peter Hampson,

Responding to the challenges

Let us take each of these worries in turn.

First, *concerning the intellectual ambition of systematic theology.* Systematic theology is only an impossible task if it is set up in such a way that its goals are unachievable. That is, if the ambition is to "write the book of the world," theologically speaking, then systematic theology is indeed practically impossible. But it need not be that way. Even recent work like that of the Finnish theologian Veli-Matti Kärkkäinen demonstrates that he is cognizant of the fact that he speaks from a certain context (he is fond of saying all theology is contextual theology), from a given tradition, and from a particular theological vantage. He writes: "Systematic/ constructive theology is an integrative discipline that continuously searches for a coherent, balanced understanding of Christian truth and faith in light of Christian tradition (biblical and historical) and in the context of the historical and contemporary thought, cultures, and living faiths. It aims at a coherent, inclusive, dialogical, and hospitable vision."[14]

The view that Kärkkäinen gives in his systematic theology is self-consciously a "view from here," that is, from a particular place and time, rather than a "view from nowhere." Whatever else one thinks of the merits of such an approach, declaring such constraints from the outset is a clear way of circumscribing the theological task and making it more manageable. It also indicates a certain intellectual humility in prosecuting theological ends that I think is a virtue all scholars should seek to maximize, along with a recognition of our own epistemic fallibilism. Theology is not only done from a particular place, theological context and tradition, and vantage, but is also subject to revision and correction by the community of scholars, that is, the professional guilds with which we are affiliated, and the more informal associations to which we subject our research for scrutiny.[15]

Second, concerning *the conceptual content of systematic theology*. Must we subscribe to a high-octane version of apophaticism? There are those who want to go down that path. I am sympathetic to apophaticism of a fairly strong sort particularly when it comes to matters touching upon the divine nature, and in this respect I think my views chime with much in historic Christian theology. Yet I worry about a kind of exaggerated or hypertrophied apophaticism, according to which we can know nothing about the divine nature. Perhaps a chastened apophaticism is in order, one that doesn't require the intellectual cost of ascribing total incomprehensibility and total ineffability to God, and which is schooled by what God reveals of himself in the revelation contained in scripture. For one thing, how are we to make any sense of the Trinity on a high-octane version of apophaticism? How are we to make any sense of the incarnation, or of Christ's teaching that he who has seen Him has seen the Father? What are we to say about the apostle John's claim that God is love? Of course those enamored of high-octane apophaticism have answers to these questions, but I for one would prefer a broader tent in which a milder apophatic theology coupled with a tolerance of real predication with respect to the divine nature is feasible. It is difficult to know exactly where to draw the line of ineffability. How can these theologians say that God is ineffable and inscrutable and incomprehensible, while simultaneously affirming that He is essentially triune? For I don't want to say that things like God is not triune, strictly speaking, or even that the Trinity is a non-fundamental aspect of the essentially ineffable, inscrutable, and incomprehensible divine nature. Instead, it seems to me that Christian theologians want to affirm that the

---

[15]Objection: Does this mean that theology is always tentative and uncertain, unable to take a stand on a given topic? What of those who come from a different standpoint, say, Judaism or even secular humanism? Does this mean theology has nothing to say to them? Response: Not necessarily. Suppose we think of theology in a critically realist way as a discipline that is truth-seeking and truth-apt, but where our grip on the truth of the matter is partial, even in principle revisable in light of further data. Then we might exercise intellectual humility in forming theological statements mindful of the fact that many, perhaps all, of our theological statements are in principle liable to revision. That is the sort of view I have in mind here.

Trinity picks out something fundamental concerning divinity; God is *essentially* triune—a cataphatic predication if ever there was one!

Nevertheless, and in keeping with my response to the previous question, I think that such a chastened Christian apophaticism (if I may be permitted that term) is consistent with a certain tentativeness in making dogmatic judgments. So, to return to the Trinity once more, my own view is that no extant model of the Trinity is adequate to the task of expressing the dogmatic content of the Nicene Creed. Perhaps some future theology will provide that for us, but until such time I think it is preferable to adopt a Trinitarian mysterianism rather like the mysterianism of Colin McGinn in philosophy of mind.[16] There the idea is that we are not sufficiently evolved to understand how the mind is related to the body, which is why we get into such conceptual knots in the philosophy of mind. Perhaps a similar way of thinking applies to the Trinity: we are not in an epistemically advantageous position when it comes to providing an account of the Trinity that adequately models the divine life. Perhaps such a model will be forever beyond human ken. At least for the present, a kind of skepticism toward Trinitarian models, and a corresponding Trinitarian mysterianism, may be one way forward that doesn't concede to the high-octane apophaticist that there is *nothing* that we can predicate of the divine nature. For with the framers of the Nicene Creed we can say that God really is one in essence and three-personed, though it is difficult to say *how* he is both at once.[17]

Third, concerning *the current state of the field of systematic theology.* Solving this matter is much thornier though not for conceptual but social and political reasons. However, although

---

[16]See Colin McGinn, *The Problem of Consciousness: Essays Toward a Resolution* (Oxford: Blackwell, 1991).

[17]For discussion of this point see James Anderson, *Paradox in Christian Theology: An Analysis of Its Presence, Character and Epistemic Status* (Milton Keynes: Paternoster Press and Eugene; OR: Wipf and Stock, 2007); Dale Tuggy, "The Unfinished Business of Trinitarian Theorizing," *Religious Studies* 39 (2003): 175–76; and Tuggy "Trinity," *Stanford Encyclopedia of Philosophy*, located at: http://plato.stanfor d.edu/entries/trinity/, first published Thursday July 23, 2009; substantive revision Friday September 13, 2013. For further development of the notion of Trinitarian mysterianism as I understand the term, see Crisp, *Analyzing Doctrine.*

resolving our various theological and sociological differences may be a rather tall order, tolerance for and charity toward "the other" are surely important intellectual virtues that are relevant at this juncture. Similarly, I think more work that is dialogical, ecumenical, and collaborative will make a difference. As someone invested in such dialogical research, I think I can say that it really does pay dividends and leads to greater understanding without playing down or smoothing over real theological differences. But there is more to be done on this score, especially in understanding where differences really exist and how to navigate them. For my own part, I have come to see that much of what passes for formulations of Christian doctrine by contemporary theologians is, like its historic counterparts, human reflection on divine revelation and witness to that revelation in scripture and tradition. Human reflection is often mistaken, partial, and in need of revision. The same is true *mutatis mutandis* with respect to our theology—which is a roundabout way of commending intellectual humility to theologians for a second time, and from a different angle.

Fourth, concerning *the integrity of systematic theology as an intellectual discipline*. It seems to me that "theological theology" (as John Webster used to call it) is something to be celebrated and pursued *ad maiorem dei gloriam*. However, unlike Webster, I am much less sanguine about the prospects of dogmatics that is for all practical purposes carried on in isolation from other, related fields of intellectual discourse. The future of systematic theology is (so it seems to me) a future engaged with the social and natural sciences, and with other humanities. This is not to parcel out the substance of theology, or to barter it away. It is rather to bring into one's storehouse things old *and new*. For all truth is God's truth. There is much hue and cry about interdisciplinary research these days. Systematic theology has been interdisciplinary from its beginnings. Theologians are always trying to bring in philosophical notions to underpin their theological claims, or to find ways in which resonances between, say, psychology and theology can bear fruit. That too seems to me to be something worth welcoming and encouraging, not something to be worried over and resisted.

Finally, systematic theology should not be ersatz theology. Either we should attempt to do the real thing, or we should give up and go and do something else. What would ersatz theology look like?

I suggest that it is theology that aims at a particular kind of effect rather than at truth.[18]

This can be done in a very sophisticated way. For instance, the revisionist systematic theologian who is a theological antirealist might think that the task of theology is to stimulate the right disposition or religious attitude in a given person. It is about producing a desired effect. It is not aimed at the truth of the matter because (so the theological antirealist thinks) there is no truth of the matter: hermeneutical universalism is the order of the day. That is, all we have is theological interpretation all the way down; there is no (access to) "truth" to which my theological judgments correspond, or that they instantiate.[19] That seems to me to be a good candidate for ersatz theology because it is not truth-apt and truth-aimed. It has given up on the task of theological realism, which is to give as accurate an account of the truth of the matter with respect to the divine nature as we are able.

Conclusion

Let me close with some words by the ecclesiastical historian Jaroslav Pelikan. Way back in 1969 he wrote this:

> Christian doctrines are ideas and concepts, but they are more. Christian doctrine is what the Church believes, teaches, and confesses as it prays and suffers, serves and obeys, celebrates and awaits the coming of the kingdom of God. It is also an expression of the broken state of Christian faith and witness, the most patent illustration of the truth of the apostolic admission in 1 Corinthians 13:12: "Now we see in a mirror dimly ... Now I know in part." The "inner logic" in the evolution of doctrine

---

[18]This notion of "aiming at effect, not truth" is, of course, a concept at the core of Harry Frankfurt's understanding of bullshit. Therefore ersatz theology is plausibly a kind of religious bullshit, for it aims at effect not truth. See Harry G. Frankfurt, *On Bullshit* (Princeton, NJ: Princeton University Press, 2005).

[19]Perhaps the hermeneutical universalist could hold onto a notion of truth, but claim that we don't have access to the truth of the matter, so that we are left with interpretation all the way down. That seems plausible. My thanks to Steven Nemes for pointing this out.

must be discerned, therefore, in the matrix of the total life of the Christian community.[20]

Systematic theology has to do with ideas and concepts that belong to a particular tradition—the various branches of the Christian tradition. It is concerned with Christian doctrine, with what the church believes, as Pelikan puts it. But it must reflect the situation in which we find ourselves, which is a state of brokenness, or of fracture—what I have called our Balkanized approaches to the discipline. Nevertheless, systematic theology has a contribution to make as an intellectual discipline that seeks better to understand the nature and purposes of God as understood from within the Christian tradition. There are significant challenges facing systematic theologians today. In this chapter I have focused on four that seem particularly pressing. These have to do with the intellectual ambition of systematic theology, the conceptual content of systematic theology, the current state of systematic theology, and the integrity of systematic theology as a discipline. In each case I have argued that there is reason to think practitioners of systematic theology have the resources with which to meet these challenges. That is not to say that systematic theologians *will* meet these challenges; time will tell. Yet I think that systematic theology still has a vital role to play in the *wissenschaft* of Christian theology, and I remain hopeful that the part it plays will be a constructive and helpful one—for both the academy and the church.

---

[20]Jaroslav Pelikan, *Development of Christian Doctrine, Some Historical Prolegomena* (New Haven, CT: Yale University Press, 1969), 143–44.

2

Receiving Calvin

John Calvin (1509–1564) is one of the most important Christian theologians in church history, and certainly one of two or three most influential Protestant thinkers to date. Yet he regarded himself as a Catholic—a reformer, yes, but as one trying to return to the piety and doctrine of an earlier age, not as an intellectual innovator. Nevertheless, like all great thinkers, he did end up innovating in some respects, perhaps despite himself. In this chapter I want to focus on four of the key theological tenets of Calvin's thought, reflecting on the way in which each of these theological notions has been influential in subsequent theology, particularly in the theology of the Reformed tradition. I will argue that in each of the areas we discuss, Calvin's theology remains salient for contemporary theological debate. He is still an interlocutor with whom theologians can fruitfully engage. Then, I shall close with some comments on deep themes of Calvin's thought, and on ways in which we may take up his insights in contemporary theological discussion as an exercise in what is now known as the project of theological retrieval.

Calvin's context

Let us begin with some words about context. Calvin was a Frenchman, born in Noyon, Picardy. For much of his life he was a refugee, and then an immigrant in the free cities of Geneva and Strasbourg, a person of increasing influence and authority, yet in several important respects without the trappings of office that usually accompany such attainments. He was a pastor of sorts and began his life in minor clerical orders as he studied Law in France.

Yet, as recent work on his context has shown, he regarded his life work as a kind of prophetic ministry, restoring Israel to its first love, and rejecting the idolatry and false worship that had overlaid her ceremonies and religious rituals.[1] He was a kind of Jeremiah born out of time. Yet he was also a man of great practical acumen and political realism. He had an organizational flair, which enabled him to significantly influence the reform of Geneva without being a citizen or a representative in its legislative bodies. He carried on an enormous correspondence with princes and potentates, leading churchmen from different branches of the Magisterial Reformation, and prelates and leaders of the Roman Church from which he (eventually) departed. Not only that, he was a person of immense energy, writing commentaries, giving sermons and lectures, and composing occasional and controversial works and tracts in response to various assaults upon the Protestant churches, as well as finding time to write and revise his magisterial account of Christian doctrine, *Institutes of the Christian Religion*. It went through numerous revisions during his lifetime, beginning as a short work in 1536 that reflected his humanist ideals, and classical learning, and focused on the Apostles' Creed and Lord's Prayer. By the time he was happy with the work in its final form (the 1559 edition), it had been transformed into a manual of Christian doctrine covering almost all the major topics of theology (the divine attributes are notably absent as a separate topic, as is theological method).[2]

Calvin is often regarded as a moral monster, someone who ensured Michael Servetus was put to the stake for his heretical beliefs about the Trinity. But this is not true: Calvin did not have the power to ensure this outcome, and, in any case, all sides in religious controversy of the period were far more willing to contemplate such ghastly acts because they honestly believed that the souls of the

---

[1]See Jon Balserak, *John Calvin as Sixteenth Century Prophet* (Oxford: Oxford University Press, 2014). The best recent critical biography of Calvin is Bruce Gordon's, *Calvin* (New Haven, CT: Yale University Press, 2009). An accessible short treatment of Calvin can be found in Randall C. Zachman, "John Calvin," in *The Cambridge Companion to Reformed Theology*, eds. Paul T. Nimmo and David A. S. Fergusson (Cambridge: Cambridge University Press, 2016), 132–47.

[2]For a recent study on the development of the *Institutes*, see Bruce Gordon, *John Calvin's Institutes of the Christian Religion: A Biography*. Lives of Great Religious Books (Princeton, NJ: Princeton University Press, 2016).

faithful were at stake.[3] (This does not excuse Calvin, of course, but it does provide some context for such oft-repeated accusations.) He was primarily a scholar scared out of his hope for a life of bookish retirement by William Farel, who charged him with the divine task of reforming the church. He was also a man who eventually settled down and married the widow of an Anabaptist. And he was a man who suffered from all sorts of ailments throughout his career, perhaps as a consequence of the punishing schedule to which he kept himself in his working life. But he was no alabaster saint. He had a temper (especially as he got older and his health didn't improve), he could be imperious, and often he didn't suffer fools gladly. But such traits are hardly unusual in a public figure with many different calls on his time such as Calvin undoubtedly became.

So, in short, Calvin was a man of many parts, not the two-dimensional cardboard cutout character that is sometimes reported. One final matter of context relevant to our concerns: Calvin was only one of a cadre of theologians whose work shaped the Reformed tradition as it grew and developed in the second half of the sixteenth century and beyond. The idea that he was some sort of Reformed "pope," or the single fountainhead of the Reformed tradition as Luther supposedly was for Lutheranism, is a fiction that recent work on the development of early Reformed theology has exploded.[4] Calvin was an influential figure. But he was a successor to the Zürich Reformer, Hulydrych Zwingli, the *protégé* of Farel and Martin Bucer (the Strasbourg Reformer and later Regius Professor of Divinity at Cambridge), and colleague to a range of other theologians such as Heinrich Bullinger, Jerome Zanchius, Peter Martyr Vermigli, Thomas Cranmer, Theodore Beza, and many others. Some later Reformed theologians, such as Jonathan Edwards, went out of their way to distance their own theological

---

[3]This claim is common coin among his biographers. See, for example, T. H. L. Parker, *Calvin: An Introduction to His Thought* (London: Geoffrey Chapman, 1995), and Gordon, *Calvin.*

[4]See, for example, Richard A. Muller, *The Unaccommodated Calvin: Studies in the Foundation of a Theological Tradition.* Oxford Studies in Historical Theology (Oxford: Oxford University Press, 2001); and Richard A. Muller, *After Calvin: Studies in the Development of a Theological Tradition.* Oxford Studies in Historical Theology (Oxford: Oxford University Press, 2003). See also David Steinmetz, *Calvin in Context* (New York: Oxford University Press, 1995).

efforts from the influence of Calvin.[5] So we need to take care to ensure we do not conflate "Reformed" with "Calvin." Similarly, it is worth noting that there is an important distinction between "Calvinist" and "Reformed" in contemporary appropriations of Calvin's work. We do better to avoid speaking of "Calvinist" in respect of the influence of Calvin's views, since today that word tends to connote someone who cherry-picks certain doctrines from the Reformed tradition, ignoring others (especially regarding ecclesiology and the sacraments). Those influenced directly by Calvin's thought we might call "Calvinians." But it would be best to speak of the Reformed as a distinct strand of Christianity, a tradition in which Calvin stands as one notable representative. In this respect, Reformed theology has a number of important luminaries, including Calvin, but also other influential theologians such as the aforementioned Jonathan Edwards, Francis Turretin, Friedrich Schleiermacher, Herman Bavinck, Abraham Kuyper, Karl Barth, and (depending on how you characterize his work) Jürgen Moltmann—the list could go on. In what follows I shall speak of Calvin as one among a number of Reformed theologians, a kind of *primus inter pares* or first among equals, perhaps, but not as *the* fountainhead of "Calvinism," though I admit that the attempt to dislodge this nomenclature—which is like a barnacle on the body ecclesiastical—is unlikely to be entirely successful.[6]

Key theological claims

What about his theology, then? What are some of the central structures of his thought and how have they been influential on subsequent theology? There is more than we can deal with in one short chapter, so I shall focus on four of what I take to be the most important contributions Calvin makes to Christian theology,

---

[5]See Edwards's preface to *Freedom of the Will*, *The Works of Jonathan Edwards*, Vol. 1, ed. Paul Ramsey (New Haven: Yale University Press, 1957).

[6]This is a point I have made elsewhere, for example, Oliver D. Crisp, *Deviant Calvinism: Broadening Reformed Theology* (Minneapolis, MN: Fortress Press, 2014), and Oliver D. Crisp, *Saving Calvinism: Expanding the Reformed Tradition* (Downers Grove, IL: IVP Academic, 2016).

concentrating especially on how these ideas have influenced subsequent theology, particularly theology of the last century, focusing on the *Institutes* since it is the major dogmatic contribution Calvin bequeathed to his theological heirs.[7]

(a) The doctrine of the knowledge of God

The first of these is the doctrine of the knowledge of God. Calvin's *Institutes* is a remarkable book for a number of reasons. One of those is that he doesn't have a long section of prolegomena, or preliminary methodological matters that he addresses prior to dealing with matters of substance in Christian doctrine. Instead, he begins by characterizing all knowledge as twofold. It is either knowledge of God or of ourselves. He then spends the first five chapters of the *Institutes* considering the natural knowledge of God, and whether we can know God independently of divine revelation. Following what he takes to be the argument of the apostle Paul in the opening chapters of the epistle to the Romans, Calvin posits what he calls the sense of the divine (*sensus divinitatis*) and seed of religion (*semen religionis*) that are implanted in us by God (*Institutes* 1.3[8]). This is something like a moral faculty or inborn awareness of the divine with which (Calvin presumes) all human beings are generated, rather like Paul speaks of the natural knowledge of God that is suppressed by human sinfulness in Romans 1:18-21. Its presence as a precondition of its suppression ensures that we

---

[7]It is often said by Calvin scholars today that one cannot fully appreciate the nuances of Calvin's thought if one restricts oneself to the *Institutes*, ignoring his commentaries, tracts, and treatises. That is true. Nevertheless, he did intend the *Institutes* as a summary of Christian doctrine that provided the doctrinal background necessary to read his commentaries with profit. And there is nothing untoward in focusing on a major synthetic work such as a summary of Christian doctrine or a systematic theology in order to understand what a particular author thought about key theological themes, especially when the author in question spent his entire adult life revising the work until it was just as he wanted it to be, as is the case with Calvin.
[8]All references to the Institutes are to John Calvin, *Institutes of the Christian Religion*, 2 Vols. ed. John T. McNeill, trans. Ford Lewis Battles (Philadelphia, PA: Westminster Press, 1960 [1559]).

are culpable for failing to act upon this knowledge in faith. Thus, according to Calvin:

> There is within the human mind, and indeed by natural instinct, an awareness of divinity. This we take to be beyond controversy. To prevent anyone from taking refuge in the presence of ignorance, God himself has implanted in all men a certain understanding of his divine majesty. Ever renewing its memory, he repeatedly sheds fresh drops. Since, therefore, men one and all perceive that there is a God and that he is their Maker, they are condemned by their own testimony because they have failed to honor him and to consecrate their lives to his will. (*Institutes* 1.3.1)

He goes on to say:

> As experience shows, God has sown a seed of religion in all men. But scarcely one man in a hundred is met with who fosters it, once received, in his heart, and none in whom it ripens—much less shows fruit in season. Besides while some may evaporate in their own superstitions and others deliberately and wickedly desert God, yet all degenerate from the true knowledge of him. And so it happens that no real piety remains in the world . . . . Finally, they entangle themselves in such a huge mass of errors that blind wickedness stifles and finally extinguishes those sparks which once flashed forth to show them God's glory. Yet that seed remains which can in no wise be uprooted: that there is some sort of divinity; but this seed is so corrupted that by itself it produces only the worst fruits. From this, my present contention is brought out with greater certainty, that a sense of divinity is by nature engraved on human hearts. (*Institutes* 1.4.1, 4)[9]

To understand Calvin's point here, consider a homely illustration. Imagine a broken, old-fashioned transistor radio. Its transistor is

---

[9]Calvin's work on the *sensus divinitatis* in the first few chapters of the first book of the *Institutes* provides a helpful doctrinal counterweight to his commentary on Romans 1. There he deals with the natural knowledge of God but in more general terms. Here, in the opening chapters of the *Institutes*, he nails down what this natural knowledge amounts to via his concept of the sense of the divine. See Calvin,

no longer able to pick up the radio signals being beamed to the device, so to speak. As a consequence, we cannot listen to radio programs on it. This is rather like Calvin's view of the sense of the divine implanted in human beings. It is something that is hardwired into us, but which has been broken by the effects of sin, including the noetic effects of sin—that is, the effects of sin upon our understanding. Now, if we were to take the radio to a repair shop we might be able to have it fixed. Perhaps it just needs a part replaced in order to work once more. Similarly, on Calvin's view, fallen human beings need some act of divine grace to "repair" our fallen human natures so that we are able to "receive" the radio signals of divine grace. Only by means of the secret work of the Holy Spirit in the heart of the believer are we regenerated so that we can receive and understand God's presence with us. And only once we are in this state can we see that the world around us is made by God for his glory. The idea is something like this: the radio waves were "there" even when the transistor was broken and unable to pick up the signals. What changed when the radio was repaired was not that the radio waves began to be beamed out once more, for they were always being beamed out. Rather, what changed is that the repaired radio could now receive the transmitted radio signals. In a similar fashion, on Calvin's way of thinking God's natural revelation of himself in creation is always there—it is written into the created order. It is just that fallen human beings are incapable of perceiving God's creative work in the natural order, so that they cannot "receive" the natural revelation of God in the world around them until and unless God's Spirit regenerates them, thereby repairing the moral and epistemological equipment needed in order for such fallen human beings to be able to pick up the signals of divine revelation all around them.

To be clear, Calvin is not saying that there is no natural revelation of God in creation independent of divine revelation in scripture. He is affirming that there is such natural revelation. It is just that fallen human beings are incapable of seeing this without the internal instigation of the Holy Spirit in regeneration. Only thereafter can

New Testament Commentaries, Vol. 8: Romans and Thessalonians, trans. Ross Mackenzie, eds. David W. Torrance and Thomas F. Torrance (Carlisle: Paternoster Press; Grand Rapids: Eerdmans, 1960), 29–32.

we "see" the hand of God in the glorious sunset, or in the great mountain range.

In twentieth-century theology this aspect of Calvin's work sparked a vituperative debate between two important modern Reformed theologians, Emil Brunner and Karl Barth. Brunner seemed to suggest that Calvin's view is consistent with natural revelation. Barth responded decisively with his infamous "Nein!" in which he repudiated such an interpretation of Calvin.[10] He believed that there was no point of contact between God and us to be found in natural revelation, and wanted to ensure that Calvin was not co-opted for such purposes. So he emphatically denied Brunner's claims to the contrary.

There are reasons why this debate in the 1930s was important—reasons having to do with the political "moment" in which both theologians were writing, and the worries Barth had about a kind of natural religion that might be assimilated to the emerging National Socialist regime in Germany. But in retrospect, and speaking just in terms of Calvin scholarship, neither theologian seems to have gotten Calvin quite right. As we have seen, Calvin did think that there is a natural knowledge of God to be had by means of natural revelation. It is just that fallen human beings no longer have the functioning sense of the divine in order to pick this up without divine grace. In this respect Calvin was no proto-Barth.

In more recent times Calvin's concept of the *sensus divinitatis* (SD) has been the subject of a rather different debate. In the early 1980s in the wake of a resurgence of interest in Christian philosophy and the philosophy of religion in Anglo-American philosophy, there developed something called Reformed Epistemology. This, very roughly, took Calvin's views on the natural knowledge of God as the point of departure for a particular way of thinking about epistemology, or the theory of knowledge, more generally. Philosophers Alvin Plantinga, Nicholas Wolterstorff, and William Alston (among others) developed variations on Reformed

---

[10]See *Natural Theology, Comprising "Nature and Grace" by Professor Dr. Emil Brunner and the Reply "No!" By Dr. Karl Barth*, with an Introduction by John Baillie (Eugene, OR: Wipf and Stock, 2002 [1946]). A helpful essay on this debate can be found in Trevor Hart, *Regarding Karl Barth: Toward a Reading of His Theology* (Eugene, OR: Wipf and Stock; Milton Keynes: Paternoster Press, 1999), ch. 7.

Epistemology that shared a common goal.[11] This was to show, in the wake of Calvin, that belief in God did not require argument to be rational. Or, more precisely, these philosophers argued that although many of our beliefs are inferred on the basis of other beliefs, belief in God may not be one such belief. It may, in some cases, be what is called a "basic" belief—one that is not inferred from something we already believe, examples of which include our belief in other minds, or our memory beliefs, or our perceptual beliefs. Thus, to return to Calvin, one might think of his work in the first few chapters of the *Institutes* as an attempt to understand belief in God as a properly basic belief, rather than as inferred on the basis of something else. We believe there is a God; we believe this because the secret work of the Holy Spirit has regenerated us enabling us to "see" that there is a God independent of arguments for his existence. Because of this work of the Spirit, my repaired sense of the divine can pick up the divine signals in the creation. Now, when I see a sunset or look at the San Gabriel mountains, I don't reason from their existence to the existence of some deity. Instead, belief in God naturally arises as I see them and think, "God made that." It is obvious, basic, primitive.

Reformed Epistemology has been an important research program in recent analytic philosophy and continues to have adherents today. But it is not clear (to me at least) that Calvin's SD is really concerned with the justification of religious beliefs. It functions more like Paul's comments in Romans 1-2, to point out human culpability for sin.[12] In any case, whether we think it rightly interprets Calvin's views or not, Calvin's understanding of the natural knowledge of God has provided an important impetus for this approach to religious epistemology, one that Plantinga and Wolterstorff in particular have claimed as a historic precedent for their own creative work.

---

[11]The *locus classicus* for Reformed Epistemology is Alvin Plantinga and Nicholas Wolterstorff, eds. *Faith and Rationality: Reason and Belief in God* (Notre Dame: University of Notre Dame Press, 1981). See also Alvin Plantinga, *Warranted Christian Belief* (New York: Oxford University Press, 2000). A more popular account of Plantinga's position is given in Alvin Plantinga, *Knowledge and Christian Belief* (Grand Rapids, MI: Eerdmans, 2015).

[12]In this I am echoing something of the view of Paul Helm. See his *Faith and Understanding* (Edinburgh: Edinburgh University Press, 1997), ch. 9.

(b) Union with Christ

Let us turn to a second theme in Calvin that has been influential in recent religious thought. This is the notion of *union with Christ*. Although the search for a central organizing principle to Calvin's work or central dogma, popular in the nineteenth century, has now (thankfully) been largely abandoned, the notion of union with Christ does do a lot of theological heavy-lifting in his thought. As Karl Barth put it at one point in his *Church Dogmatics*, the notion of union with Christ "has a comprehensive and basic significance for Calvin. Indeed, we might almost call it his conception of the essence of Christianity."[13] Others have taken up this call in more recent commentary on Calvin's work, Charles Partee being one of the best-known examples, following in the footsteps of Thomas and James Torrance.[14] This theme is not merely a notion or idea; it is comprised of a cluster of concepts having to do with Calvin's understanding of the nature of salvation.

Not only is union with Christ an important theme in Calvin's thought. It has also generated a great deal of scholarly dispute. Two issues are at stake. The first concerns the right interpretation of Calvin himself, which is the preserve of the Calvinians as we are calling them. The second has to do with the theological legacy Calvin bequeathed his intellectual heirs, that is, the Reformed theologians who have come after him. Let us tackle these two problems in turn. In so doing we will give some account of the cluster of notions making up union with Christ as we survey the lie of the interpretive landscape, so to speak.

As to the first of these scholarly disputes about union with Christ, that is, the right understanding of Calvin himself, there are basically three sorts of approach in the current scholarly literature. The first emphasizes forensic aspects of Calvin's doctrine of justification by faith and minimizes those places where he speaks in ways that reflect more organic language of union with Christ. The

---

[13]Karl Barth, Church Dogmatics IV/3, 551.
[14]See Charles Partee, *The Theology of John Calvin* (Louisville, KY: Westminster John Knox, 2008). He is associated with the Thomas Torrance-inspired trajectory in contemporary Reformed theology called Evangelical Calvinism. See Myk Habets and Robert Grow, eds. *Evangelical Calvinism: Essays Resourcing the Continuing Reformation of the Church* (Eugene, OR: Wipf and Stock, 2012).

second approach takes the opposite view, playing up the language of union and minimizing or even denying the forensic component of Calvin's work. The final sort of view is a *via media* that places the forensic language of justification within the broader context of his references to union with Christ.[15] Where one finds oneself on the spectrum of views in this matter depends in large measure on what one makes of the relationship between the doctrine of justification and sanctification in Calvin's thought alongside the related notion of regeneration, that is, the moment at which an individual is brought to salvation through the secret work of the Holy Spirit (as Calvin puts it).

Calvin's understanding of justification was similar in basic outline to that of the German Reformer, Martin Luther. Like Luther, though with different nuances, Calvin thought that fallen human beings have to be justified in the sight of God by means of the alien righteousness of Christ, which is ascribed, or imputed, to the given individual. He writes, "Therefore, we explain justification simply as the acceptance with which God receives us into his favor as righteous men. And we say that it consists in the remission of sins and the imputation of Christ's righteousness" (*Institutes* 3.11.2). God treats the fallen individual *as if* she or he were clothed with the righteousness of Christ, so that he may declare the person righteous, or justified. Because the person is justified by this declarative act, the believer may then be sanctified by the secret working of the Holy Spirit, a lifelong process. In this way, Calvin's thought takes up broadly Augustinian themes about the way in which salvation is entirely a work of divine grace, but makes a distinction not shared by Augustine, treating justification as a quasi-judicial declarative act whereupon the fallen human person may begin the lifelong task of growing in grace, which is sanctification. Although these two things are intimately related, on Calvin's way of thinking, they are conceptually distinct. Augustine did not make such a distinction, preferring instead to think of justification and sanctification

---

[15]An excellent overview of the literature is given in Michael Horton's essay, "Calvin's Theology of Union with Christ and the Double Grace: Modern Reception and Contemporary Possibilities," in *Calvin's Theology and Its Reception: Disputes, Developments and New Possibilities*, eds. J. Todd Billings and I. John Hesselink (Louisville, KY: Westminster John Knox, 2012), ch. 4.

together as one divine act in the human heart that takes place over a lifetime. In this way, Calvin and the other Magisterial Reformers might be regarded as the heirs to Augustine's understanding of unmerited divine grace received through faith in Christ, whereas the Tridentine decision on justification may be regarded as the heir to Augustine's particular account of the trajectory of justification in the Christian life. Both drew upon Augustine's thought, but in rather different ways, yielding rather different theological conclusions as a consequence.

Let us call this Calvinian understanding of justification by grace through faith *the forensic justification doctrine*, since the idea is that God declares the individual righteous on the basis of Christ's work, not through some infusion of grace. She or he is simply declared to be right before God, and consequently accepted into his favor.

Now, it may be thought that a declaration of this sort, as a kind of divine speech act, could bring about the relevant change to the person about whom this declaration is made, so that by means of this very declaration of righteousness in justification the person's status is changed.[16] This is an analogy with legal situations in which a judge declares a person free to go, dropping all charges, whereupon the person who had been in custody may now walk free from the court. We might say that the declarative act of the judge changes the status of the person accused. But for Calvin, although the declarative act of justification does change our status before God, bringing us into his favor, it is not equivalent to the moral change that is brought about in the human individual by means of the secret working of the Holy Spirit in regeneration. There is, in Calvin's language, a "wondrous exchange" between the believer and Christ so that the sin of the believer is imputed to Christ on the cross and the righteousness of Christ is imputed to the believer by God in forensic justification. Because of this declarative act, the

---

[16]This point is made in the recent literature by Bruce McCormack. See "What's at Stake in Current Debates about Justification?" in *Justification: What's at Stake in The Current Debates*, eds. Mark Husbands and Daniel J. Treier (Downers Grove, IL: IVP Academic, 2004), 64.

Holy Spirit may regenerate the individual, thereby uniting them with Christ in more than a forensic sense. Calvin writes:

> Therefore, that joining together of Head and members, that indwelling of Christ in our hearts—in short, that mystical union—are accorded by us the highest degree of importance, so that Christ, having been made ours, makes us sharers with him in the gifts with which he has been endowed. We do not, therefore, contemplate him outside ourselves from afar in order that his righteousness may be imputed to us but because we put on Christ and are engrafted into his body—in short, because he deigns to make us one with him. (*Institutes* 3.11.10)

There is, then, strong language about union with Christ that Calvin approves. But he does not like the idea, which he finds in the Lutheran renegade Andreas Osiander, that the forensic aspect of justification gets swallowed up, as it were, by language of union and participation. The order in the purposes of God seems to be justification first, then union with Christ by means of the regenerative action of the Holy Spirit. Or, to put it another way, it looks like we are really and truly and mystically united to Christ (to use Calvin's language) by the Holy Spirit because we have been accounted righteous by means of the wonderful exchange with Christ ascribed or attributed to us by God the Father.

Earlier I said that Calvin's views on union with Christ have been the subject of much debate in recent Reformed theology, depending on whether one finds the forensic side of his approach or the organic metaphors of union more appealing. This really goes to the heart of an important fault line in modern Reformed thought, a disagreement about where the emphasis should lie in discussing the nature of salvation. For some modern theologians, like the Princeton Barth scholar Bruce McCormack, this is a debate about the soul of the Reformation. The issue as he sees it is whether modern Protestants wish to hold on to their heritage or give way to Platonizing tendencies that are fundamentally inimical to the concerns of the Reformation.

However, I am more sympathetic to the views of Osiander—and, strange to say—there are resources in Reformed theology that press in that direction as well. Axiomatic to the exposition of justification in the theology of the eighteenth-century New England Reformed theologian Jonathan Edwards is the notion that the real metaphysical union of the believer to Christ is the foundation of the legal or forensic declaration of God. He writes:

> what is real in the union between Christ and his people, is the foundation of what is legal; that is, it is something really in them, and between them, uniting them, that is the ground of the suitableness of their being accounted as one by the Judge: and if there is any act, or qualification in believers, that is of that uniting nature, that it is meet on that account that the Judge should look upon 'em, and accept 'em as one, no wonder that upon the account of the same act or qualification, he should accept the satisfaction and merits of the one, for the other, as if it were their satisfaction and merits: it necessarily follows, or rather is implied.[17]

But clearly Edwards has inverted Calvin's distinction between justification and union. For whereas for Calvin it seems that justification is logically prior to union in regeneration, for Edwards it is the other way around. The real union between Christ and his elect is logically prior to the ascription of Christ's righteousness in justification.

Edwards is not a modern theologian, of course. Nevertheless, he is a significant voice in the Reformed tradition, a thinker whose work is increasingly consulted as a resource for constructive theology today. Importantly for our purposes, Edwards's position seems to be precisely the opposite of Calvin's, representing the triumph of union with Christ and full-blown participation language over the forensic. And yet, recent work on Calvin has suggested that the language of participation plays a more fundamental role in his theology than is often thought. Thus, for instance, Julie Canlis and Carl Mosser[18] have

---

[17]Jonathan Edwards, "Justification by Faith," in *Sermons and Discourses, 1734-1738: The Works of Jonathan Edwards*, Vol. 19, ed. M. X. Lesser (New Haven, CT: Yale University Press, 2001), 158.

[18]See Carl Mosser "The Greatest Possible Blessing: Calvin and Deification," *Scottish Journal of Theology* 55.1 (2002): 36–57; and Julie Canlis, "Calvin, Osiander and Participation in God," *International Journal of Systematic Theology* 6.2 (2004): 169–84. See also Julie Canlis, *Calvin's Ladder: A Spiritual Theology of Ascent and Ascension* (Grand Rapids, MI: Eerdmans, 2010); Todd Billings, *Calvin,*

argued that Calvin, like a number of other Western theologians, has a doctrine of theosis or deification as part of his understanding of union with Christ in sanctification. If that is right, then the picture is rather more complicated than has previously been thought—and a lot closer to the sort of view one finds in later Reformed theologians like Edwards, who most certainly defended a doctrine of theosis and participation in the divine life.

(c) Election

We turn now to the "dreadful decree" (*decretum horribilis*) as Calvin called it (*Institutes* 3.23.7), that is, the doctrine of election. This doctrine is often thought to be synonymous with Calvin's thought, even though his thinking in this area, as in so many others, was really "borrowed" from Augustine rather than made up whole cloth by Calvin himself. Although it is commonplace in treatments of Calvin's doctrine to start by saying that his account of election was not a central and defining doctrine for his theology, it bears repeating. He doesn't treat election in detail until Book 3 of the *Institutes* in the context of the Christian life, not, as it is in the work of much later Reformed theology, as something contained within the doctrine of God, or in protology (the doctrine of first things). It was Karl Barth that took Calvin's doctrine of election and revolutionized it. This is so much the case that really all post-Barthian treatments of the doctrine are living in the shadow of his monumental theological achievement in this area.

But we begin to get ahead of ourselves. Before saying more about Barth's transformation of the Calvinian doctrine, we must say something more about Calvin's position itself. Let us describe it as *Calvin's Fork*. This is the view that God ordains the salvation of some number of human beings less than the total number according to his

---

Participation, and the Gift: The Activity of Believers in Union with Christ. Changing Paradigms in Historical and Systematic Theology (Oxford: Oxford University Press, 2007); and Mark A. Garcia, *Life in Christ: Union with Christ and Twofold Grace in Calvin's Theology*. Studies in Christian History and Thought (Milton Keynes: Paternoster, 2008). Also of value in this connection is William B. Evans, *Imputation and Impartation: Union with Christ in American Reformed Theology*. Studies in Christian History and Thought (Milton Keynes: Paternoster, 2009).

good pleasure and will, as the letter to the Ephesians tells us. These people are elect according to the will of God. Those who are not elect are passed over by divine saving grace. They perish in their sins, suffering punishment in hell that is inevitable without the interposition of divine grace. These are the reprobate. Calvin puts it starkly:

> We call predestination God's eternal decree, by which he compacted with himself what he will to become of each man. For all are not created in equal condition; rather eternal life is foreordained for some, eternal damnation for others. Therefore, as any man has been created to one or other of these ends, we speak of him as being predestined to life or to death. (*Institutes*, 3.21.5)

So, on Calvin's way of thinking, the eternal divine decision in election results in a bifurcation of the human race into two groups, hence the metaphor of the fork. More often, this is referred to as the doctrine of double predestination. For some, it offers great comfort, which was Calvin's aim and the reason why it is placed where it is in the *Institutes*, after discussion about the nature of faith and salvation, and in the context of the Christian life. I prefer to call it his Fork because it is the means by which humanity is divided into two groups that are definitive of the eternal destiny of the individual members of those groups, irrespective of anything they do that might be thought to merit them a place among the elect or the reprobate. Thus Calvin writes in his Commentary on Ephesians 1:

> In adopting us, therefore, the Lord does not look at what we are, and is not reconciled to us by any personal worth. His single motive is the eternal and good pleasure, by which he predestinated us. Why, then, are the Sophists not ashamed to mingle with it other considerations, when Paul so strongly forbids us to look at anything else than the good pleasure of God?[19]

Two questions immediately arise in the discussion of Calvin's doctrine of election. The first is this: Doesn't it make me a puppet in

---

[19]John Calvin, *New Testament Commentaries, Vol. 11: Commentaries on Galatians, Ephesians, Philippians and Colossians*, trans. T. H. L. Parker, eds. David W. Torrance and Thomas F. Torrance (Carlisle: Paternoster Press; Grand Rapids, MI: Eerdmans, 1965), 127.

the hands of the divine puppet master, depriving me of control over my eternal destination? And isn't that an intolerable outcome for the Calvinist? The second question is this: What does this say about the deity who arranges matters thus? What kind of moral monster would Calvin have us worship?

As to the first question, Calvin's doctrine does not deprive human beings of moral agency. His doctrine of total depravity, according to which all human beings are fallen and incapable of saving themselves because of the noetic effects of sin upon our minds, is not a means of tying off human moral agency but of circumscribing its limits. A quick illustration will make the point. Consider someone addicted to some sort of substance, like alcohol or cocaine. The addict is able to make all sorts of moral choices for which she is responsible. However, because she is an addict, certain choices are now beyond her metaphysical purview. They are off-limits, choices she is incapable of making because of her addicted state. Thus, she cannot choose to kick her habit forthwith and without further ado. That choice is beyond her reach and she cannot attain it without external help. In a similar manner, Calvin argues that our fallen moral state is such that certain choices are off-limits: we are incapable of making them. We cannot choose to serve and love God from this moment forward without the interposition of divine grace. Indeed, salvation is entirely a work of grace for Calvin because it is a matter that is beyond our purview in a fallen state. How does this address election? In this way: Calvin's position is consistent with human beings having responsibility for all sorts of actions, including important and significant actions. However, I cannot choose my salvation. That has to be the decision of God. But God cannot select me for inclusion within the number of the elect on the basis of any good he sees in me, any character virtues or prospective goods I may decide upon or bring about, because then my salvation would be due, at least in part, to my own good works; and that is semi-pelagian. Instead, says Calvin, God ordains salvation independent of any merit I may or may not have, or any actions I may or may not bring about according to his good pleasure and will—and nothing else.

But this takes us straight to our second question, which has to do with the moral character of a deity that arranges matters thus. Calvin, like the apostle Paul before him, may punt to mystery at this point: "But who are you, a human being, to talk back to God?" (Rom. 9:20, NIV). But this is not a very satisfactory answer, if it is an answer at all. For, if nothing prevents God from willing the salvation of all humanity, why does he allow any to remain reprobate?

It is at this juncture that we may return to Barth's response to Calvin. In *Church Dogmatics* II/2 Barth sets out a magisterial account of election that is predicated on inverting Calvin's Fork so as to answer this problem about divine grace and the scope of salvation. Instead of starting with the eternal purposes of God that yield two predestined groups of human beings, the elect and the reprobate, we might begin with the rejection of God by fallen human beings and the need for their salvation. That is, we might begin, as it were, with the problem of the reprobate and elect, these two groups of predestined humans. Now, what if we think of them not as *two distinct groups* of humans but as two ways of describing *one* human—two ways of being human that meet in the life of one individual? What if, in his grace, God sees that no human being will ever come to salvation absent divine grace and provides that grace for all? And what if, the means by which this is brought about is the election and reprobation, not of one or other group of humanity, but of *one individual*, whose action is on behalf of the whole? That is exactly what God has done in Christ: he has elected Christ to be the True Human, the one who is the Elect of God, and the one who is also Reprobate. He is chosen to bring about salvation for humanity, but he is chosen to bring this about by being rejected on behalf of the rest of humanity. Thus, the two prongs of Calvin's Fork don't divide humanity into two. Instead, they meet together in the person of Christ. Moreover, because Christ is the Elect One and the Reprobate One, he is able to act in a vicarious manner for all humanity. Sin is still dealt with; its seriousness is acknowledged. But its presence in creation is no longer a reason for rejecting any. Rejection of God, on Barth's reckoning, must now be regarded as a kind of surd element, an "impossible possibility," as he puts it.

Whereas the second question we asked Calvin was how the deity could allow some to be reprobate and what this said about the divine character, with Barth, the question has changed to become like this: Why are any rejected at all if Christ has taken the place of all? Although he is often accused of universalism, Barth's response is hopeful but not finally definitive. We can hope that all will be saved, but we cannot be dogmatic about it. This, he thinks, better tracks with the New Testament witness to Christ. For this reason, Barth says of universalism, "I do not teach it, but I also do not *not* teach it." That is, he does not affirm it (for who can know the scope of God's salvation?). Yet he does not deny it either (for the same reason). This may be the best that we can hope for—it certainly seems to be an improvement on Calvin's doctrine even if it is not without shortcomings.[20]

(d) The Eucharist

Our final topic is Calvin's doctrine of the Eucharist. Calvin's way of thinking about the Eucharist is sometimes referred to as "receptionism," because a key element of the view is that the believer receives Christ in the elements of communion and that these elements are the means by which the human soul is drawn into mystical union with Christ so that if they are received with faith, then a real and "wonderful exchange" takes place. In this context, however, the exchange is one whereby the believer truly communicates with Christ who is really, though not corporeally, presented to the faithful by means of the elements. Hence, we might characterize Calvin's view as a doctrine of real presence, but not of corporeal presence.[21]

David Steinmetz makes the point that there is an important leitmotif in Calvin's thought that occurs in his natural theology and recurs here in his Eucharistic theology as well. This has to do with

---

[20]For a helpful recent discussion of this point, see David W. Congdon, "*Apokatastasis* and Apostolicity: A Response to Oliver Crisp on the Question of Barth's Universalism," *Scottish Journal of Theology* 67.4 (2014): 464–80.

[21]A classic (and to my mind, reliable) treatment of Calvin's doctrine of the sacraments can be found in B. A. Gerrish, *Grace and Gratitude: The Eucharistic Theology of John Calvin* (Minneapolis, MN: Augsburg Fortress, 1993). Also of interest is the more recent volume by Matthew Myer Boulton, *Life in God: John Calvin, Practical Formation, and the Future of Protestant Theology* (Grand Rapids, MI: Eerdmans, 2011).

the distinction between what is offered by God and what is received by fallen human beings. He writes:

> Calvin argues that the substance of Christ's body and blood is offered to the congregation in the eucharist, whenever it is celebrated, but can only be received by faith. Men and women who lack faith participate in the simple meal of bread and wine and not in the spiritual real presence of Christ. Christ is truly offered, whether faith is present or absent; Christ is truly received, only when faith is present.[22]

In nineteenth-century American Presbyterian theology, there was some dispute about the reception of Calvin's doctrine. Although the Princetonian Charles Hodge thought himself the guardian of Reformed orthodoxy, in a heated dispute with his former pupil and sometime colleague, John Williamson Nevin, it became clear that his view was, in fact, more Zwinglian than Calvinian. Nevin's book *The Mystical Presence* set forth a high-Reformed doctrine of the Eucharist, but one that reflected the teaching of Calvin as a version of real, non-corporeal mysticism that included the Calvinian emphasis upon union with Christ as well. By contrast, Hodge thought of the Eucharist as an ordinance. He worried about any inroads being made into Reformed thought by what he thought of as the excesses of idealist thought and resisted language of "mysticism" accordingly.[23]

Today we find a similar sort of pattern emerging. There are those, often called the New Calvinists, who think of themselves as the heirs of Calvinism. They favor the so-called Five Points of Calvinism that can be traced to the Synod of Dort in the early seventeenth century and are summarized in the TULIP acrostic: Total depravity (of fallen humans); Unconditional election; Limited atonement (for the elect);

---

[22]David C. Steinmetz, "Calvin and the Natural Knowledge of God," in *Calvin in Context* (New York: Oxford University Press, 1995), 32.

[23]See John Williamson Nevin, *The Mystical Presence: And The Doctrine of the Reformed Church on the Lord's Supper.* The Mercersburg Theology Study Series, ed. Linden J. DeBie (Eugene, OR: Wipf and Stock, 2012). See also, W. Bradford Littlejohn, *The Mercersburg Theology and the Quest for Reformed Catholicity* (Eugene, OR: Wipf and Stock, 2009). I have discussed this dispute in "John Williamson Nevin on the Church" in *Retrieving Doctrine*, ch. 8.

Irresistible grace; and the Perseverance of the saints. Although there is much to be said in favor of the theological zeal with which some of these New Calvinists have pursued their theological agenda in the churches today, it is a rather truncated form of Calvinism that they espouse, and one that I think would have puzzled Calvin. One obvious example of this has to do with the nature of the church and sacraments. To return to the Eucharist, many of these New Calvinists, like Hodge in nineteenth-century Princeton, think of their view of the sacrament as Calvinist though in fact their view is really Zwinglian in nature. In other words, they tend to think that the Eucharist is a memorial feast, where Christ may be present by his Spirit, but not in any way that implies some quasi-magical event that takes place when the elements are blessed and manducated.

Yet Calvin's position on the Eucharist, which, as we have already noted, reflects themes to be found elsewhere in his theology about union with Christ and about receiving the presence of God by faith, is much more than a matter of mere remembrance. Christ is truly present to the faithful; he is communicated to those receiving the elements by faith by the power of the Holy Spirit so that they may be nourished in their faith by Christ and drawn into ever greater and more intimate union with him. They are united with him by the power of the Spirit in this event.

The influence of Calvin's theology

The influence of Calvin's thought on subsequent theology, especially (though not exclusively) Reformed theology, has been enormous. We have only been able to scratch the surface in this chapter. Nevertheless, even in this cursory glance at several nodal issues in his work, we have seen how his views have influenced subsequent thought right up to the present day. To have one's ideas discussed as the subject of live theological debate 500 years after they were first articulated is an indication of just how formative his views have been. In closing, I want to offer some comments on the deep themes that our discussion of Calvin's work has touched upon in passing. Then I shall end with some remarks about theological retrieval.

The four topics we considered reflect several key themes in Calvin's thought. These are his emphasis on absolute divine sovereignty over the created order and human destiny in particular; the hopeless

state of fallen humankind without divine grace; the way in which
God has fashioned us for fellowship and communion with Godself;
and the way in which God provides the means by which we may be
united with him in fellowship, participating in matters divine both
in the declaration of justification and secret working of the Holy
Spirit in the human heart and in the nourishment of the Eucharistic
meal. No wonder these themes have resonated with subsequent
theologians—they get to the very heart of the Christian faith. But
they have also been influential on the shape of subsequent Reformed
theology. At the start of this chapter I said that Calvin is one of a
number of important voices in the early Reformed tradition, which
is true. Nevertheless, his place as a source for Reformed theology
has meant that the four themes we have considered, and the deeper
ideas to which they are connected, form a coherent theological
framework that was built upon and adapted by many subsequent
Reformed theologians. Aside from the clarity and simplicity with
which he writes, the way in which he conveys the outline of his
theological edifice to his readers with direct, immediate images and
clear, unadorned prose is testimony to the power and clarity of his
theological vision. That is something that marks out the greatest
thinkers, including the greatest Christian theologians.

I close with a note on the resourcing of contemporary theology
with theology of the past. One common trope in contemporary
systematic theology is the notion of retrieval, that is, reaching back
to bring past ideas and arguments into present religious debate.
Theology is always *traditioned* in some manner; it is always the
case that theologians are in conversation with those who have gone
before us, whose ideas have helped fashion the edifice of the church
in different ways across time. We might say that theologians are in
communion with the dead. W. David Buschart and Kent Eilers, in
writing about theological retrieval, put it like this:

> Theology as a task or craft requires discernment—a form of
> discernment that is as much art as science. . . . As we use the term,
> "retrieval" names *a mode or style of theological discernment*
> that looks back in order to move forward. It is a particular way
> of carrying out theological work—what John Webster calls "an
> attitude of mind"—in which resources from the past are found
> distinctly advantageous for the present situation. Such resources
> might include doctrines, practices, a metaphysic or ontology,

traditions of the Great Tradition more generally. Theologies of retrieval seek to recover these resources in order to seize an opportunity or respond to a particular change.[24]

But theology is neither necromancy nor intellectual archeology. The conversations we have with thinkers of the past are never of *merely* historical interest. They are always a means of resourcing our current theological concerns with the arguments of the past. That is what theological retrieval is about: fructifying the work of today with the best of the past as a means of pursuing a constructive theological project. Calvin is one of the greatest minds in Christian history. Not everything he says will be serviceable today and not all of it will be helpful. Yet, much of what he says resonates because he was able to speak beyond his own context and into ours. For as long as human beings care about God's relationship to his creation, his fashioning of us, and his plans for us and for our salvation, as understood in scripture and tradition, I venture to say that Calvin's thought will be the subject of debate, and his theological vision will be a resource to which theologians will continue to turn, with great benefit.

---

[24]W. David Buschart and Kent D. Eilers, *Theology as Retrieval: Receiving the Past, Renewing the Church* (Downers Grove, IL: IVP Academic, 2015), 12–13, emphasis in the original.

PART TWO

God and Creation

3

Edwards on Creation
and Divine Ideas

It is often said that Jonathan Edwards was a Christian Neoplatonist.[1] It is not hard to see why. He was influenced early on in his intellectual development by the philosophy of Henry More and the Cambridge Platonists and attracted to the Augustinian vision of theology that was inherited by the Reformed Orthodox whose works he imbibed at Yale.[2] He even framed his account of the doctrine of creation at the end of his career with the traditional Neoplatonic language of *exitus* and *reditus*, describing the world as a divine emanation or communication.[3] Edwards was also an idealist, who thought of the world as comprising minds and their ideas.[4] Even apparently physical objects were actually mental objects, on the Edwardsian way of thinking—including human brains![5] But how far did that

---

[1]This is a common trope in Edwards scholarship. But one recent example can be found in Michael J. McClymond and Gerald R. McDermott, *The Theology of Jonathan Edwards* (New York: Oxford University Press, 2012), ch. 26.

[2]For discussion of this point, see Adrian Neele, *Before Jonathan Edwards: Sources of New England Theology* (New York: Oxford University Press, 2019).

[3]See Jonathan Edwards, *God's End in Creation* in WJE8. (All references are to the Yale edition of Edwards's Works, cited as "WJE" followed by volume and, where relevant, page number.)

[4]See, for example, the works collected together in WJE6. For discussion of this point, see Oliver D. Crisp, *Jonathan Edwards on God and Creation* (New York: Oxford University Press, 2012).

[5]In his early unpublished notebook on "The Mind," §35 Edwards writes, "Seeing the brain exists only mentally, I therefore acknowledge that I speak improperly when I say, the soul is in the brain only as to its operations. For to speak yet more strictly

immaterialist way of thinking extend? Was he an idealist all the way down, so to speak? What about abstract objects like properties and numbers? Did Edwards think they are, in fact, mental entities as well? And if he did, what relation did he think that they bear to the divine being who thinks them?

In this chapter I will argue that Edwards did indeed think that abstract objects are divine ideas, a view that is often called *divine conceptualism*. But he was a divine conceptualist of a particular sort, one that depends in important respects on his broader theological and philosophical views. His is a kind of hypertrophied divine conceptualism given his commitment to idealism and more particularly to immaterialism, the doctrine according to which all that exists are minds and their ideas. When set within the broader context of his philosophical vision, it turns out that Edwards's version of divine conceptualism solves certain worries that beset other, non-immaterialist versions of divine conceptualism, though it is not without its own theological cost, as we shall see.

The argument of the chapter is as follows. In the first section, I provide a brief account of divine conceptualism. The second section considers some historical background on the Augustinian understanding of the divine ideas that informs Edwards's view. The third section considers Edwards's version of divine conceptualism. Then, in the fourth and final section I close with an aporia his view raises that, strange to say, Edwards does not appear to have considered.

Divine conceptualism

According to divine conceptualism, when we read in scripture that "In the beginning, God created the heavens and the earth" (Gen. 1:1), we should understand by this the claim that *every contingent thing other than Godself* was generated by God. This is underlined

---

and abstractly, 'tis nothing but the connection of the operations of the soul with these and those modes of its own ideas, or those mental acts of the Deity, seeing the brain exists only in idea. But we have got so far beyond those things for which language was chiefly contrived, that unless we use extreme caution we cannot speak, except we speak exceeding unintelligibly, without literally contradicting ourselves." WJE6, 355.

in the prologue to the Fourth Gospel, which reads, "In the beginning was the Word, and the Word was with God, and the Word was God. He was in the beginning with God. All things came into being through him, and without him not one thing came into being" (Jn. 1:1-3, NRSV). It would be pressing matters a little too far to suggest that by the phrase translated here "came into being" the writer of the Fourth Gospel meant *literally* all things came into by God's creative Word—including what we think of as paradigmatic abstract objects like properties or numbers. Yet it seems natural to understand it, like the opening verse of Genesis which it echoes, to mean that somehow by means of a single generative divine speech act all *contingent created* things came into existence.[6]

This immediately raises an important concern, however. For how are we to understand the generation of abstract objects given that they are usually thought to be, like the platonic forms, things that are necessary, immutable, and *uncreated*—and thus, independent of God? This is a concern because if such entities exist, then they appear to undercut claims about divine aseity or independence from everything else, and divine sovereignty over all that God has made. The divine conceptualist thinks that the answer to this worry is to suggest that what we think of as abstract objects are in fact divine ideas. They are uncreated, necessary beings. That much is shared in common with the Platonists. But they exist as "concepts" in the mind of God—some of his eternal, immutable thoughts, if you will. In this way, the divine conceptualist relocates the platonic forms to the divine mind, making important changes in the process so as to protect divine aseity and sovereignty. Let us unpack this way of thinking a little more carefully, looking briefly at four central characteristics of these divine ideas. We shall see that central to the divine conceptualist understanding of God's relation to the divine ideas are that they are necessary and immutable, and yet also dependent and uncreated concrete things. Let us consider these qualities in two pairs.

---

[6]This is how William Lane Craig understands the Johannine Prologue, and his argument for this conclusion, which draws on recent biblical scholarship, seems to me to be sound. See Craig, *God Over All: Divine Aseity and the Challenge of Platonism* (Oxford: Oxford University Press, 2016), ch. 1.

First, the divine ideas are necessary and immutable. Given that God is a necessary being who is strongly immutable—both of which are traditional theological claims Edwards endorses[7]—God's ideas will also be necessary beings. For the content of his mind is necessary and strongly immutable. His thoughts do not fluctuate or change as do our thoughts (Is. 55:8-9). For, so the divine conceptualist presumes, the content of the mind of a necessary being who is strongly immutable is itself necessary and strongly immutable.

Second, the divine ideas are dependent though uncreated. In a sense, God's ideas are dependent on the fact that he thinks them and depend on his continuing to think them. They cannot persist without God thinking them, according to Edwards.[8] So, somewhat paradoxically, the divine ideas are necessary beings in one sense, and yet are also radically dependent on God for their existence as the one who thinks them and continues to think them.[9] What the Platonists thought of as abstract objects like propositions or numbers are necessary, uncreated beings that are divine ideas for the divine conceptualist. Because they are the content of the divine mind, they are concrete objects, not abstract ones as the Platonists presumed, existing in some heavenly realm of Forms independent of anything else. So we have an odd situation in which what we often think of as abstract objects, like propositions or numbers,

---

[7]"But as God is immutable, and so it is utterly and infinitely impossible that his view should be changed; so 'tis, for the same reason, just so impossible that the foreknown event should not exist: and that is to be impossible in the highest degree: and therefore the contrary is necessary. Nothing is more impossible than that the immutable God should be changed, by the succession of time; who comprehends all things, from eternity to eternity, in one, most perfect, and unalterable view; so that his whole eternal duration is *vitae interminabilis, tota, simul,* and *perfecta possessio.*" WJE1, 268.

[8]"Thus it appears, if we consider matters strictly, there is no such thing as any identity or oneness in created objects, existing at different times, but what depends on *God's sovereign constitution* . . . for it appears, that a divine constitution is the thing which *makes truth,* in affairs of this nature." WJE1, 404.

[9]Are they causally dependent on God? That is a source of some discomfort to the divine conceptualist, as Craig points out in *God Over All,* ch. 5. However, there is at least one other relation that Christians have traditionally thought to be an eternal act that is generative without being causal, namely, the eternal generation of the Second Person of the Trinity. Perhaps, like that act, divine ideas are eternally generated yet without being caused. Edwards appears to have fewer worries about ascribing causation to God than some historic, orthodox Christian theologians however.

are thought of on this view as concrete divine ideas rather than as abstract platonic forms independent of God.

Why think that divine ideas cannot exist as necessary beings independent of God? As I have already indicated, three closely interrelated traditional reasons for thinking this have to do with preserving God's ultimacy, his aseity, and his absolute sovereignty over all things. Divine ultimacy is a claim about ontological priority. God has ultimacy just in case all things depend on him for their existence because he is the source of all things other than Godself, and in some sense "causes" them to exist or otherwise brings them about.[10] But God cannot have ultimacy where there are abstract objects like the platonic forms that exist as necessary beings independent of God's agency.

Relatedly, if God exists *a se*, he exists as independent of all other things—both psychologically and metaphysically independent. (And, so the thought goes, surely God, being a perfect being, will possess aseity.) That means that he cannot be dependent for his existence on something else (this is metaphysical dependence). It also means that he cannot be psychologically dependent on anything else either, in the way that an addict may be psychologically dependent on a particular substance. However, if abstract objects exist independent of God, then there is a sense in which God does depend on things outside himself, namely, the platonic forms or abstract objects which he instantiates as do the creatures he generates.

What about divine sovereignty? It is a traditional theological claim rooted in scripture that God is an absolute sovereign (see, e.g., Is. 40:25). The advocate of divine conceptualism, wishing to uphold this aspect of a classical picture of the divine life, endorses a very strong version of divine sovereignty. For on this way of thinking everything, including what we conventionally think of as abstract objects, depend for their existence upon God in some important, and substantive, sense as dependent, though uncreated, necessary, and immutable, mental entities. So God is literally a sovereign

---

[10]For a helpful discussion of divine ultimacy, aseity, and sovereignty, see Sandra Visser and Thomas Williams, *Anselm*. Great Medieval Thinkers (Oxford: Oxford University Press, 2009), ch. 6. I put "causes" in quotes because God's creative agency is often thought to be significantly unlike creaturely causal agency. I have discussed this further in "Meticulous Providence," in *Divine Action and Providence: Explorations in Constructive Theology*, Oliver D. Crisp and Fred Sanders (Grand Rapids, MI: Zondervan Academic, 2019), ch. 1.

over all things, even those supposedly abstract things like forms or abstract objects that the Platonists thought existed independently of any divinity.

This brings us to the matter of the generation of creatures. The divine conceptualist thinks that contingent creatures like humans, horses, or hydrogen atoms are created on the basis of eternal ideas or exemplars God has of these things in his mind. Perhaps creatures are the exemplification or instantiation of the ideas of them that God has in his mind. Then, it would seem that there is God, the divine ideas, and the instantiation of at least some of those ideas in the created world. (This is a matter to which we shall return later in the chapter.)

Clearly, such a view is a way of holding onto some of the intuitive power of Platonism, without commitment to the infinite horde of abstract entities that Platonism must presume. We might say that for Christians attracted to the vision of Plato's theory of Forms, but worried about how this appears to infringe divine ultimacy, aseity, and absolute sovereignty (by granting necessary eternal existence to the abstract horde independent of God), divine conceptualism is a natural view to adopt.

Augustinian divine ideas

Discussion of the doctrine of divine ideas has a long history in Christian theology, especially in that strand of Christian theology indebted to Neoplatonic thought. For instance, in his *Confessions*, Augustine writes that God does not create heaven and earth by means of some preexisting matter, or via some other medium. Rather, "you spoke and they were made. In your Word alone you created them." God creates the world ex nihilo in a single divine eternal act so that "there was no material thing before heaven and earth; or, if there was, you must certainly have created it by an utterance outside time, so that you could use it as the mouthpiece for your decree, uttered in time, that heaven and earth should be made." Indeed, as he goes on to say, "In your Word all is uttered at one and the same time, yet eternally."[11] In the course of his discussion of these

---

[11]Saint Augustine, *Confessions*, trans. R. S. Pine-Coffin (Harmondsworth: Penguin Classics, 1961), Bk XII. 5–7, 257–59.

arcane matters of God's relation to time and creation, Augustine distinguishes between the earth, which is all visible created things, and the heavens above, as well as what he calls the "Heaven of Heavens," which is not a visible part of creation, but something more like a kind of divine archetype existing in God's mind. He writes, "Clearly the Heaven of Heavens, which you created 'in the Beginning', that is, before the days began, *is some kind of intellectual creature*. Although it is in no way co-eternal with you, the Trinity, nevertheless it partakes in your eternity."[12] Commenting on this passage, the British philosopher Paul Helm writes, "The heaven in question appears to be a sort of ideal, divinely-willed archetype which exists in complete form in the mind of God."[13] He goes on to suggest that one plausible interpretation of Augustine's rather obscure notion of the Heaven of Heavens is as a kind of template or conceptual framework—something like a blueprint for the created order—on the basis of which God brings about the creation. This sounds rather like the notion that in creating all things, God brings into existence everything apart from himself. These things are all divine ideas, so that God creates on the basis of an existing eternal blueprint, something like a collection of ideas or forms, that exists eternally in his mind.

Later Christian thinkers took up and developed the sort of picture of God's relation to the things he creates bequeathed to them by Augustine. One particularly interesting example of this can be found in the work of Anselm of Canterbury. Although his view is rather different from Augustine, it is clearly indebted to an Augustinian picture of God's act of creation, and God's relation to the ideas he has of the things he creates. This can be seen in his account of creation in the *Monologion*. In that work Anselm reasons that the Word of God, which he personifies as does Augustine, is the exemplar of all that is created. By that he means, the Word of God somehow "contains" within himself in a single exemplar the myriad ideas of all that is created. To put it in more familiar language, it is as if the Word of God "contains" within himself like a single zipped computer file, all the data necessary to generate every single possible creature. In eternally generating the Word, God also

---

[12]Augustine, *Confessions* Bk. XII. 9, 286. Emphasis added.
[13]Helm, *Faith and Understanding*, 95–96.

in the very same act eternally generates the exemplar of all possible divine ideas as well, which are somehow "contained" in the Word. Anselm's argument is subtle and complex, and developed over a number of chapters in *Monologion*. One of the central arguments can be found in chapter 33. There he reasons as follows:

1. "When the supreme understands himself by uttering himself, he begets a likeness of himself that is consubstantial with himself: that is his Word."

2. This Word "is not a likeness of creation but rather its paradigmatic essence."

3. Hence, "he does not utter creation by a word of creation."

4. "Now, if he utters nothing other than himself and creation, he cannot utter anything except by his own Word or by a word of creation."

5. He utters nothing by a word of creation.

6. So "whatever he utters, he utters by his own Word."

7. "Therefore, he utters both himself and whatever he made by one and the same Word."[14]

This, as Sandra Visser and Thomas Williams note,[15] transforms rather than transmits the doctrine of divine ideas. For on this view the exemplar from which God creates the world is identical with the Word, the second divine hypostasis, and is somehow eternally generated in the self-same act in which the Word is eternally generated.

This is rather intoxicating. My concern here is not Anselm-exegesis, however, fascinating though that is. My point is rather to indicate that Edwards's treatment of divine ideas, as the central component of his divine conceptualism, stands in a tradition going back at least to Augustine. It is important to see that this tradition is not monolithic, however. There is not one single view on the

---

[14]From Anselm *Monologion* in *Anselm*, 43–44; cf. *S. Anselmi cantuariensis archiepiscopi opera omnia, volumen primum*, ed. Francis. S. Schmitt (Edinburgh: Thomas Nelson & Sons, 1946 [1938]), 52–53.
[15]See Sandra Visser and Thomas Williams, *Anselm*. Great Medieval Thinkers (Oxford: Oxford University Press, 2009), 124.

topic shared between all the heirs of Augustine's position, as the example of Anselm (hardly a liminal or eccentric figure) suggests. Consequently, it should not be that surprising to find that Edwards's views share important affinities with others in the Augustinian tradition on this topic while exhibiting important differences from what has gone before him. This is in fact what we find to be the case upon examination.

Edwards on divine ideas

Well then, what is Edwards's position on the divine ideas? Does he stand in the Augustinian tradition as we might expect him to do, given his broadly Neoplatonist philosophical inclinations? Does his idealism have a bearing on this? Let us turn to consider the shape of Edwards's view.

Readers who are historians may well cringe at what comes next. For, rather than going carefully through various works by Edwards, plotting the development of his ideas, and any changes that may have occurred during his career, I want to present a kind of synthetic view that represents what I take to be the position of the mature Edwardsian theology.[16] The historians will cringe because such a synthetic Edwards is, of course, a kind of theological golem formed out of the clay of various aspects of Edwards's thought, but given life by the one who fashions it. In other words, the worry is that such an account is not actually the position of the Jonathan of history, but more like the creation of an Edwards of faith—an Edwards more in the likeness of the theologian writing about Edwards's thought than the historical Jonathan.

This is a right and proper concern. Distortions to our understanding of a historic figure can creep in much more easily when attempting such synthesis. What is more, synthetic pictures tend to smooth out apparent inconsistencies and tensions rather than preserving them. However, there is surely a place for presenting

---

[16]I have given a more sustained treatment of the development of Edwards's thought, and of the relative importance of different aspects of his larger and diffuse corpus, in the Introduction to Crisp, *Jonathan Edwards on God and Creation.*

an Edwardsian picture, even if, like Augustine, Edwards's corpus is
sprawling, diffuse, and replete with tensions and difficulties.

There are several aspects of Edwards's thought that bear on
the question of divine ideas. These are his idealism, especially
his immaterialism; his conception of the divine nature, especially
his views on ultimacy, aseity, and divine sovereignty; and his
understanding of the radical dependence of the creation on God,
especially his views on continuous creation and occasionalism. Let
us consider each of these in turn.

Idealism and immaterialism

First, his idealism and immaterialism. Perhaps the clearest
expression of Edwards's idealism is found in his early unpublished
philosophical works. Here, for example, is a familiar passage from
his notebook "The Mind," that indicates how Edwards thought of
the world as ideal:

> And indeed, the secret lies here: that which truly is the substance
> of all bodies is the infinitely exact and precise and perfectly
> stable idea in God's mind, together with his stable will that the
> same shall gradually be communicated to us, and to other minds,
> according to certain fixed and exact established methods and
> laws: or in somewhat different language, the infinitely exact
> and precise divine idea, together with an answerable, perfectly
> exact, precise and stable will with respect to correspondent
> communications to created minds, and effects on their minds.[17]

Note that here, as elsewhere in his work right through to his
latest treatises, Edwards thinks of the created order as a *divine
communication*. This has led some recent commentators to suggest
that Edwards does not really have a principled distinction between
minds and their ideas. For instance, Marc Cortez writes, "Thus,
at the most basic level, there is no ontological difference between
the mind and the body. Neither are proper substances, and both
are equally and continuously the result of God's creative activity.

---

[17]WJE6, 344.

Indeed, Edwards spends far more time discussing the relationship between God and creation because he seems to view this as the only fundamental ontological distinction."[18] The reason for this, according to Cortez, is that Edwards developed an event-based metaphysics, which, when coupled with his expressed idealism, does not provide him with a principled distinction between minds and ideas. For both are basically events communicated directly by God.

But I am not sure that is quite right.[19] For one thing, Edwards does distinguish minds and their ideas in this way: he thinks of minds as ephemeral created divine communications, yet as in some qualified sense, created substances. But he thinks that ideas are not. Thus, for Edwards, a table is not a substance as such because it is not a mind. Rather, it is a collocated collection of percepts communicated moment-by-moment by God. Creaturely minds, which are also communicated from God, are nevertheless in some qualified sense property-bearers and centers of will and intellect. Still, Cortez is right when he says that creatures and ideas are neither proper substances for Edwards. Creatures are only substances in an attenuated sense.[20] So one might press Edwards in such a way that his event ontology leads to the collapse of a real distinction between created minds and their ideas, in which case there is only the divine substance, and the ephemeral and

---

[18]Marc Cortez, "The Human Person as Communicative Event: Jonathan Edwards on the Mind/Body Relationship," in *The Ashgate Companion to Theological Anthropology*, eds. Joshua R. Farris and Charles Taliaferro (Aldershot: Ashgate, 2015), 139–50; 145.

[19]As I previously indicated in Oliver D. Crisp, "Jonathan Edwards on God's Relation to Creation," *Jonathan Edwards Studies* 8.1 (2018): 2–16; 11, n. 31.

[20]Compare Edwards in "['Notes on Knowledge and Existence']," which includes the following: "How God is as it were the only substance, or rather, the perfection and steadfastness of his knowledge, wisdom, power and will." WJE6, 398. Similarly in his notes on atoms he writes, "the substance of bodies at last becomes either nothing, or nothing but the Deity acting in that particular manner in those parts of space where he thinks fit. So that, speaking most strictly, there is no proper substance but God himself (we speak at present with respect to bodies only). How truly, then, is he said to be *ens entium*." WJE6, 215.

momentary communications from God in creaturely minds and their ideas.[21]

Edwards clearly does think that ideas are mind-dependent in a radical way. Thus, on the question of immaterialism he says this:

> Since all material existence is only idea, this question may be asked: In what sense may those things be said to exist which are supposed, and yet are in no actual idea of any created minds? I answer, they exist only in uncreated idea. But how do they exist otherwise than they did from all eternity, for they always were in uncreated idea and divine appointment? I answer, they did exist from all eternity in uncreated idea, as did everything else and as they do at present, but not in created idea.[22]

This is important for our purposes because of its clear statement of a doctrine of divine ideas as (some of the) uncreated and immutable content of the divine mind. There is an exemplar of all created things in God's mind, and even if a thing is not instantiated as an idea in a created mind, it nevertheless exists as an uncreated idea as it has "from all eternity." There are also several places in his "Miscellanies" notebooks where Edwards refers to the divine ideas in connection with his doctrine of God. For instance, in entry 955, entitled "TRADITIONS OF THE TRINITY AMONGST THE ANCIENT HEATHEN," he writes,

> Plato, speaking of the divine ideas, speaks of one that is 'self-subsisting, or independent, eternal, indivisible, immaterial, and simple'; but 'besides this original simple Idea, Plato brings in *Timaeus* discoursing of another kind of Idea, which he calls παραδειγμα and εικονα, an exemplar or image, which he makes to be the first fetus, impress, or offspring of the former, original Idea. . . . So likewise it is a lively delineation or representation of the future work or thing to be made, whence the divine agent, having got his exemplar, proceeds to the production of his work answerable thereto.'[23]

---

[21]This is not a new problem. Charles Hodge made similar claims about Edwards in the nineteenth century, accusing him of pantheism for this very reason. I discuss this in Oliver D. Crisp, *Jonathan Edwards Among the Theologians* (Grand Rapids, MI: Eerdmans, 2015), ch. 9.

[22]"The Mind," (40), in WJE6, 356.

[23]WJE20, 228. Cf. WJE23, 683 for a similar citation.

This sounds very much in the tradition of Augustine's notion of divine exemplars on the basis of which God creates the world, which Edwards presumes to find in embryonic form in Plato's *Timaeus*.[24]

So it appears that Edwards thinks there are the following: minds of two sorts, one uncreated and many that are created; and the ideas had by these minds. Yet it is not as if there are these two sorts of minds existing in space both of which have ideas communicated to them like an adult and a group of schoolchildren all sitting in a movie theater watching the same film together. Rather, God is the one true and stable substance who communicates created minds and their ideas on the basis of uncreated exemplars that exist eternally in the divine mind. So in a very real sense, for Edwards, all of creation, including creaturely minds, is a divine communication. It is as if we creatures are characters in the movie which is being projected onto the screen from God outwards. Ideas are perceived by creaturely minds where they are communicated by God rather like the various props and scenery in the film are perceived and used by the characters in the movie. But there are also ideas that are not communicated or perhaps not perceived by creaturely minds. These exist as divine ideas, along with the exemplars of all creaturely ideas. It would seem that the doctrine of divine ideas is doing quite a bit of work here in explaining the relationship between God, created minds, and the ideas that God has aboriginally, as it were, and which he communicates in creation.[25]

Ultimacy, aseity, and sovereignty

This brings us to the matters of divine ultimacy, aseity, and sovereignty.[26] Edwards's whole metaphysical vision could be

---

[24]Edwards was enamored of the idea that an ancient theology, the *prisca theologica*, had been transmitted to ancient thinkers like Plato, so that it is not surprising to him to find echoes of what he takes to be Christian theological tropes about the Deity in the work of apparently pagan philosophers. For discussion of this matter in Edwards's thought see Gerald R. McDermott, *Jonathan Edwards Confronts the Gods: Christian Theology, Enlightenment Religion, and Non-Christian Faiths* (New York: Oxford University Press, 2000), especially ch. 5.

[25]Edwards's idealism is also discussed in Oliver D. Crisp and Kyle C. Strobel, *Jonathan Edwards: An Introduction to His Thought* (Grand Rapids, MI: Eerdmans, 2018).

[26]I have tackled this matter elsewhere at greater length. See Crisp, *Jonathan Edwards on God and Creation*.

construed as a statement of divine ultimacy. There are several
reasons for this. First, as we have seen, he thinks that the whole
of creation is an immaterial divine communication. He denies
Platonism. He clearly endorses a doctrine of divine ideas, albeit an
idealist version thereof. And, as we shall see in the next section, he
endorses a strong doctrine of continuous creation coupled with a
version of occasionalism. What is more, for Edwards, only God is
a true substance. All creaturely existence is fleeting and ephemeral.
Thus Edwards in his early philosophical notebook "Of Atoms"
writes:

> The substance of bodies at last becomes either nothing, or nothing
> but the Deity acting in that particular manner in those parts of
> space where he thinks fit. So that, speaking most strictly, there
> is no proper substance but God himself (we speak at present
> with respect to bodies only). How truly, then, is he said to be *ens
> entium*.[27]

And in another of his early notebooks, called "Things to Be
Considered an[d] Written Fully About" (long series), entry 44,
Edwards says: "Bodies have no substance of their own, so neither is
solidity, strictly speaking, a property belonging to a body. . . . And if
solidity is not so, neither are the other properties of a body. . . . So that
there is neither real substance nor property belonging to bodies; but
all that is real, it is immediately the first being." And, "God is . . . *ens
entium*; or if there was nothing else in the world but bodies, the
only real being. . . . The nearer in nature beings are to God, so much
the more properly they are beings, and more substantial; and that
spirits are much more properly beings, and more substantial, than
bodies."[28] This seems to imply an unequivocal divine ultimacy.

On divine aseity, Edwards says this in his dissertation *God's End
in Creation*:

> That no notion of God's last end in the creation of the world
> is agreeable to reason which would truly imply or infer any

---

[27]WJE6, 215.
[28]WJE6, 238. Edwards says substantially the same thing in "[Notes on Knowledge
and Existence]" in WJE6, 398.

indigence, insufficiency and mutability in God; or any dependence of the Creator on the creature, for any part of his perfection or happiness. Because it is evident, by both Scripture and reason, that God is infinitely, eternally, unchangeably, and independently glorious and happy: that he stands in no need of, cannot be profited by, or receive anything from the creature; or be truly hurt, or be the subject of any sufferings or impair of his glory and felicity from any other being. . . . [Moreover] if the creature receives its all from God entirely and perfectly, how is it possible that it should have anything to add to God, to make him in any respect more than he was before, and so the Creator become dependent on the creature?[29]

God is absolutely independent of his creatures, according to Edwards. We can add nothing to the divine life or divine happiness because God is infinitely happy and delighted with himself. This must be the case, for Edwards, because God is a perfect being. It would, in fact, be a vice in a perfect being not to delight in himself in this way. Similarly, it would be a failing that would ensure he was not a perfect being if his happiness was, in fact, dependent in some sense on things outside himself, such as the lives of his creatures. So God is psychologically independent of his creatures (he does not need us to be happy). But he is also metaphysically independent of his creatures (his existence does not depend on us).[30]

It is well known that Edwards thought of God as an absolute sovereign, in keeping with his Reformed proclivities. If anything, his particular idealist vision of the relation between God as the only true substance, and everything that is created, including creaturely substances, only underlines this fact. For if we, and everything else in creation, when taken together, constitute an immediate divine communication like the movie projected onto the silver screen in the theater, then God really is sovereign over all in a very important

---

[29]WJE8, 421. He says similar things elsewhere. Even when making passing remarks about the divine nature he speaks in terms of God being "self-sufficient, immutable and independent." WJE8, 47.

[30]Edwards does think the creation is a necessary product of God's creativity. But that does not mean he needs *us in particular*. It just means that it is necessary that a creative God create.

ontological sense. For we and the ideas we possess are all literally divinely transmitted. It is difficult to see how one could have a more exalted understanding of divine sovereignty than that.

Edwards also clearly thinks that God's nature is strongly immutable, as befits a perfect being.[31] Thus, in discussing God's knowledge in his treatise *Freedom of the Will*, Edwards writes,

> If all created beings were taken away, all possibility of any mutation or succession of one thing to another would appear to be also removed. Abstract succession in eternity is scarce to be understood. What is it that succeeds? One minute to another perhaps, *velut unda supervenit undam* ["Follows upon" or "succeeds the other."] But when we imagine this, we fancy that the minutes are things separately existing. This is the common notion; and yet it is a manifest prejudice. Time is nothing but the existence of created successive beings, and eternity the necessary existence of the Deity. Therefore, if this necessary Being hath no change or succession in his nature, his existence must of course be unsuccessive.[32]

Later in the same passage, he concludes, "If once we allow an all-perfect Mind, which hath an eternal immutable and infinite comprehension of all things, always (and allow it we must) the distinction of past and future vanishes with respect to such a mind."[33] God's life is timeless, and as a consequence strongly immutable. And, as Edwards observes, such a "necessary Being hath no change or succession in his nature"—ideas included.

So, in short, the whole of creation is radically dependent on God as the one divinely communicating minds and their ideas from himself. God creates and communicates these things on the basis of exemplars within himself, so to speak—that is, on the basis of divine ideas. These divine ideas are uncreated, necessary, and immutable for they exist "in" the divine mind, as it were, and are dependent on God continuing to think them.

---

[31]As was mentioned previously. See above n. 6.
[32]WJE1, 386.
[33]WJE1, 386.

Continuous creation and occasionalism

This segues rather nicely into what Edwards says about continuous creation and occasionalism. On the matter of continuous creation, Edwards says this in his treatise on *Original Sin*: "It will certainly follow from these things [i.e., from the consideration of whether God is constantly upholding the world by his power], that God's *preserving* created things in being is perfectly equivalent to a *continued creation*, or to his creating those things out of nothing at *each moment* of their existence." He goes on, "It will follow from what has been observed, that God's upholding created substance, or causing its existence in each successive moment, is altogether equivalent to an *immediate production out of nothing*, at each moment."[34]

As I have pointed out elsewhere, Edwards thinks of this world not so much as something that he creates like a massive Lego diorama with many moving parts, and then sustains in being interacting and "playing" with what he has formed. Rather, God is continuously creating. The "world" as we call it is not a single persisting thing like the Lego model. It is a collection of momentary communications from God. Returning to our analogy of the movie, on this way of thinking the world as we know it is really a series of momentary stages created by God, just as old celluloid movies were composed of a series of photographic stills run together in the projection room, the images being transmitted onto the silver screen so that it appears to the naked eye as if the same action is taking place across time. That is very like how Edwards thinks God continuously creates the world. And given that he also thinks the world is an immaterial divine communication, it is even more like the ephemeral, flickering images we see at the theater. For Edwards we literally are the communication of divine ideas.

A final aspect to Edwards's vision of the way God creates underscores this last point. In various places Edwards indicates his endorsement of the doctrine of occasionalism. This is the view that God is the only real cause of what takes place in the world.

---

[34] WJE3, 401, 402. Emphasis in the original. For further discussion of this, see Crisp, *Jonathan Edwards on God and Creation*, and Crisp, *Jonathan Edwards among the Theologians*, ch. 4.

Creatures are not properly causal agents, but only the occasions of God's action. Thus, when I scratch my nose it is God that causes me to scratch my nose. I am the occasion of God causing that action to take place. There is some debate in Edwardsian scholarship about the extent of Edwards's occasionalism, and some interesting recent work has been done in this area.[35] For my own part, I think that Edwards is a consistent occasionalist, and that he believes God directly and singularly causes all that takes place. Some commentators have suggested that Edwards believed creaturely minds are real causes, so that Edwards holds to a kind of qualified occasionalism.[36] But it seems to me that there is good evidence that Edwards thinks that even creaturely minds are not capable of acting in this way. For Edwards's God is an absolute sovereign. In addition, the world, including the created minds it contains, does not exist for long enough to cause anything to obtain. As Edwards says in "Miscellanies" entry 267 on God's existence:

> The mere exertion of a new thought is a certain proof of a God. For certainly there is something that immediately produces and upholds that thought; here is a new thing, and there is a necessity of a cause. It is not antecedent thoughts, for they are vanished and gone; they are past, and what is past is not. But if we say 'tis the substance of the soul (if we mean that there is some substance besides that thought, that brings that thought forth), if it be God, I acknowledge; but if there be meant something else that has no properties, it seems to me absurd. If the removal of

---

[35] See for example Crisp, *Jonathan Edwards on God and Creation*; Crisp, "Jonathan Edwards on God's Relation to Creation"; S. Mark Hamilton, *A Treatise on Jonathan Edwards, Continuous Creation and Christology* (N.P.: Jonathan Edwards Society Press, 2017); Stephen H. Daniel, "Edwards' Occasionalism," in *Jonathan Edward as Contemporary: Essays in Honor of Sang Hyun Lee*, ed. Don Schweitzer (New York: Peter Lang, 2010), 1–14; and Steven Nadler, *Occasionalism: Causation among the Cartesians* (Oxford: Oxford University Press, 2011). For a recent attempt to take up an Edwardsian way of thinking about this matter in a constructive direction, see Walter J. Schultz and Lisanne D'Andrea-Winslow, "Divine Compositionalism as Occasionalism," in *Occasionalism Revisited: New Essays from the Islamic and Western Philosophical Tradition*, ed. Nazif Muhtaroglu (N.P.: Kalam Research and Media, 2017), 219–36.

[36] This is Hamilton's view drawing on Nadler's research in early modern accounts of occasionalism more broadly speaking.

all properties, such as extendedness, solidity, thought, etc. leaves nothing, it seems to me that no substance is anything but them; for if there be anything besides, there might remain something when these are removed.

In other words, all created beings are momentary, fleeting things that vanish. Consequently, it is in the nature of things that nothing at one moment can cause what occurs at the next because it doesn't exist for long enough to do so. God alone exists for more than a moment, continuously creating the world, which is an immediate divine communication or "projection" from Godself outwards, so to speak. So God causes all that takes place.

Let us take stock. Having briefly surveyed some of the most salient aspects of Edwards's thought, we can draw some provisional conclusions. These are that he clearly does hold to a doctrine of divine ideas, which is a core component of divine conceptualism; and that Edwards does think that divine ideas are uncaused, necessary, dependent, immutable, and concrete things. Thus, he appears to be a divine conceptualist. If anything, he is a kind of hypertrophied divine conceptualist because he thinks that there are only minds and their ideas, with God being the only true substance and the creation being the direct and continuous communication of divine ideas, which are based on eternal, uncaused, necessary exemplars within God's mind. This is divine conceptualism of a very strong sort indeed.

An aporia

Naturally, there are a number of problems with divine conceptualism generally as a philosophical view, as well as with Edwards's particular version of it. However, rather than tackling these in detail here, I will close with what I take to be an important conceptual aporia with Edwards's account. It is this: Does Edwards's idealism remove an important motivation for thinking that the created order is *real*? Edwards could say that God is the only real substance, and that all creatures are merely divine thoughts that do not exist "outside" God, so to speak. Why go to the bother of speaking of the created order as a divine communication—for *to whom* is the created order communicated? This is hardly a new objection. Many years ago, the doyen of a previous generation of Edwards scholars, Thomas Schafer, in reflecting on just this issue in Edwards's philosophy, wrote, "One way of reading this metaphysical analysis is that, instead of guaranteeing the value and immortality of intelligent creatures, Edwards' doctrine of perception leaves God finally alone, talking to a reflection of himself in a mirror. That, of course, was not Edwards' intention, but it is curious that he never seems to have been aware of this potential objection."[37] The worry is that Edwards's idealism, together with his doctrine of divine ideas, has provided a powerful argument for a kind of *theological antirealism*. In this case, the antirealism in question pertains to the created order, which, as Schafer points out, seems to be so transient and fleeting in Edwards's thinking that it is not clear it has any real existence. It would indeed be ironic if, in an effort to safeguard divine aseity and sovereignty, Edwards's idealist twist on an Augustinian theme about divine ideas provided an argument for theological antirealism about the existence of creation.

---

[37]WJE13, 49.

4

Girardeau on Human Free Will

In recent Reformed theology the topic of human free will has once more moved to the top of the agenda.[1] There has been some discussion in the literature about the shape of the Reformed understanding of human free will, and how this doctrine developed in post-Reformation theology.[2] One focus of attention has been on the work of the New England theologian, Jonathan Edwards, and whether there is a step-change in the way Reformed theologians thought about the matter as a consequence of Edwards's contribution

---

[1]The recent debate has been stimulated in large measure by Willem Van Asselt, J. Martin Bac, and Roelf T. te Velde, eds. *Reformed Thought on Freedom: The Concept of Free Choice in Early Modern Reformed Theology* (Grand Rapids, MI: Baker Academic, 2010). Richard A. Muller has also weighed in with his book *Divine Will and Human Choice: Freedom, Contingency, and Necessity in Early Modern Reformed Thought* (Grand Rapids, MI: Baker Academic, 2017).

[2]See, for example, Paul Helm, "Synchronic Contingency in Reformed Scholasticism: A Note of Caution," *Nederlands Theologisch Tijdschrift* 57 (2003): 207–22 and reply by A. J. Beck and Antonie Vos "Conceptual Patterns Related to Reformed Scholasticism," *Nederlands Theologisch Tijdschrift* 57 (2003): 223–33 and a rejoinder from Helm, "Synchronic Contingency Again," *Nederlands Theologisch Tijdschrift* 57 (2003): 234–38; Paul Helm, "Reformed Thought on Freedom: Some Further Thoughts," *Journal of Reformed Theology* 4.3 (2010): 185–207; and Paul Helm, "'Structural Indifference' and Compatibilism in Reformed Orthodoxy," *Journal of Reformed Theology* 5.2 (2011): 184–205. See also the commentary by Dolf te Velde, *The Doctrine of God in Reformed Orthodox, Karl Barth, and The Utrecht School: A Study in Method and Content* (Leiden: E. J. Briill, 2013), 670–76.

to the debate.[3] His treatise *Freedom of the Will* contains one of the most important discussions of the topic in the history of Christian thought. In it he argued for a version of theological compatibilism (roughly, the thesis that God's determining all that takes place in creation is compatible with human free will), and against all forms of theological freethinking and what he called "Arminianism."[4] Edwards's influence on anglophone Reformed theology in this matter in the century after his death was considerable and can still be felt today.[5] Nevertheless, his views did not sway every nineteenth-century Reformed theologian.

In this chapter we shall consider the work of the American Southern Presbyterian John L. Girardeau on the matter of human free will. Although he is not widely known in theological circles today, Girardeau was an important representative of an American Presbyterian alternative to the legacy of Edwards, whose work in this area is interesting for several reasons.[6] The first of these is that, unlike Edwards, he was a confessionally Reformed theologian who

---

[3]In this regard see Paul Helm, "Jonathan Edwards and the Parting of the Ways?" *Jonathan Edwards Studies* 4.1 (2014): 21–41; and Richard A. Muller, "Jonathan Edwards and The Absence of Free Choice: A Parting of The Ways in the Reformed Tradition," *Jonathan Edwards Studies* 1.1 (2011): 3–22. For a helpful account of the influence of Edwards's arguments about free will, see Allen C. Guelzo, *Edwards on the Will: A Century of American Theological Debate* (Eugene, OR: Wipf and Stock, 2008 [1989]).

[4]In this connection, "Arminianism" was a cypher for those opponents of his that were theologically libertarian. They believed that moral responsibility and free will are incompatible with divine determinism, and denied that God determines all that takes place in the world. For discussion see the editorial introduction to WJE1. However, in what follows, I use the term "libertarian" and "libertarian choice" in a more restricted sense to mean a choice that is free in the sense of originating with the agent, not God. A libertarian choice is one for which the agent is morally responsible at least in part because he has an alternative possibility he could actualize at the moment of choice. This is a term of art that is consistent with what John L. Girardeau says (and with much of Edwards' concern about 'uncaused' free actions), although he doesn't use the term itself.

[5]See, Guelzo, *Edwards on the Will*, and the influence of Edwards upon the "young, restless, and Reformed" movement in the United States, reported on in Colin Hanson, *Young, Restless, Reformed: A Journalist's Journey with the New Calvinists* (Wheaton, IL: Crossway, 2008).

[6]An account of Girardeau's life can be found in George A. Blackburn, ed. *Life Work of John L. Girardeau, D.D. LL.D.* (Columbia, SC: The State Company, 1916).

sought to defend the dogmatic deposit of Reformed theology in his doctrinal and controversial works. He was not a theological innovator, but more of an expositor and transmitter of Southern Presbyterianism.[7] Second, and in light of this, he sets out a vision of the relationship between human free will and divine ordination very different from that of Edwards. Indeed, as we shall see, he claims that his own more moderate position is commensurate with confessional Reformed theology, and with the views of Calvin, in a way that is not true of Edwards's views. Whether or not one finds Girardeau's account convincing, he does provide an alternative to the unrelenting determinism that characterizes the Edwardsian brand of Calvinism. His is a more moderate theological account of human freedom, one which demonstrates that Edwardsianism is not the only available option within the bounds of Reformed theology. One of the most controversial aspects of Girardeau's position, one that resonates with some of the recent historiographical work on the development of Reformed views of human freedom, is that Girardeau countenances the possibility of something like libertarian choices in certain mundane decisions for human beings—which would have been anathema to Edwards.

We shall proceed as follows. The first section of the chapter offers a critical exposition of Girardeau's account of human free will in conversation with Edwards, who was his principal interlocutor. Here I shall proceed according to what Scott MacDonald has recently called the method of *philosophical clarification*. On this way of thinking, the theological task is conceived as a matter of articulating and developing the views found in (say) the work of a particular historic thinker, "probing their internal coherence, joint consistency, and systematic connections, and exploring their relations to other theological and non-theological doctrines."[8] Such a method might be thought commensurate with a species of retrieval theology, which seeks to engage with thinkers of the past in

---

[7]This is not to suggest Edwards set out to be a theological innovator. He thought his views were consistent with Reformed orthodoxy. However, the conclusions he reached did, in fact, have implications that were innovative in a number of respects. I have discussed this in more detail in Oliver D. Crisp, "On the Orthodoxy of Jonathan Edwards," *Scottish Journal of Theology* 67.3 (2014): 304–22.

[8]Scott MacDonald, "What Is Philosophical Theology?" in *Arguing about Religion*, ed. Kevin Timpe (New York: Routledge, 2009), 24–25.

a collegial manner in order to furnish theologians with arguments and concepts that may be of use in contemporary constructive theology. In a second, shorter section of the chapter, I segue from philosophical and theological clarification to retrieval by offering some reflections on the place of Girardeau's arguments in the wider debate about the shape of Reformed views about human free will and contemporary Christian philosophy.

John Girardeau on free will

Girardeau's main work on the subject is his monograph *The Will in Its Theological Relations*, although he makes mention of the same issues in passing in other writings, and we shall have cause to touch upon those as well. At the very beginning of this study, Girardeau stakes out his own position against that of Edwards. He writes that the publication of Edwards's treatise on free will "was attended by singular and apparently contradictory results."[9] On the one hand, there were those who were skeptical about the theological determinism for which it argued, and who used it to fortify their own opposition. On the other hand, there were Reformed theologians in both the United States and Great Britain that "absorbed from it a powerful influence," leading to the incorporation of "its principle of Determinism as a component element of its structure" in order to "vindicate the sovereignty of God and the dependence of man."[10] Warming to his theme, Girardeau goes on to say that "it is still a matter of serious inquiry whether there were not tendencies in his system legitimately leading to an unhappy result, and whether the Calvinistic theology has not injured itself and crippled its rightful influence, to the extent of their appropriation." In short, he is persuaded that the Edwardsian doctrine of theological determinism

---

[9]John L. Girardeau, *The Will in Its Theological Relations* (Columbia, SC: W. J. Duffie; New York: The Baker & Taylor Co., 1891), 18. Hereinafter, cited as TWTR, followed by page reference.
[10]Ibid., 18–19. This claim is also argued for by Richard Muller in "Jonathan Edwards and the Absence of Free Choice."

presents a theory that is "radically defective," so that he "cannot but regret its continued prevalence, even in a modified form."[11]

According to Girardeau, the will is "precisely the power through which the freedom of the man expresses itself. To affirm or deny the freedom of the will is the same thing as to affirm or deny the freedom of the man."[12] He thinks of the will as one of several intellectual faculties that human persons normally possess.[13] This means that willing a particular thing is really a matter of the person engaging the relevant faculty. Hence his reference to the will as the power through which the freedom of the person is expressed. The "elements of the Will," as he puts it, include: (1) the power to choose in virtue of possessing causal efficiency; (2) choice, which obtains in a given act of will in keeping with the other human mental powers; (3) conation, or a "chosen nisus to action"; (4) the determinate choice of action, whether for one thing or another. He has no separate account of volition, which is assimilated to willing.[14] It should be clear from this that Girardeau, in common with many other nineteenth-century Southern Presbyterian theologians, owes a debt to the Scottish commonsense tradition.[15]

By contrast, Edwards, following John Locke, regards talk of the will as a *façon de parler*. By his lights it is the human person that wills; there is no distinct faculty or mental power by means of which the person chooses one thing or another. Thus, at the beginning of his treatise *Freedom of the Will*, he writes, "I observe, that the will

---

[11]TWTR, 19.

[12]John L. Girardeau, *Calvinism and Evangelical Arminianism* (Harrisburg, PA: Sprinkle Publications, 1984 [1890]), 397. Hereinafter, cited as CEA, followed by page reference.

[13]He distributes human mental powers into (1) intellect or understanding, (2) the feelings, including desire, (3) the will, and (4) conscience or the moral faculty. TWTR, 39.

[14]TWTR, 43–44.

[15]Girardeau was schooled in the commonsense tradition of nineteenth-century American Presbyterianism, which shaped the way he approached Edwards's more speculative philosophical theology. This can be seen in Girardeau's *Philosophical Questions*, ed. George A. Blackburn (Richmond, VA: The Presbyterian Committee of Publication, 1900), which, his editor writes in the Introduction, may be read as having as their "main purpose to advance the Scottish school of philosophy. They are not intended to be a system in themselves." Indeed "This book is really a supplement to Hamilton's *Metaphysics*, in connection with which it ought to be studied" (7).

(without any metaphysical refining) is plainly, that by which the mind chooses anything. The faculty of the will is that faculty or power or principle of mind by which it is capable of choosing: an act of the will is the same as an act of choosing or choice."[16] The fundamental matter for Edwards is choice. The will might properly be said to be "that by which the soul chooses"[17] on his way of thinking.

Girardeau distinguishes between what he calls *freedom of deliberate election* and *freedom of spontaneity*. "The freedom of deliberate election," he says, "is the freedom of the will to determine itself to either of two opposing alternatives—the power of otherwise determining, and is inconsistent with causal necessity."[18] Such freedom has built into it a principle of alternate possibilities, that is, the notion that at the moment of choice an agent has an alternative that he could choose, other than the one he does choose. By contrast, freedom of spontaneity is "the freedom of the will to do as the man pleases, to pursue his inclinations in any one, definite direction, and is consistent with necessity."[19] This view does not include a principle of alternate possibilities. Doing as one pleases is, after all, consistent with having no alternative.[20] Consequently, it is commensurate with determinism. Girardeau resists the assimilation of freedom of deliberate election to the liberty of indifference, because he denies that choices are made in a state of moral equilibrium, or without

---

[16]Edwards, *Freedom of The Will*, *WJE1*, 137.

[17]Ibid.

[18]TWTR, 401. Compare what he says elsewhere in CEA: the freedom of deliberate action is "between opposing alternatives, of going in either of two directions, the freedom, as it is sometimes denominated, of otherwise determining." (397–98). Quite clearly this includes a notion of alternate possibilities at the moment of choice.

[19]TWTR, 401. In CEA he speaks of freedom of spontaneity as "the freedom of a fixed and determined spontaneity" (398), and complains (in the same passage) that freedom should really only be applied to the freedom of deliberate action, whereas freedom of spontaneity should be denominated merely "spontaneity." The implication is that only the former properly applies to freedom of the will. This is not an insignificant concession coming from a Reformed theologian.

[20]Suppose Jones has a microchip in his brain that stimulates certain nodes each evening effectively "programming" him to eat rhubarb and custard for dessert. Nevertheless, he reports that he loves rhubarb and custard and wants to have it every evening for dessert. According to Girardeau's way of thinking, Jones enjoys liberty of spontaneity, because he is doing "as he pleases" even though he has no alternative.

motive. The freedom of deliberate election has to do with the freedom of the soul to choose between alternatives, nothing more. It is freedom from causal necessity in making a free and morally responsible choice.[21]

Girardeau avers that the aboriginal human pair had the freedom of deliberate election in the state of innocence. This, he maintains, the church has universally believed.[22] Unsurprisingly, therefore, it is a view reflected in the Confessions of the Reformed churches. He remarks somewhat dryly, "The Calvinistic Confessions, which surely ought to be accepted as exponents of Calvinism, affirm that man before the Fall was possessed of the freedom of deliberate election between the alternatives of sin and holiness; and they also teach that God decreed to permit—they do not asset that he efficiently decreed—the first sin."[23] We shall return to this matter of the theological authority for his position presently.

After the Fall, a distinction can be made between what he calls natural and spiritual ability. (Here he offers a "correction" to the Edwardsian distinction between moral and natural ability set forth in *Freedom of the Will*.) According to postlapsarian natural ability, fallen humans continue to enjoy freedom of spontaneity. "It is obvious that the liberty of spontaneity was not lost" at the Fall. However, the liberty of contrary choice involved in the freedom of deliberate election was lost as a consequence of the Fall.[24] "In man's fallen and unregenerate state, the will has no self-determining power in relation to the contrasts between holiness and sin. The free decision for sin destroyed man's holy spontaneity, and originated, in its place, a sinful spontaneity."[25] That is, the "freedom of deliberate election between the alternatives of sinfulness and holiness no

---

[21]TWTR, 45–46; 132–33.
[22]CEA, 398.
[23]CEA, 400. Compare TWTR, where he makes this case at greater length, and the *Westminster Confession*, ch. 9. I–II on free will: "God has endued the will of man with that natural liberty, that is neither forced, nor, by any absolute necessity of nature, determined good, or evil. Man, in his state of innocency, had freedom, and power to will and to do that which was good and well pleasing to God; but yet, mutably, so that he might fall from it."
[24]TWTR, 134–35.
[25]TWTR, 403.

longer exists." The will, "in the spiritual sphere, is under *bondage to sin*."[26]

It is unfortunate that Girardeau muddies the waters by speaking of a holy spontaneity and a sinful spontaneity, given his initial distinction between freedom of deliberate election and freedom of spontaneity. What he seems to mean is this: Prior to the Fall the moral orientation of human beings was such that if they acted in accordance with their natural moral orientation, they would remain sinless. Nevertheless, it was possible for such prelapsarian humans to act against this moral orientation, by sinning. As he puts it earlier in his study, unfallen Adam was "able to stand, liable to fall."[27] This is because the original human pair enjoyed both a sinless moral orientation and the ability to act contrary to that moral orientation (Girardeau's freedom of deliberate election). "The specific difference of such a case is the possession of the power of contrary choice—of the will's power to determine itself *in utramque partem*."[28]

However, after the Fall, this was no longer the case. The moral orientation of humanity had been altered by the primal sin of the first human pair so that post-Fall, human beings act on the basis of a vitiated moral condition, "under bondage to sin," as Girardeau puts it. Fallen human beings still have a natural ability to make all sorts of choices consistent with the freedom of deliberate election. What they lack is such freedom with respect to choices pertaining to their salvation; it is the ability to make appropriate *spiritual choices* that has been impaired in fallen human beings. This is a consequence of vitiating the moral orientation with which the first human pair were endowed. He writes, "But while, in the spiritual sphere, the will of man in his unregenerate condition has by its own fatal act lost all self-determining power, it still possesses that

---

[26]Ibid. Emphasis original. He goes on to say, "But while, in the spiritual sphere, the will of man in his unregenerate condition has by its own fatal act lost all self-determining power, it still possesses that power in the merely natural sphere" (404). Interestingly, this is substantially the view of Martin Luther in his *Bondage of the Will*, trans. J. I. Packer and O. R. Johnston (London: James Clarke, 1957, reissued by Baker Academic in 2012), although Girardeau does not discuss Luther's position in any detail.

[27]TWTR, 83.

[28]TWTR, 83.

power in the merely natural sphere."[29] The following are indicative examples Girardeau offers by way of illustrating this important point. Fallen human beings may exercise freedom of deliberate election in choosing between choices tainted by sin; in external and civil matters (i.e., matters that are mundane, having no personal soteriological significance); with respect to "moral culture" (e.g., refraining from blaspheming); and with respect to certain sorts of actions that "tend towards religion," without making a permanent soteriological change in the sinner, for example, the arguments of natural theology, acknowledging the divine origin of scripture, attending to the ordinances of the church, and so forth.[30] It is even in the power of a fallen human being to "call on God to show him the truth, to reveal to him his real spiritual condition, to extend to him mercy, and to deliver him from bondage to sin."[31]

At times Girardeau's views are not as pellucid as one might like. For instance, in *Calvinism and Evangelical Arminianism*, he says that fallen humanity "sins freely, in the sense of spontaneity; in sinning he is urged by no compulsory force exerted by a divine influence either upon him or through him, but follows the bent of his own inclination—in a word, does as he pleases. He is not, however, free to be holy or to do holy acts."[32] So when speaking of free will with respect to fallen human beings in an unregenerate condition, Girardeau thinks that what is in view is merely "the freedom which is implied by a fixed spontaneity in accordance with which he pleases to sin. Only in that sense is he a free agent, as to spiritual things."[33] On a cursory reading, this suggests that he thinks of human freedom in two distinct phases: a first, unfallen phase in which human beings have libertarian freedom including a principle of alternate possibilities; and a second, fallen phase in which human beings are enslaved to sin and incapable of acting in a holy manner. The unwary reader might be led by such reasoning into thinking that Girardeau is affirming something like theological compatibilism with respect to the free and morally responsible

---

[29]TWTR, 404.
[30]TWTR, 404–5.
[31]TWTR, 405.
[32]CEA, 401.
[33]CEA, 401.

decisions of fallen humanity. I am free to continue to make sinful choices but, given that I am bound to sin (being in bondage to sin through original sin), this is consistent with my being determined to act as I do because of my sinful disposition.

However, a more careful analysis of what he says in this passage of *Calvinism and Evangelical Arminianism* shows that what he says here, though less precisely articulated than in *The Will in Its Theological Relations*, is nevertheless consistent with it. For what he means by the "fixed spontaneity" in accordance with which fallen human beings are pleased to sin is precisely a moral orientation that places a life of uninterrupted holiness beyond the reach of fallen human beings. But a fallen human being may still make all sorts of mundane choices that include alternate possibilities while possessing a sinful disposition. Girardeau's account stipulates that fallen human beings do act from a certain moral constraint (what he calls, somewhat unhelpfully, a "moral necessity") as a consequence of the change of moral orientation consequent upon the primal sin of the first human pair. If we are now in bondage to sin, then there is a factor that restricts the choices available to me, because I am no longer free to act sinlessly, from an untainted moral orientation.

To see this, consider the case of the fictional, high-functioning consulting detective and cocaine addict, Sherlock Holmes. He makes all sorts of mundane choices on a daily basis, for many of which he is morally responsible, including the solving of many crimes that baffle conventional law enforcement agencies. Of course, his moral purview is tainted, as it were, by the fact that he is a substance abuser. This puts certain sorts of moral choices beyond his reach. For instance, he is unable to decide forthwith and without any deleterious effects to give up his addiction to the coca leaf. Even if he decides he must rid himself of his physical and psychological dependence on the drug, he cannot do so immediately or at least he cannot rid himself of his addiction immediately, even if he resolves to begin the long process of rehabilitation forthwith. Nevertheless, we would not think that the mundane choices he makes that are within the ambit of what he is capable of doing immediately are less free because he has an addiction to cocaine. His decision to have tea rather than coffee or to solve a crime rather than sitting and sawing at his violin in his rooms on Baker Street is evidence of this.

From this I conclude that Holmes's addiction is not immaterial to the question of the scope of his free choices. Yet, in any given circumstance, if he has "significant moral freedom" (i.e., freedom of deliberate election) to choose one thing or another, he has free will in the relevant sense. Girardeau's contribution, then, is to show that libertarian free choices are consistent with a sinful moral orientation (i.e., bondage to sin), although being in bondage to sin means that a certain class of action, those pertaining to the salvation of the individual concerned, are no longer within reach.[34] His is what we might call a chastened libertarianism, or a libertarianism within certain (theological) constraints. This is not all that strange, given that all careful accounts of libertarianism are versions of the doctrine that allow for certain constraints, including things like addiction and moral failure. However, his view would appear to require a hybrid view of moral responsibility. This is somewhat unorthodox, since it makes room for a class of actions for which an agent is morally responsible *though determined by God*. This will be regarded as an important cost—or alternatively a benefit—of his view, depending on whether one is sympathetic to his basic strategy.

As was mentioned earlier, Girardeau also maintains that his view, which includes a species of libertarianism for at least some mundane choices, is consistent with the Reformed faith, unlike Edwardsianism. This strand of his reasoning has several parts. Negatively, this includes his attack upon the moral consequences of Edwardsian determinism. Positively, it involves an appeal to various authorities as theological precedent for (something very like) his own view. The latter includes detailed exposition of the view of John Calvin as well as reference to the Reformed confessions. Let us take each aspect in turn, beginning with the negative.

According to Girardeau, the question between himself and Edwards is this: "Did [God], in the instance of the first sin, causally determine the will of Adam?" To which he responds,

> There are but two alternatives: either God efficiently determined Adam's will in the first sin, or he did not. There is no middle ground. If he did, the sin was unavoidable, and could not have

---

[34]Recall that "libertarian," or "libertarian choice," is used here to mean a choice that is free in the sense of originating with the agent, not God. Moreover, a libertarian choice is one for which the agent is morally responsible at least in part because he has an alternative possibility he could actualize at the moment of choice.

been attended with just liability to punishment. If he did not, as no other being could have efficiently determined Adam's agency, the sin was avoidable. If avoidable, there was no causal necessity which operated to its production. For, if a thing is causally necessary, it is not avoidable. To suppose that it is, is self-contradictory.[35]

Matters are made worse when we turn to the covenant of works, that covenant between God and human beings that many historic Reformed theologians thought provided the moral framework for the original human pair in the primordial garden. Suppose that there was such a covenant, the condition of which was continued obedience to the divine moral law (symbolized in the command not to eat of the tree of the knowledge of good and evil). Failure to meet this condition would lead to punishment. Some Reformed theologians (including Girardeau) also speculated that had Adam (and Eve) remained upright, resisting the temptation of the serpent, they would have been "confirmed" in their moral orientation, so that they would be incapable of sinning thereafter, like the saints in heaven and the elect angels. This is usually referred to as Adam's "probation." However, if the Edwardsians are right, then the covenant of works becomes a "mockery." For "it stipulated conditions which could not be fulfilled, and tendered rewards that could not be secured."[36] That is, if Adam's sin was somehow divinely determined, then holding out the prospect of moral "confirmation" upon fulfillment of the period of probation that was usually thought to be part and parcel of the covenant of works was insincere. Adam (and Eve) could not fulfill the condition of the covenant because they were determined to act as they did by God "efficiently" bringing about that end.

We turn to Girardeau's positive appeal to theological authority in order to trump Edwardsianism on the will. Two in particular draw our attention. These are his appeal to Calvin and his appeal to the Confessions. Calvin's views do not have the status of the confessions as subordinate standards within particular Reformed communions. Nevertheless, his standing as arguably the preeminent

---

[35]TWTR, 84.
[36]TWTR, 85.

Reformed theologian of the sixteenth century meant that appealing to his views over Edwards and arguing that Edwards's position deviated substantially from that of Calvin was a way of calling into question the bona fides of Edwardsianism as a species of Reformed theology. As Sean Lucas writes, "By claiming Calvin's authority for his position, Girardeau was doing more than simply balancing one cultural authority with another. He was signaling Edwards' deviation from the Reformed tradition through doctrinal novelty."[37]

He cites from a range of Calvin's works, including commentaries, the *Bondage and Liberation of the Will*, and the *Institutes of the Christian Religion*. For instance, in *Institutes* 2.3.10, Calvin seems to endorse the idea that in his unfallen state Adam had freedom including a principle of alternate possibilities: "We admit that man's condition while he still remained upright was such that he could incline to either side."[38] Earlier in *Institutes* 2.15.8, Calvin says something similar,

> In this integrity man by free will had the power, if he so willed, to attain eternal life. . . . Therefore Adam could have stood if he wished, seeing that he fell solely by his own will. But it was because his will was capable of being bent to one side or the other, and was not given to the constancy to persevere, that he fell so easily. Yet his choice of good and evil was free, and not that alone, but the highest rectitude was in his mind and will, and all the organic parts were rightly composed to obedience, until in destroying himself he corrupted his own blessings.[39]

According to Girardeau these passages (and others like them, for he cites Calvin copiously and at length) "clearly prove that Calvin affirmed for man in innocence the power of contrary choice— the liberty of inclining to either of opposing alternatives. He

---

[37]Sean Michael Lucas, "'He Cuts up Edwardsism by the Roots': Robert Lewis Dabney and the Edwardsian Legacy in the Nineteenth-Century South," in D. G. Hart, Sean Michael Lucas, and Stephen J. Nichols, eds., *The Legacy of Jonathan Edwards: American Religion and the Evangelical Tradition* (Grand Rapids, MI: Baker Academic, 2003), 206.

[38]From John Calvin, *Institutes* 2.3.10. Compare TWTR, 151 where Girardeau cites the same passage.

[39]*Inst.* 1. 15. 8, p. 195. Compare TWTR, 150–51.

plainly . . . declares that, although Adam freely elected to sin, he might have done otherwise—he might have elected to stand."[40] Support for Girardeau's account of Calvin's views can be found in the recent philosophical-theological literature on the subject. Paul Helm, who regards Calvin as, in a qualified sense, a theological compatibilist, *not* a theological libertarian, nevertheless addresses himself to the question of whether Calvin thinks humans have free will in the following way: "Yes, he [Calvin] believes that we have on appropriate occasions the power to choose between alternatives in a way which is uncoerced. No, he does not believe that we naturally possess free will in the sense of the power to choose what is good, at present; but yes, unfallen man had free will in that sense."[41] But if that is right, then this actually provides support for Girardeau's claim to be defending a Calvinian doctrine of the will—at least in terms of how Girardeau understands the exercise of free will in the primal sin of Adam and Eve. What is more, if this is right, then Edwards's position is different from that of Calvin in an important respect, for Calvin allows for something very like libertarian free will in at least the paradigm case of primal sin. Edwards emphatically denies this.

What of the Reformed confessions? These Girardeau treats more quickly. He provides gobbets from the *Gallic* and *Scots Confessions*, the *Canons of the Synod of Dordt*, the *Second Helvetic Confession*, the *Formula Consensus Helvetica*, and the *Westminster Confession*. In each case there appears to be good prima facie evidence for the view that these confessions, like Calvin, allow for libertarianism with respect to the primal sin of our first human parents. Representative citations from the *Westminster Confession* may serve to indicate

---

[40]TWTR, 152, cf. 158.

[41]Paul Helm, *John Calvin's Ideas* (Oxford: Oxford University Press, 2005), 161. In the sequel to this volume, Helm writes, "Calvin's doctrine of the bondage of the will . . . has no necessary connection with the issue of the metaphysics of agency." He goes on to say, "When Calvin and Luther deny free will, therefore, they chiefly have in mind not the metaphysical issues being discussed in this chapter, but a spiritual disposition stemming from sin which is, logically speaking, neutral on the question of determinism and libertarianism." Paul Helm, *Calvin at the Centre* (Oxford: Oxford University Press, 2010), 228–29. A very useful resource on the wider debate about Calvin and the Reformation understanding of the bondage of the will can be found in Kivin S. K. Choy "Calvin's Defense and Reformulation of Luther's Early Reformation Doctrine of the Bondage of the Will," PhD dissertation, Calvin Theological Seminary, January 2010.

the sort of evidence he has in mind. What is more, given that this is the historic subordinate standard for the Southern Presbyterians among whom Girardeau was numbered, and given that Edwards had acceded to the *Confession* in order to become president of The College of New Jersey (now Princeton), this symbol is particularly pertinent. The fourth chapter on creation says the following:

> II. After God had made all other creatures, He created man, male and female, with reasonable and immortal souls, endued with knowledge, righteousness, and true holiness, after His own image; having the law of God written in their hearts, and power to fulfil it; and yet under a possibility of transgressing, being left to the liberty of their own will, which was subject unto change.

In the ninth chapter on free will, we read this:

> II. Man, in his state of innocency, had freedom, and power to will and to do that which was good and well pleasing to God; but yet, mutably, so that he might fall from it.

> III. Man, by his fall into a state of sin, has wholly lost all ability of will to any spiritual good accompanying salvation: so as, a natural man, being altogether averse from that good, and dead in sin, is not able, by his own strength, to convert himself, or to prepare himself thereunto.

Finally, in the nineteenth chapter on the Law of God we are told:

> I. God gave to Adam a law, as a covenant of works, by which He bound him and all his posterity, to personal, entire, exact, and perpetual obedience, promised life upon the fulfilling, and threatened death upon the breach of it, and endued him with power and ability to keep it.

Manifestly, these statements are consistent with Girardeau's claims about prelapsarian human free will. (I do not say they *require* it.) What is more, and importantly for our purposes, these statements do *not* appear to be consistent with the Edwardsian position, which is not a little odd, given the fact that Edwards is on record as saying that he had no qualms about signing the Confession.[42] "To sum up the matter," says Girardeau, "the standards say that Adam in innocence had the power of otherwise determining than he did; the Determinist says that he had not that power. The two doctrines are contradictory and mutually exclusive."[43]

Let us take stock: it would appear that Girardeau's account of human freedom is able to accommodate what we might call a species of "chastened" or circumscribed libertarianism. His account of freedom of deliberate election allows that choices falling under this description originate with the agent; are actions for which the human agent is morally responsible; are actions that are not determined by any agents or factors other than the human agent in question; are actions that are not determined by any factors "internal" to the psychology or character of the agent him or herself at the moment of choice; are actions that the agent could refrain from; and are actions which include some alternative state of affairs that the agent could have chosen to bring about at the moment of choice, but did not. He remains staunchly Reformed in his account of the bondage of the human will after the Fall. And he is able to show that his views are consistent with some of the major Reformed symbols as well as with the views of Calvin—which, he thinks, Edwards is incapable of doing.

The promise of libertarian Calvinism

Girardeau thinks that his position is not merely theologically permissible within the bounds of Reformed confessionalism, but *just is* the historic Reformed position on the subject. It is Edwards and his followers that have departed from the moderation of historic Reformed thought by insisting upon an unrelieved divine determinism. I have not defended this stronger claim, though it is

---

[42]In a letter to his Scottish correspondent, John Erskine in 1750, Edwards writes, "You are pleased, dear Sir, very kindly to ask me whether I could sign the Westminster Confession of Faith, and submit to the Presbyterian form of church government. . . . As to my subscribing to the substance of the Westminster Confession, there would be no difficulty." *WJE16*, 355.

[43]TWTR, 177.

an interesting one that (I think) merits closer scrutiny. Much turns on whether sense can be made of the notion of libertarian free choices. For Edwards, there is no real alternative to determinism. "Arminianism," which in his mind is synonymous with what today we would call theological libertarianism, is not so much a poor relative to determinism as it is a thesis that is utterly incoherent. However, for those who, like Girardeau, are willing to allow that libertarian choices are both coherent and obtain in at least some instances, matters are not quite so stark. If Girardeau is right about the pedigree of his own views, then not only is his position consistent with Reformed confessionalism in a way that Edwards's is not; his view is also *Calvinian* in a way that Edwardsianism is not. One of the lessons that Girardeau strives hard to teach his readers is that it is the defender of what we might call a circumscribed libertarian Calvinism that has the stronger claim to being the natural heir to the mantle of Calvin and the Reformed confessions. Even if we are not willing to grant him that much, a more modest result would still be significant. Like another nineteenth-century luminary, the Scottish Reformed theologian and father of the Free Church of Scotland, William Cunningham, we might allow that confessional Reformed theology is metaphysically underdetermined.[44] In that case, one might opt for either the Edwardsian or the Girardean position and still be within the bounds of Reformed orthodoxy.

But there is more. If Girardeau is right, then it looks like the Reformed may avail themselves of the apologetic benefits that go along with theological libertarianism. In the recent philosophical literature, the vast majority of work done toward solving various problems of evil depend on versions of libertarianism. Not all of these will be commensurate with libertarian Calvinism of the sort envisaged by Girardeau. But no doubt some will. Many Reformed thinkers committed to compatibilist accounts of human freedom have found themselves on the back foot, trying to offer alternatives

---

[44]Cunningham writes, "1st, there is nothing in the Calvinistic system of theology, or in the Westminster Confession of Faith, which precludes men from holding the doctrine of philosophical necessity. 2d, There is nothing in the Calvinistic system of theology, or in the Westminster Confession, which requires men to hold the doctrine of philosophical necessity." William Cunningham, "The Doctrine of Philosophical Necessity," in *The Reformation and the Theology of the Reformers* (Edinburgh: T&T Clark, 1862), 483. His essay repays careful scrutiny.

to the preponderation of work being done among Christian philosophers in this area. If Reformed thought turns out to be consistent with a circumscribed libertarianism, then it may be that at least some of these wider philosophical resources are available to them in their bid to provide defenses and theodicies consistent with their particular theological commitments.

5

Zwingli on Original Sin

Thanks in part to his early and violent death on October 11, 1531, Huldrych Zwingli's theology was eclipsed by the more fulsome work of other leaders in the Reformed branch of the Magisterial Reformation, particularly by the work of Calvin in Geneva and Heinrich Bullinger, Zwingli's successor in Zürich. Even today, when historical theologians have begun to recover the work of a number of early Reformed divines such as Peter Martyr Vermigli and Girolamo Zanchi, there is still considerably less systematic-theological engagement with the work of Zwingli.[1] Much of his literary remains are scattered and occasional pieces, the writings of a man on the move—both physically (as a church leader trying to establish a Reforming movement in Zürich) and intellectually. Even his most systematic work, *Commentary on True and False Religion*, which was published six years before his death, was composed in a hurry (he labored "for three and a half months night and day" in its composition) and in response to pressure from French and Italian scholars to publish his own account of the Christian faith.[2]

---

[1]There is the journal *Zwingliana* (which mainly showcases historical work connected to Zwingli and his legacy), and several notable works, including English-language studies (see note below) of a previous generation of scholarship. However, Zwingli is seldom the subject of theological *ressourcement* today in a way analogous to Luther, Calvin, or Cranmer.

[2]See Huldrych Zwingli, *Commentary on True and False Religion*, ed. Samuel Macauley Jackson and Clarence Nevin Heller (Durham, NC: Labyrinth Press, 1981 [1929]), 54 and 51, respectively, as well as the editorial introduction to the volume. A new critical edition of the works of Zwingli is being produced at present, but older editions are easily available. See, for example, *Huldreich Zwinglis Sämtliche Werke, Corpus Reformatorum*, Vols. 88–101, ed. Emil Egli and Georg Finsler et al. (Berlin:

Consequently, those interested in his views must sift through his *corpus* in order to reconstruct his position on a given topic.[3] The results are often tantalizing, leaving one wondering what might have been if he had lived longer, and some of his late work—preeminently, his sermon *On the Providence of God*—show evidence of a more careful and sustained engagement with both the tradition and substantive issues in theology and philosophy.[4]

One of these tantalizing strands of his thinking has to do with his doctrine of original sin. Zwingli's version of the doctrine represents a rather different view from that often reported as the "classic" Reformed position.[5] He did not side with many in the later Reformed tradition (particularly, in the period of Reformed

---

Schwetschke und Sohn, 1905–1963). I shall refer to this edition in what follows as *Sämtliche Werke*, followed by volume number, and page number, for example, *Sämtliche Werke* 1, 105.

[3]The best treatment of his theology in English is W. P. Stephens, *The Theology of Huldrych Zwingli* (Oxford: Oxford University Press, 1986). See also W. P. Stephens, *Zwingli: An Introduction to His Thought* (Oxford: Oxford University Press, 1992). There is a useful bibliography at the end of this work. A more recent summary of Stephens's work with a useful final section on interpretations of Zwingli can be found in his essay, "The Theology of Zwingli," in David Bagchi and David C. Steinmetz, eds. *The Cambridge Companion to Reformation Theology* (Cambridge: Cambridge University Press, 2004), ch. 8. Gottfried W. Locher's collection of essays, *Zwingli's Thought: New Perspectives* (Leiden: E. J. Brill, 1981) also repays careful study. George R. Potter's intellectual biography, *Zwingli* (Cambridge: Cambridge University Press, 1977) is still the most thorough account of his life in English. Two recent short essays on his life and work are Bruce Gordon, "Huldrych Zwingli," *Expository Times* 126.4 (January, 2015): 156–68, and Peter Opitz, "Ulrich Zwingli," *Religion Compass* 2.6 (2008): 949–60. Opitz has also produced a short recent biography in German, entitled *Ulrich Zwingli: Prophet, Ketzer, Pionier des Protestantismus* (Zürich: TVZ-Verlag, 2015). Perhaps the most substantial recent engagement with Zwingli's theology is Daniel Bolliger's treatment of Zwingli's reception of Scotism in *Infiniti contemplatio: Grundzüge der Scotus und Scotismusrezeption im Werk Huldrych Zwinglis* (Leiden: E. J. Brill, 2003).

[4]An English translation of *On the Providence of God* can be found in Samuel Macauley Jackson, ed. *On Providence and Other Essays* (Durham, NC: The Labyrinth Press, 1983 [1922]), 128–234. (Compare *Sämtliche Werke* 6.3, 64–230.)

[5]There have been Reformed theologians since the nineteenth century that have offered revisionist accounts of original sin, such as Friedrich Schleiermacher, Reinhold Niebuhr, and Karl Barth. However, whatever the merits of their views, they don't represent the classic Reformed position that can be found in confessional documents such as the Westminster Confession, and in the work of the Reformed Orthodox thinkers of the post-Reformation.

Orthodoxy) who thought that Adam's primal sin and his guilt is transmitted to his progeny so that they are guilty for the sin of their forebear.[6] Rather, he thought that no fallen human being is culpable merely for possessing original sin; we are only culpable for the actual sins we commit. This has led to a history of interpreting Zwingli's doctrine of original sin as a sort of aberration in Reformed thought that was only a step away from unorthodoxy. Typical of such commentators is the nineteenth-century historian of Christian symbols, Philip Schaff. He is of the view that, in the matters of original sin and guilt,

> Zwingli departed from the Augustinian and Catholic system, and prepared the way for Arminian and Socinian opinions. He was far from denying the terrible curse of the fall and the fact of original sin; but he regarded original sin as a calamity, a disease, a natural defect, which involves no personal guilt, and is not punishable until it reveals itself in actual transgression.[7]

In contrast to the sort of view espoused by Schaff and others, the present work offers a fresh look at Zwingli's doctrine of sin, as a creative and potentially fruitful resource for constructive theology today. I shall offer an outline of some of the central dogmatic features of Zwingli's account of original sin. Then, I shall attempt to use these materials to provide a moderate Reformed account of original sin, which modifies Zwingli's position in several respects in order to overcome certain shortcomings with his view. The result is shaped by central structures in Zwingli's doctrine, though it is not the same as Zwingli's doctrine: it is a piece of retrieval theology in a Zwinglian key.[8] We shall see that this moderate

---

[6]See, for example, references that can be found in Heinrich Heppe, *Reformed Dogmatics*, ed. Ernst Bizer, trans. G. T. Thomson (London: Collins, 1950), ch. xv.

[7]Schaff, *History of the Christian Church, Vol. VIII: Modern Christianity. The Swiss Reformation*. Third Edition (Grand Rapids, MI: Eerdmans, 1976 [1910]), §29. Compare Locher who says that since Luther there has been a recurring claim in textbook literature that Zwingli denied the doctrine of original sin because for him it meant only a defect. *Zwingli's Thought: New Perspectives*, 53.

[8]As I intimated in a previous chapter, following David Buschart and Kent Eilers, I construe "retrieval theology" as "a *mode or style of theological discernment* that looks back in order to move forward. It is a particular way of carrying out theological

Reformed doctrine of original sin is able to avoid certain significant theological objections that have dogged other Reformed varieties of original sin that include the notion of original guilt. It may also be a doctrine that has promise as a resource for ecumenical theology where rapprochement with other Christian traditions on this vital matter would be greatly helped by the omission of original guilt as a constituent of original sin.

A reading of Zwingli's doctrine of original sin (and baptism)

Zwingli's doctrine of original sin is closely wrapped up with his sacramental theology, particularly his doctrine of baptism. The two notions developed side-by-side in his controversial writings. In setting forth his positive doctrine for baptism, he rejected the two traditional justifications: that the rite removed original guilt and that it regenerated the infant, who is given an embryonic faith that develops as the child grows, provided she or he eschews mortal sin. Instead, he avers that baptism is a "covenant sign which indicates that all those who receive it are willing to amend their lives and to follow Christ. In short," he says, "it is an initiation to new life" like the monastic cowl is a sign of initiation into a religious order.[9] This position, outlined in his 1525 work *On Baptism*, led him to offer a more sustained account of original sin in his *Declaration Regarding*

---

work . . . in which resources from the past are found particularly advantageous for the present situation. Such resources might include doctrines, practices, a metaphysic or ontology, traditions or the Great Tradition more generally. Theologies of retrieval seek to recover these resources in order to seize an opportunity to respond to a particular challenge." W. David Buschart and Kent D. Eilers, *Theology as Retrieval: Recovering the Past, Renewing the Church* (DownersGrove, IL: IVP Academic, 2015), 12–13, emphasis original. Here the challenge is a doctrinal one, posed by the particular difficulties that original sin raises for contemporary theology in a post-Darwinian world.

[9]Huldrych Zwingli, "*On Baptism*" [1525], in Geoffrey Bromiley, ed. and trans. *Zwingli and Bullinger*. Library of Christian Classics, Vol. 24 (Philadelphia, PA: Westminster Press, 1953), 141. The German text can be found in *Sämtliche Werke* 4, 206–337.

Original Sin Addressed to Urbanus Rhegius[10] published a year later. The conclusions he reached in that work were distilled, along with his settled views on baptism, in his summary statement of his theological views called *Account of the Faith to Charles V,* which went to press in 1530, the year before his death. These are not the only places where Zwingli deals with baptism and original sin, but they may be said to fairly represent his developed views, alongside what he says in his *Commentary on True and False Religion.* As we shall see, in order to give a sense of the dogmatic shape of this thought, these need to be set into the context of his understanding of the divine decrees and God's purposes in creation, given in his sermon *On the Providence of God.* It is to these works that we now turn, in order to get a sense of the development of his mature thought on these related topics.[11]

Zwingli's most sustained treatment of original sin is to be found in the *Declaration* of 1526, though his *Commentary* of 1525 also displays the hallmarks of his view.[12] He divides the *Declaration*

---

[10]All references to the English translation of the *Declaration* are to the version published in *On Providence and Other Essays,* cited parenthetically in the body of the text as *D,* followed by page reference, for example (D, 45). The Latin text can be found in *Sämtliche Werke* 5, 369–396.

[11]Zwingli's views changed in significant respects in his controversy with the Anabaptists. However, our concern is with his mature position. I take it an uncontroversial hermeneutical principle is that for the purposes of establishing a person's views on a particular topic one should normally privilege settled or mature views over earlier, more immature views. Zwingli was intellectually restless and is a good example of an early Protestant whose views changed as he came to a more evangelical position. Hence, I think that it is appropriate to privilege his later, settled views on a topic if one is interested in probing "Zwingli's distinctive view" on that topic. W. P. Stephens charts some of the important changes in Zwingli's position on the sacraments in "Zwingli's Sacramental Views," in *Prophet, Pastor, Protestant: The Work of Huldrych Zwingli after Five Hundred Years,* eds. E. J. Furcha and H. Wayne Pipkin (Allison Park, PA: Pickwick Publications, 1984), 155–70. David Steinmetz offers a helpful comparison between Zwingli's developing views in dialogue with Balthasar Hubmaier, and Calvin, with particular reference to the interpretation of Acts 19 in "Calvin and the Baptism of John," *Calvin in Context* (New York: Oxford University Press, 1995), ch. 11. Ulrich Gäbler also has a useful account in *Huldrych Zwingli: Leben und Werk* (Zürich: Theologischer Verlag, 2004 [1983]), ch. VIII.

[12]The *Commentary* (hereinafter, cited parenthetically in the body of the text as *C,* followed by page reference) deals with sin principally under the topics of "Man" and "Sin" (75–86, and 138–52 in the English translation edited by Samuel Macauley Jackson; compare *Sämtliche Werke* 3, 628–912). Characteristic motifs in his account

between two questions that offer a framework for his development of the doctrine, in conversation with the biblical and ecclesiastical traditions as well. The first question concerns the nature of sin and original sin. The second question has to do with the effects of original sin, and in particular, whether possession of original sin condemns all those who have it to perdition. We shall examine both questions in turn.

First, there is the matter of the nature of sin and original sin. At the beginning of the *Declaration*, he states the substance of his own position as follows:

> For what could be said more briefly and plainly than that original sin is not sin but disease, and that the children of Christians are not condemned to eternal punishment on account of that disease? On the other hand, what could be said more feebly or more at variance with the canonical Scriptures than that this disaster was relieved by the water of baptism, while through want thereof it was intensified, and that it was not only a disease but even a crime? (D, 3)

Sin, he says, is "a wrong committed through negligence or thoughtlessness" (D, 4). The primal sin of Adam was *philautia*, or (excessive) self-love, on account of which he fell (D, 9; Compare C, 78). Because of this, all subsequent humans (barring Christ) are born with a propensity or disposition to sin, though this disposition is itself not properly a sin so-called, but more of a source of sin (D, 9). Sin is an act; it is for actions of sin that we are culpable, not for possession of the condition of original sin which gives rise to acts of sin (he cites various New Testament passages in support of this claim, especially Rom. 7). (See D, 9.) Similarly, in the *Commentary*, he observes that sin has a twofold sense in the Gospels. First, it has to do with "that disease which we contract from the author

---

of sin make an appearance here, including sin as self-love or *philautia*, sin as disease, and the juxtaposition of this with his rather pessimistic account of human beings post-Fall. But the emphasis is decidedly on the narrative of Genesis 1-3, Romans, and the practical implications of sin, as well as castigating thinkers with a more optimistic estimation of the moral condition of fallen human beings. His humanistic impulses are also on display, for example, in his approving references to Cicero's account of the "inner nature of man" (83–84 in Samuel Jackson's translation).

of our race, in consequence of which we are given over to love of ourselves" (C, 138). Secondly, "sin is . . . that which is contrary to the [moral] Law as through the Law comes knowledge of sin, Rom. 7:7. Any course of action, therefore, which is contrary to the Law is called sin" (C, 139). There is a clear bifurcation here between sin as inherited disease or condition, and sin as immoral action—that is, between original and actual sin, respectively.

On the characterization of sin as a disease, Zwingli says, "I use it as combined with a defect and that a lasting one, as when stammering blindness, or gout is hereditary in a family" (D, 4). "On account of such a thing no one is thought the worse or the more vicious. For things which come from nature cannot be put down as crimes or guilt" (D, 4-5). For this reason, he says, "the original contamination of man is a disease, not a sin, because sin implies guilt, and guilt comes from a transgression or trespass on the part of one who designedly perpetrates a deed" (D, 5). Later in the same passage he says original sin is "a condition and penalty, the disaster and misery of corrupted human nature, not a crime of guilt on the part of those who are born in the condition of sin and death" (D, 6).[13] A particularly vivid example Zwingli uses in the *Declaration* and elsewhere is of a person born into slavery. No doubt a sin was committed when the ancestor of the slave was deprived of his freedom, yet the slave born into this condition as a consequence of this ancestral sin is not himself guilty of the condition in which he finds himself. In a similar fashion, the individual born in sin, born, that is, with the condition of original sin, is not himself guilty of the ancestral sin that gave rise to his unfortunate condition.[14]

---

[13]Cf. his *Account of the Faith to Charles V* (hereinafter, *Account*), where he states "original sin, as it is in the children of Adam, is not properly sin . . . for it is not a misdeed contrary to law. It is, therefore, properly a disease and condition—a disease, because just as he fell through self-love, so do we also; a condition, because just as he became a slave and liable to death, so also are we both slaves and children of wrath . . . and liable to death." *On Providence and Other Essays*, 40. (Compare *Fidei Ratio* in *Sämtliche Werke* 6.2, 796–97.) Similar ideas can be found in his *Commentary* (for example, C, 138–38.) Admittedly, Zwingli's language is sometimes unhelpful (for example, saying that original sin "is a disease, not a sin") but taken in the round, so to speak, it is clear that he is not denying original sin despite some ill-advised ways of expressing himself.

[14]The example of slavery is a common Zwinglian trope. For instance, his *Account* says, "This condition [of original sin] neither Adam himself nor anyone born of

When possession of the condition of original sin is described as itself being sin in scripture, Zwingli thinks such biblical occurrences to be examples of metonymy (D, 5). So, when St. Paul says, "All have sinned" in Rom. 3:23, Zwingli glosses this in the following figurative manner: "All are in the wretched condition of having been deprived of the glory of God through the fault of their first parent" (D, 6).

We come to the second framing question, concerning the consequences of original sin for those that possess it. The ground for the ascription of sin and of condemnation as a consequence of sin is divine election (D, 10-11). For this reason, Zwingli does not link original sin with condemnation apart from circumcision or baptism, the covenant signs of inclusion within the ambit of the church in the Old Testament and New Testament respectively (D, 11). He says, "blessedness and grace are from election, so also is rejection, not from the participation in signs or sacraments" (D, 20). God chooses whom he will, irrespective of such covenant signs, so that an individual is not necessarily damned just because she perishes before receiving the sign of covenant inclusion (D, 12).[15] He gives the example of Seneca (another recurring trope[16]) as one whose life implies election, despite not being part of the covenant community (D, 12). "In a word," he says, "election is unshaken and the law written on the hearts of men, but so that those who are elect and do the works of the law in accordance with the law written on their hearts come to God through Christ alone" (D, 13). Here is an early indication of Zwingli's characteristically inclusive account of the scope of salvation, developed elsewhere in his sermon *On Divine Providence*.

Nevertheless, as far "as the force of sin is concerned, the first man and all who are descended from him are damned by it" (D, 14-15). Yet "a very present remedy saves . . . and it has been applied not too late but just in time"—that is, the work of Christ, imputed to

---

him could remove, for a slave can beget nothing but a slave," 40. Compare the *Commentary*, 80–81.

[15]He is clear that the sacraments are covenant signs on a par with circumcision and the Passover meal in the Old Testament. "The external things, therefore, are symbols of spiritual things, but they are by no means themselves spiritual, nor do they perfect anything spiritual in us, but they are the badges, as it were, of those who are of the spirit" (D, 29).

[16]Zwingli also refers to Seneca in *On the Providence of God*.

us by means of the Holy Spirit (D, 15). Later, in summing up this point, he remarks, "we must admit the great power for damnation that sin would have had, and we must likewise recognize how much its strength has been taken from it by the remedy which God has provided" (D, 18). Who then is damned? Not the children of believers (a point he had already made in *On Baptism*). They are included within the ambit of the covenant community and are elect. As to the children of non-Christians, he says, "we have no right to pronounce rashly about the children even of Gentiles and those who do the works of the law according to the law written in their hearts by the finger of God" (D, 18-19). He even entertains the notion—without finally embracing it—that the work of Christ has a similar scope to the sin of Adam (D, 23), bringing about universal atonement. He does not approve this view, though he is clearly attracted to it, because, he says, some things seem to contradict it, and "because I do not know whether anybody has held it" (D, 23).

Zwingli is also of the view that those born with original sin are in a state of innocence while they are too young to know the law, relying on Rom. 4:15 where St. Paul says, "For where there is no law, there is no transgression" (D, 25). He reasons, "those of tender years who know not the law are just as much without the law as Paul was. Therefore, they do not transgress, and consequently are not damned" (D, 25).

In summarizing his views at the end of the *Declaration*, he says this: that original sin is a defect and disease inflicted on our first parents as a penalty (D, 29); and that it so polluted the progeny of Adam and Eve that all subsequent humans are born with the inclination to sin, which will lead to damnation apart from divine grace in salvation. Though the remnant of original sin, that is, self-love, remains in us, those who are in Christ are saved. He has removed the poison of sin (D, 30).

To this account we may add remarks made in Zwingli's sermon *On the Providence of God* (hereinafter, PG). There he provides a theological backstory to his doctrine of original sin. Not only does God determine all that comes to pass so that, as he says repeatedly in the course of his sermon, God is the only real cause of what obtains in the cosmos and "nothing happens by chance or at random" (PG, 158). "Other things," he remarks, "are not truly causes any more than the representative of a potentate is truly the potentate" (PG, 154). Moreover, "since all things have their being, existence, life, movement and activity from One and in One, that One is the only real cause of all things, and those nearer things which we call causes, are not properly causes, but the agents and instruments with which the eternal mind works, and in which it manifests itself to be enjoyed" (PG, 157-158).[17] In an incautious moment he even goes as far as to wonder whether God "took from Himself this existence which he gave to His works and creatures" so that "everything that is, is in Him and through Him and a part of Him" (PG, 143).[18] This fits with Zwingli's rather strong version of theological voluntarism according to which God is not bound by any law because "what is law to us is not law to God" so that "when He slays according to His will, He is no murderer because He is not under the law, and not being under the law He does not sin" (PG, 169). Indeed, "the Deity is Himself the author of that which to us is unrighteousness, though not in the least so to Him" (PG, 176). So, according to Zwingli, God is the determiner of all things, and nothing stands in the way of his will because only his will is causally efficacious, strictly speaking; no other thing is a real cause of events in creation.

This does raise a significant concern about the integrity of his doctrine of sin. Unlike much later Reformed thought that attempts to avoid imputing the authorship of sin to God by appealing to the divine permissive will in allowing creaturely sin, Zwingli embraces the consequent of his view: God determines all things, sin included. It is just that it is not sin for him. Along with this goes his advocacy

---

[17]Compare this to Calvin's endorsement of secondary causation: "What I have maintained about the diversity of causes must not be forgotten: the proximate cause is one thing, the remote cause another. Then we shall know how great is the distinction between the equitable providence of God and the stormy assaults of men. Certain shameless and illiberal people charge us with calumny by maintaining that God is made the author of sin, if His will is made first cause of all that happens. For what man wickedly perpetrates, incited by ambition or avarice or lust or some other depraved motive, since God does it by his hand with a righteous though perhaps hidden purpose—this cannot be equated with the term sin. Sin in man is made by perfidy, cruelty, pride, intemperance, envy, blind love of self, and kind of depraved lust. Nothing like this is to be found in God." *Concerning the Eternal Predestination of God* trans. J. K. S. Reid (London: James Clarke, 1961), 181.

[18]It is not clear how the reader should take these remarks. It might just be a poorly phrased attempt to reiterate a basically Christian Neoplatonist account of creation, and it is not clear to me that Zwingli means to endorse a significantly stronger view than this without qualification, despite his hypertrophied account of divine determinism and—what appears to be—incipient occasionalism.

of a version of the *felix culpa* or "happy sin" theodicy. On this supralapsarian ordering of the divine decrees, God determines to create a world of creatures that he knows will sin because this brings about a greater good state of affairs that could not otherwise be actualized. He says,

> Since the fall brought disaster, the fall itself was evidently not a blessing, nor can the disaster which followed from it be called a blessing either. But when we consider that which dawned upon man in consequence of the fall, namely, the knowledge of righteousness, which could not be learned except by gazing upon the face of unrighteousness, and this God could not show in His own person, we see that the fall was imposed upon our race for our good, that we might learn by the fall and by erring what could not have been done by earnest striving and endeavor. (PG, 227)

This theological backstory certainly places the doctrine of original sin Zwingli develops in his *Declaration* (and elsewhere, such as his *Commentary*) in a rather different light. For he cannot claim that the primal sin of our first ancestors was an undetermined act that might not have happened. Nor are particular sins acts for which we are responsible because they are freely chosen. Rather, all actions, including all sinful actions, proceed directly from the divine decision to create this particular world, for God's own glorious purposes.

Zwingli appears to entertain a strange concatenation of ideas in this area of his thought. On the one hand, his expressed views on the nature and transmission of original sin place him much closer to the Western Catholic tradition than to his Reformed *confrères*. On the other hand, the theological backstory in which he situates this doctrine is, if anything, more unrelenting in its adherence to a doctrine of absolute divine sovereignty than any of the other Magisterial Reformers, and is perhaps only equaled in Reformed thought by the decidedly philosophical brand of determinism that Jonathan Edwards brought to bear upon these matters in his treatise *Freedom of the Will*, published over two centuries later in 1754.[19]

---

[19]Among the Magisterial Reformers, Luther is sometimes even more incautious in his remarks about human freedom than Zwingli. Nevertheless, it seems to me that *The Bondage of the Will*, trans. J. I. Packer and O. R. Johnson (Cambridge:

Critical issues in Zwingli's doctrine of original sin (and baptism)

There is disagreement among Zwingli scholars about the upshot of his doctrine of original sin. Does it represent a legitimate expression of Reformation theology, or is it a sort of hangover from late medieval religion? Is Zwingli's doctrine a coherent whole, or does the fact that his views are expressed in occasional and polemical works often in a piecemeal fashion, developing over time and in response to various immediate problems, cast doubt on the value and consistency of his works? Is his doctrine of original sin of a piece with his views about theodicy in *On the Providence of God*? Gottfried Locher sums up the findings of twentieth-century work on Zwingli's doctrine like this:

> Today the result of the discussion [about whether Zwingli held to the doctrine of original sin in twentieth century Zwingli scholarship] may be stated as follows: according to Zwingli, *morbus* or "presten" characterizes sin as "sickness unto death," as the necessity which is laid upon every man a) to sin, and b) to die; and noetically it involves c) our complete blindness to revelation. However, man becomes "guilty" only when he actually commits sin. The intention of this purely theoretical distinction between original sin and original guilt is to deprive the sinner of the possibility of representing his actions as the consequence of some fateful destiny, and so passing himself off as innocent, in the last analysis. When understood in this way, Zwingli's formulations do not constitute a weakening but rather a Reformation sharpening of the conception of original sin.[20]

James Clarke & Co., 1957 [1525]) is not as unrelenting in its divine determinism as is Zwingli's *On The Providence of God*. In some respects Zwingli's theological backstory anticipates the exotic metaphysics with which Edwards endows his doctrine in *Freedom of the Will*, for example, in the matter of causation. See Edwards, *Freedom of the Will, The Works of Jonathan Edwards*, Vol. 1, ed. Paul Ramsey (New Haven, CT: Yale University Press, 1957).

[20]Locher, *Zwingli: New Perspectives*, 54.

Rather more hesitant are the views of W. P. Stephens. He writes that Zwingli

> gave a varied response to the question whether original sin damns us. We are sinners as we are descendants of a sinner. However, if we are sinners, we are enemies of God and therefore damned. But Zwingli qualifies this apparently clear statement by reference to Jacob who was beloved of God before he was born, so that original sin could not have damned him. He supports this with reference to the covenant with Abraham's seed in Gen. 17:7, which includes the children of Christian parents. "If therefore, he promises that he will be a god to Abraham's seed, that seed cannot have been damned because of original guilt." Besides these arguments which relate to election Zwingli also developed an argument relating to Christ's work as making good the evil done by Adam, a point made in relation to Rom. 5:19-21. Zwingli applied this to the children of Christian parents, but held back from applying it to the whole human race.[21]

Given these scholarly assessments, it appears that there are several interrelated issues that an adequate account of Zwingli doctrine must address. These are: the question of the internal coherence of his understanding of original sin; the relation of his account of baptism to his doctrine of original sin; and, whether the conclusions he reached on the topic of original sin (and baptism) represent truly Reformation doctrines. Let us consider each of these matters in turn.

To begin with, there is the question of whether Zwingli's position on original sin is incoherent. Perhaps the best way to assess this is to reconstruct the logical form of Zwingli's reasoning in two stages: looking at his doctrine of original sin, and then considering its relation to the wider concerns about baptism and predestination. Here is an outline of the first stage:

1. All human beings after Adam's primal sin (barring Christ) possess original sin.

---

[21]Stephens, *Zwingli: An Introduction*, 74.

2. Original sin is an inherited moral disease, defect, or corruption of nature, a condition with which every fallen human being is created that stems from inordinate, disordered self-love.

3. Fallen humans are not culpable for being created in this morally vitiated condition.

4. Fallen humans are not culpable for Adam's sin either. That is, they do not bear original guilt (i.e., the guilt of Adam's sin being imputed to them along with original sin).

5. This morally vitiated condition inevitably yields actual sin. That is, a person born with this defect will inevitably commit actual sin on at least one occasion provided that person lives long enough to be able to commit such sin.

6. Fallen human beings are culpable for their actual sin and condemned for it, in the absence of atonement.

7. Possession of original sin leads to death and separation from God irrespective of actual sin.

In essence, Zwingli's doctrine involves an inherited moral defect or disease, but not inherited guilt. Culpability is restricted to actual sin. Yet all humans in possession of the moral defect of original sin will inevitably perform at least one act of actual sin provided they live long enough to do so. However, he does not appear to share the view, common in much post-Reformation Reformed theology, that original sin is imputed from Adam to his progeny on the basis of a federal union instituted by God. There is little evidence that Zwingli regarded Adam's role in original sin as somehow representative for the whole race, as the natural head of the race, or as the public person acting on behalf of the rest of humanity—all theological terms important in post-Reformation Reformed views on original sin. Instead, according to Zwingli, Adam's primal sin brings about a moral corruption that is inherited, not imputed. It is a morally vitiated condition that Adam passes on to his progeny, one that is transmitted via natural generation. In this connection, his appeal to slavery as an analog to original sin is instructive. It is clear that Zwingli sees original sin as a sort of inherited blight for which fallen human beings bear no culpability, though it will lead to perdition without the interposition of divine grace.

This means that Zwingli's doctrine avoids some of the besetting problems of later Reformed views of original sin. Two traditional objections to the doctrine are that it is immoral and that it is unjust. Immoral because God ascribes the sin of one guilty individual to an innocent race; and unjust because the mechanism by means of which this is brought about trades upon a legal fiction. God treats Adam's offspring *as if* they had committed Adam's sin and bore the guilt of a perpetrator when neither of these things is in fact the case. This sort of view, which may fairly be called the majority view in much later Reformed thought, is known as federalism or representationalism.[22] There is an alternative, minority report in Reformed theology. This is often called Augustinian realism, because it maintains that there is a real connection between Adam and his offspring such that they together form a metaphysical whole—a doctrine often thought to originate with St. Augustine of Hippo, hence *Augustinian* realism. God transmits the sin and guilt accompanying Adam's primal sin to his progeny because they are either present with him at the moment of sin or are so united to him that his sin transfers to them as a property that is had by numerous parts of one metaphysical whole, namely, fallen humanity. But this too has trouble addressing the moral and legal worries besetting federalism. For it is difficult to find some plausible account of the metaphysics capable of making Adam and all his progeny one entity for the purposes of the transmission of original sin.[23]

Zwingli's view elides the problems these two traditional Reformed positions raise in two ways. First, by excising original guilt from original sin, so that none of Adam's progeny is culpable for his sin. Second, by reframing original sin so that it is not the sin of Adam for which I am punishable, but rather a disease or defect that Adam's action instantiates in every subsequent individuation of human nature. Zwingli's position is similar in some respects to debilitating diseases that develop because a person has two parents

---

[22]For a recent defense of this federalist view, see Donald Macleod, "Original Sin in Reformed Theology," in Hans Madueme and Michael Reeves, eds. *Adam, the Fall, and Original Sin: Theological, Biblical, and Scientific Perspectives* (Grand Rapids, MI: Baker Academic, 2014), 129–46.

[23]A recent attempt to do just this can be found in Oliver D. Crisp, "Original Sin and Atonement," in Thomas P. Flint and Michael C. Rea, eds. *The Oxford Handbook of Philosophical Theology* (Oxford: Oxford University Press, 2009), ch. 19.

with a recessive gene that they pass on to their offspring. Although Zwingli does not suggest that original sin is something like a recessive gene, or that it is physical in nature, what he does say is similar to such medical conditions in that (a) they require two parents with the gene to generate a child with the gene, (b) they are chronic and sometimes debilitating conditions, and (c) the sufferer is not culpable for having inherited the condition.

So in answer to the immorality objection to the transmission of original sin, the Zwinglian can say that it is not immoral for God to allow Adam to freely choose to commit the primal sin.[24] Nor is it immoral that the moral consequences of this act are transferred to all his progeny as a spiritual disease, moral defect, and inherited condition on analogy with the inheritance of serious medical conditions that are recessive in nature. This is just the natural outworking of Adam's primal sin, just as, in a different context, the selling of oneself into slavery is the reason why one's offspring and their offspring, and so on, are all born into sin—it is the natural outworking of an initial, immoral act. For, in a sense, and metaphorically speaking, that is just what Adam has done: he has sold his offspring into a condition of bondage to sin. This means that each of his offspring (barring Christ) is generated with original sin, a condition that will lead to spiritual death if it is not addressed.

What about the injustice objection to the transmission of original sin? Here too, Zwingli's position has distinct advantages. On the federalist/representational view, it seems that it is unjust that I suffer for the sin and guilt of another, one that I never authorized to act on my behalf, and one whose actions I cannot influence or change, because they are wholly in the past. On the Augustinian realist view it may be just that I suffer the sin and guilt of another because I am somehow metaphysically united with that person in a whole where many of the parts share the property of original sin; or, I was somehow present with Adam when he sinned. The problem with this solution is that it is counterintuitive and requires a fairly sophisticated argument in its defense, one that many will find too

---

[24]However, in order to do this the Zwinglian would have to disavow the Zwinglian notion of global divine causation—what seems to be an incipient occasionalism.

exotic to be a plausible solution.[25] Zwingli can say something different from both these views. God justly transmits Adam's sinful condition to me through natural inheritance. (Perhaps, we might think, God does this via some sort of spiritually recessive "gene" that both parents of any fallen person possess—though this would be to go beyond what Zwingli actually says.) He does not transmit Adam's guilt to me, so the condition in which I find myself—that is, being born with the condition of original sin—is not one for which I am culpable though it will lead to my death without the interposition of divine grace just as some inherited conditions lead to death without medical intervention.

Note that Zwingli clearly does endorse original sin. He is not a Pelagian (*pace* Luther), for Pelagians deny the doctrine of inherited sin, opting instead for the view that sin obtains by imitation, not imputation, nor inheritance. Clearly, Zwingli does think sin obtains through inheritance, the inheritance of a vitiated moral condition that leads inevitably to acts of sin. Is he semi-Pelagian? Semi-Pelagians hold to a doctrine of synergism in the matter of salvation. That is, they teach that human beings are able to exercise their free will independent of divine grace in order to cooperate with divine grace in bringing about their own salvation. But as we have seen, Zwingli emphatically denies this. He does not think that creaturely causes are true causes, and he believes that God determines all that takes place to the exclusion of chance and randomness in the created order. So he is clearly not semi-Pelagian. In fact, his position commits him to monergism of a rather strong sort: only divine grace can bring about personal salvation, the human will being impotent to do so, because it is in bondage to inherited sin.

With this in mind, we can proceed to a second stage assessment of the coherence of Zwingli's doctrine with reference to his teaching on baptism and predestination. Recall that his baptismal views, which changed in important respects after engaging the theology

---

[25]William Shedd is perhaps the best-known historic Reformed advocate of Augustinian realism. His views are set forth in his *Dogmatic Theology, Third Edition,* ed. Alan Gomes (Phillipsburg, NJ: Presbyterian and Reformed, 2003 [1888–1894]). I expound and criticize his views in Oliver D. Crisp, *An American Augustinian: Sin and Salvation in the Dogmatic Theology of William G. T. Shedd* (Milton Keynes and Eugene, OR: Paternoster Press and Wipf and Stock, 2009).

of the Swiss Brethren, amount to a denial of the medieval rationale for paedobaptism. It does not remove original sin or guilt, it does not regenerate, and it is not a sacrament, strictly speaking, for it is not a rite that confers some special grace. Rather, it is an ordinance which signifies covenantal inclusion on the part of the children of Christian parents. As Geoffrey Bromiley points out, "Zwingli refused absolutely to base infant baptism upon the alleged guilt of original sin. He allowed an inherited frailty of our nature which inevitably gives rise to sin, but he did not believe that any guilt attaches to that frailty, at any rate in the case of Christians."[26] Bromiley thinks this indicates a weakness in Zwingli's argument. He "seems to lack the beliefs or presuppositions which make infant baptism logically necessary."[27] By this he means that Zwingli's rejection of both the doctrine of original guilt and the notion of infant faith makes of baptism a purely covenantal sign, which does not represent the more developed sacramentalism of later Reformed thought. It is not clear to me why Zwingli's revision to the justification for infant baptism weakens his case for infant baptism as Bromiley seems to think. One could adopt the view that baptism is a covenantal sign; that it signifies inclusion in the covenant community; and that it brings about no ontological or moral change in the person to whom it is administered. These are different reasons for adopting infant baptism as the conventional means of entry into the visible church than those espoused in late medieval Western Christianity, to be sure. But it is odd for Bromiley, himself an evangelical Anglican, to admonish Zwingli for denying the doctrine of baptismal regeneration, which most paedobaptist evangelicals are quite happy to shrug off. More concerning, perhaps, is Zwingli's decoupling of the sign from its sacramental efficacy, something later Reformed theology refused to countenance. But this too is no objection to the *internal coherence* of his reasoning, or of the "fit" between what he says about baptism on the one hand, and original sin on the other. It is a worry about the implications of Zwingli's sacramentalism—and we are not here concerned with the implications of his sacramentalism beyond the

---

[26]Bromiley, *Zwingli and Bullinger,* Introduction, 124.
[27]Bromiley, *Zwingli and Bullinger,* 125–26.

immediate issue of the relation between it and his understanding of original sin.[28]

The contribution of Zwingli's mature views on the nature of baptism to his mature understanding of original sin is, therefore, an important indicator of the coherence of his thinking. The fact that original sin doesn't include original guilt and doesn't condemn the children of believers in the absence of actual sin fits rather well with his claim that baptism doesn't remove original sin or original guilt, and that it doesn't regenerate a person either. The two doctrines mutually reinforce each other.

Perhaps surprisingly, similar things can be said about the consonance between Zwingli's views on predestination and original sin. Granted, it is strange that he holds to milder views on original sin than many in the Reformed tradition while defending stronger views on divine determinism than most Reformed theologians. Nevertheless, these two sorts of claim are not necessarily inconsistent. For surely God can create a world in which he ordains that the sin of humanity that he foresees will be atoned for by the work of Christ, where all that obtains is the consequence of divine determinism, and where there is really no creaturely causal agency. Such a world could be one where original sin is a non-culpable disease or defect introduced by Adam that spreads to all of his progeny, and where creatures inevitably fall into actual sin because they possess vitiated moral natures.

In fact, although Zwingli does have significant obstacles to overcome in his understanding of divine predestination and providence, these are concerns that are independent of his doctrine of original sin. The worry is that his account of divine determinism removes from creatures any real agency. For on the one hand, his views imply that creatures are not really causal agents, but merely the occasions of divine action. And on the other hand, this seems

---

[28]In this connection, it is strange to find John B. Endres, OP, claiming that the tone of the Lutheran Augsburg Confession of 1530 is decidedly anti-Zwinglian, "containing a strong affirmation of the reality of original sin which will condemn one without baptism, and that no justification is possible by one's own powers." Endres, "The Council of Trent and Original Sin," *Proceedings of the Catholic Theological Society of America* 22 (1967): 64. Although Zwingli does not link baptism and original sin with regeneration as do the Lutherans and Roman Catholics, it is hardly fair to imply that Zwingli denies the reality of original sin.

to imply that God is morally as well as causally responsible for all creaturely actions, which is theologically intolerable. This does have the further implication (when applied to the particular example of original sin) that God is causally and morally responsible for Adam's primal sin, for the ascription of original sin to human beings after Adam, and for any actual sins they commit. However, although this makes matters worse in one respect, this is really only a particular application of a wider theological principle derived from Zwingli's understanding of God's determining of all things. The arguments he provides for the material content of his doctrine of original sin can, it seems, be decoupled from these more problematic commitments in his doctrine of predestination and his doctrine of providence. If we do so, then his doctrine of sin becomes much more interesting as a potential contribution to ecumenical theology.

But is this Zwinglian position really a *Reformation doctrine*? Recall that this is our third objection. The Council of Trent, which postdated Zwingli's demise, taught that original sin is a condition of being deprived of the grace of original justice and holiness, which gives rise to the death of the soul (*mors anima*). Original sin, the state of moral corruption into which Adam fell upon committing the primal sin, is transmitted via natural generation. But it is fundamentally a privative state,[29] a matter that is underlined by the much more recent *Catechism of the Catholic Church*, which makes it clear that original sin "is called 'sin' only in an analogical sense: it

---

[29]The text of the Tridentine decree on original sin is given in several places. See, for example, John Leith, *Creeds of the Churches, A Reader in Christian Doctrine from the Bible to the Present, Third Edition* (Louisville: John Knox Press, 1982 [1963]), 405–408. See also, Ludwig Ott, *Fundamentals of Catholic Dogma*, trans. James Bastible (Rockford, IL: Tan Books, 1955), 106–14; Endres, "The Council of Trent and Original Sin"; *Catechism of the Catholic Church* (New York: Doubleday, 1995), Part 1, Sect 2. Ch. 1, para. 7. III, 111–18. Compare Ian A. McFarland, "in [Roman] Catholic theology, beginning in the medieval period, original sin is defined in terms of a lack." By contrast, "Theologians in the Reformed tradition differed sharply from [the Roman] Catholics, in that they viewed original sin as an active resistance to God that evoked no less active condemnation in human beings by God." *In Adam's Fall, A Meditation on the Christian Doctrine of Original Sin* (Oxford: Wiley-Blackwell, 2010), 37, 39. From a Roman Catholic perspective, the Lutherans and Reformed conflated concupiscence (disordered desire) with original sin (the privation of original righteousness).

is a sin 'contracted' and not 'committed'—a state and not an act."[30] This does sound rather like Zwingli's doctrine. However, differences quickly emerge when this is set alongside the sacramental doctrine of Roman Catholicism, and its views on baptismal regeneration. Nevertheless, the convergence is striking. Is his position really a Reformation doctrine, then?

I think it is. Consider Article 9 of the Anglican *Thirty Nine Articles of Religion* (1563). It states,

> Original sin . . . is the fault and corruption of the Nature of every man, that naturally is engendered of the offspring of Adam; whereby man is very far gone from original righteousness, and is of his own nature inclined to evil, so that the flesh lusteth always contrary to the Spirit; and therefore in every person born into this world, it deserveth God's wrath and damnation. And this infection of nature doth remain, yea in them that are regenerated; whereby the lust of the flesh, called in Greek, *phronema sarkos* . . . is not subject to the Law of God. And although there is no condemnation for them that believe and are baptized; yet the Apostle doth confess, that concupiscence and lust hath of itself the nature of sin.

Now, compare this with Article 15 of the *Belgic Confession* (1561). Like the *Thirty Nine Articles*, it has no clearly articulated doctrine of original guilt. But, like Zwingli, it states that original sin is a state of turpitude, not merely privation. Original sin, according to this symbol,

> is a corruption of the whole human nature—an inherited depravity which even infects small infants in their mother's womb, and the root which produces in humanity every sort of sin. It is therefore so vile and enormous in God's sight that it is enough to condemn the human race, and it is not abolished or wholly uprooted even by baptism, seeing that sin constantly boils forth as though from a contaminated spring.

---

[30]Endres, *Catechism of the Catholic Church*, 114.

It goes on, "Nevertheless, it is not imputed to God's children for their condemnation but is forgiven by his grace and mercy."[31]

Although much later Reformed teaching included the doctrine of original guilt thereby moving decisively beyond Zwingli's account, it is noteworthy that these two important Reformed symbols, both composed in the latter half of the sixteenth century, and therefore some decades after Zwingli's death, enunciate rather moderate accounts of the doctrine. Both provide views which, though perhaps not identical to Zwingli's position, are very similar in doctrinal tone and content. Both symbols agree with Zwingli's mature position that original sin is a corruption introduced by our first parents that is inherited, not imputed. They agree that if this corruption remains untreated, it will lead to destruction. They also agree that this state inclines fallen human beings to actual sin. Finally, both symbols affirm that baptism does not wholly remove original sin. Although this may suggest a more sacramental understanding of baptism than Zwingli embraces, it is a lot closer to the Zürich Reformer's position than, say, Roman Catholicism or Lutheranism.[32]

---

[31]I have used the translation of the Confession located at the website of the *Christian Reformed Church*, http://www.crcna.org/sites/default/files/BelgicConfession_2.pdf. The claim in the *Belgic Confession* that original sin "is enough to condemn the human race" might suggest something stronger than Zwingli or the *Thirty Nine Articles*, namely, that original sin itself condemns absent actual sin. That may be. However, the point here is that the *Belgic Confession* does not have a clear doctrine of original guilt like Zwingli and the *Thirty Nine Articles*, and that its language is more moderate than some later Reformed symbols, placing it much closer to Zwingli's position. The same is true of ch. 3 of the *Scots Confession*, which dates from the same period (1560).

[32]Article II of the Lutheran *Augsburg Confession* (1530) states, "since the fall of Adam, all men begotten in the natural way are born with sin, that is, without the fear of God, without trust in God, and with concupiscence; and . . . this disease, or vice of origin, is truly sin, even now condemning and bringing eternal death upon those not born again through Baptism and the Holy Ghost." The Latin text reads: "*quod post lapsum Adae omens homines, secundum natural propagati, nascantur cum peccato, hoc est, sine metu Dei, sine fiducia erga Deum et cum concupiscientia, quodque hic morbus sue vitium originis vere sit peccatum, damnans et afferent nunc quoque aeternam mortem his, qui non renascuntur per baptismum et Spiritum Sanctum.*" See *Triglot Concordia: The Symbolical Books of the Evangelical Lutheran Church: German-Latin-English.* Published as a memorial of the quadricentenary jubilee of the Reformation anno Domini 1917 by resolution of the Evangelical Lutheran Synod of Missouri, Ohio, and Other States (St. Louis, MO: Concordia Publishing House,

Not only that: the moderate doctrine of original sin found in the *Thirty Nine Articles,* the *Belgic Confession,* and in Zwingli's later work, represent a rather different trajectory in Reformed theology even if they do not all agree on every point of detail. To see just how different they are from much later Reformed thought, compare the *Westminster Confession,* composed in 1646, well over a century after Zwingli's death and almost a century after the promulgation of the *Articles of Religion,* and the *Belgic Confession.* It affirms that the corruption of original sin leads to death, affecting all the faculties of soul and body (ch. VI. II). Moreover, since our original parents were "the root of all mankind, the guilt of this sin was imputed; and the same death in sin, and corrupted nature, [was] conveyed to all their posterity descending from them by ordinary generation" (VI. III). Actual sin proceeds from this corruption of nature (VI. IV). What is more, "Every sin, both original and actual, being a transgression of the righteous law of God, and contrary thereunto, does in its own nature, bring guilt upon the sinner" (VI. VI).

Even this cursory summary of the Westminster doctrine of original sin makes clear that the difference between it and the doctrine of Zwingli, the *Articles of Religion,* and the *Belgic Confession* is much more than a matter of tone or emphasis. Even if this is understandable in terms of the doctrinal development in the intervening period between the Reformation and post-Reformation context of these different symbols, it is nevertheless an important change. What is more significant for our purposes, however, is what this suggests about a *third* doctrine of original sin within the Reformed tradition, which is distinct from federalism and Augustinian realism, and might properly be called Zwinglian. (Although, as we have seen, a very similar view is found in the Anglican *Articles of Religion* and the *Belgic Confession.*) Given the problems that attend the other two Reformed doctrines of sin—problems to which the Zwinglian position is immune—there may be good reasons for revisiting a Zwinglian account. What is more, as we have seen, the Zwinglian view has at least some prima facie confessional support, which is an important consideration when weighing its merits as a contribution

---

1921), Vol. II, 42–45. Clearly, Zwingli could not affirm the doctrine of baptismal regeneration implied in this article of the *Augsburg Confession.*

to Reformed theology. But in addition, there is also an ecumenical consideration. His is a moderate doctrine that does not fall foul of the traditional worries about Pelagian and semi-Pelagian notions of sin. For these reasons it may provide a more conducive Reformed contribution to the dialogue across the splintered traditions of the Western churches on this vital anthropological matter.

PART THREE

Christ and Salvation

6

Assuming Human Flesh

The prologue to the Fourth Gospel tells us that "the Word became flesh and made his dwelling among us. We have seen his glory, the glory of the one and only Son, who came from the Father, full of grace and truth" (Jn. 1:14). Following the author of the Fourth Gospel, let us call this divine action *the assumption of human flesh*. Strictly speaking, the doctrine of the assumption of human flesh (AHF) that eventually became part of classical Christology is the assumption by the Word of a complete human nature. This is consistent with what the Fourth Gospel affirms, but makes explicit what is intimated in the statement here in John 1 as understood by the fathers of later ecumenical councils of the church, especially those of Chalcedon in 451 AD. There the two natures doctrine was canonized, which consists in the claim that in the incarnation the Word assumed a complete human nature, in addition to the divine nature he already possessed, in order to bring about human salvation. With these considerations in mind, we might restate the AHF principle a little more carefully, thus:

> (AHF) The divine act of incarnation by means of which the Word assumes a complete human nature in addition to his divine nature.

According to the classical Christology of historic Christian orthodoxy, when we read these words in the Johannine Prologue we should understand them in a way consistent with AHF to mean that the Word, that is, God the Son, assumes human "flesh" (i.e., a complete human nature, which is how I shall understand the term "flesh" in what follows), in addition to his divine nature in the incarnation—the human nature of Jesus of Nazareth. But what is meant by a "human nature" in this connection? Could the Word have assumed any particular human nature? Could he have assumed *your* human nature or *mine*?

It is my contention that in principle the Word could have assumed *any particular* human nature because all human natures are configured such that they may be assumed by a divine person. Indeed, on my way of thinking, this is an important constituent of the concept of the divine image in human beings.[1] However, in a recent paper, James T. Turner, Jr. has challenged this view. He argues for two substantive conclusions that bear upon my contention. The first of these is that the Word cannot be possibly hypostatically united to just any human nature. The second of these is that human natures cannot be configured such that they may be assumed by a divine person, given a metaphysics of human persons that "deploys an identity relation between a person and her concrete human nature or else some essential component of her concrete human nature."[2] Call the conjunction of these two claims, *Turner's objection.*

This chapter offers a response to Turner's objection. We shall begin with a brief overview of some central issues in the metaphysics of the incarnation that are salient for addressing Turner's objection, focusing on the terms "person" and "nature." Then, in a second section, we shall recapitulate Turner's objection. The third section will offer a response to Turner drawing on the metaphysical picture of the incarnation set forth in the first section of the paper. Finally, I shall draw together the different strands of the foregoing reasoning in a concluding section.

---

[1]In an earlier publication, I wrote, "All human beings have a nature that is capable of such hypostatic union, in principle. And all human beings are given a nature that has the requisite image of God so that God the Son may unite himself with that nature." Oliver D. Crisp, *The Word Enfleshed: Exploring the Person and Work of Christ* (Grand Rapids, MI: Baker Academic, 2016), 63.

[2]James T. Turner, Jr., "Identity, Incarnation, and the *Imago Dei*," *International Journal of Philosophy and Theology* (2019), https://doi.org/10.1007/s11153-019-09716-z.

The metaphysics of incarnation

Let us begin by making some remarks about the way in which the terms "person" and "nature" are used in the argument that follows, in the context of the doctrine of the incarnation.

First, some remarks focusing on the notion of "person." Many medieval and post-Reformation scholastic theologians follow the Roman theologian Boethius in maintaining that the metaphysical definition of a *persona* is *an individual substance of a rational nature*. In this context, we want to say that "individual substance" is equivalent to a substance that *subsists*, the scholastic term of art for a substance that is fundamental, being independent of other entities. Sometimes such substances are called *supposits*, from the Latin term for fundamental substance. So a fundamental substance or supposit is a particular individual substance, independent of other substances. Such substances cannot be composed with other substances without ceasing to be fundamental (i.e., independent) substances. Persons are such substances: they are fundamental and cannot be composed with other substances without ceasing to be supposits. Thus, echoing Boethius, we might say that a good metaphysical starting point for thinking about persons is to say that they are fundamental substances of a rational nature, adding to this the claim that particular substances that are fundamental substances cannot be composed with other substances.[3] Notice that on this way of thinking, being a supposit is not necessarily an essential property of a given substance. It is possible for a substance like a human nature to fail to be a fundamental substance—provided some action blocks the human nature in question from becoming a fundamental substance. It is my contention that this is exactly what happens when a human nature is assumed by a divine person from the first moment of its existence.[4]

---

[3]This is how I have characterized matters in Crisp, *The Word Enfleshed*, ch. 5.

[4]Objection: does this entail that there is a "moment" in which the human nature is not yet a substance and thus not personalized? Response: the issue here is a conceptual, not temporal, one. The claim is that in principle, human natures, which are substances, only become fundamental substances upon being instantiated *provided at the very moment of instantiation that human nature is not assumed by a divine nature.*

Now, in the case of the incarnation, we want to say that there is only *one* person "in" Christ, so to speak. For we do not want to affirm Nestorianism, the heresy according to which there are two persons "in" Christ, the divine person of the Word plus the human person he assumes in the incarnation. The model I favor in this connection is sometimes called the "model S" ("S" for Scotus, whose work provides the impetus for this view).[5] On this way of thinking, the divine person of the Son assumes a concrete particular, that is a human nature (human body + soul, rightly related), at the first moment of incarnation. The result is a three-part Christology, wherein Christ comprises the person of the Word and the human nature he assumes, that is, his human body plus soul, rightly related. Now, according to model S, the person of the Word never *inheres* in the human nature he assumes. That is, the Word is never an *essential component* of his human nature, because the assumption relation is an accidental or contingent relation. Nor is it the case that his divine person is *composed* with his human nature, strictly speaking. By this I mean, the Word is never a *proper part* of his human nature. The "part" of Christ that is the Word is not a proper part of his human nature; and his human nature is not a proper part of his divine nature. (For present purposes a proper part of a thing is some part less than the whole entity.) The two natures of Christ are, as Catholic Christology puts it, distinct and without confusion. They remain intact though personally united in the hypostatic union that results from the act of assuming human flesh on the part of the Word.

But also note that on this model S view, the Word is only one "part" of a larger metaphysical whole, the other parts being his human body and soul, rightly related. So on this version of three-part Christology, the Word is not identical to Christ. No doubt some will see this as a metaphysical "cost" of model S. I think it is a potential advantage, for on this view the AHF brings about no substantive change to the Word, and does not jeopardize

---

[5]This model is set forth and discussed by Thomas P. Flint in "Should concretists part with mereological models of the incarnation?" in Anna Marmadoro and Jonathan Hill, eds. *The Metaphysics of the Incarnation* (Oxford: Oxford University Press, 2011), ch. 4. It is also discussed in James M. Arcadi, "Recent Developments in Analytic Christology," *Philosophy Compass* 13.4 (2018): 1–12.

the doctrine of divine simplicity—for the Word may remain a metaphysically simple "part" of a composite Christ, so to speak. He does not expand, as it were, to include a human nature from the first moment of incarnation onwards.

This three-part compositional Christology is the Scotist (model S) metaphysical "gloss" on our AHN principle. The human nature of Christ is not a fundamental substance, although it is the natural endowment of a fundamental substance—one that, absent assumption by a divine person, would normally form a fundamental substance independent of a divine person. Thus, on this way of thinking, the person "in" Christ, that is, the Word, is an independent substance of a rational nature as per Boethius. He is joined with a dependent substance (his human nature) in the hypostatic union. This is an *accidental* union, that is, one that is not essential to the Word, one that he takes up voluntarily and may in principle relinquish at any moment thereafter by de-coupling from his human nature. And this accidental union effectively "blocks" the human nature of Christ from becoming a fundamental substance because it is a union that obtains from the first moment at which the human nature begins to exist. As I have said elsewhere, rather like the connecting of one computer to another in a network may mean that the first computer, once properly synched, no longer works independently of the second computer to which it is united, so the human nature of Christ is so united to the Word from the first moment of its generation that it never exists independently of the Word, and, in virtue of being "synched" with a divine person from the first moment of its creation, never forms a fundamental substance independent of the Word.

Next, some remarks focused on the notion of a "nature." There are many ways in which this term is used in theology and philosophy, and there is now a sophisticated literature that discusses these different accounts.[6] For present purposes I will zero in on one family of views on this matter, which I shall call the *concrete*

---

[6]My own view can be found in Oliver D. Crisp, *Divinity and Humanity: The Incarnation Reconsidered* (Cambridge: Cambridge University Press, 2007), chs. 2–3. The best recent treatment of these matters can be found in Tim Pawl, *In Defense of Conciliar Christology: A Philosophical Essay* (Oxford: Oxford University Press, 2016), ch. 2.

nature view. On this way of thinking, a human nature, including the human nature of Christ, is a concrete particular of some sort. It could be a human body, or human body plus soul, or (perhaps, for idealists) just a soul. The competing view is the *abstract nature view*, according to which human nature is a property (or cluster of properties) necessary and sufficient for being human. I think that Christ's human nature is a concrete particular. Most Christians have thought that human natures normally comprise a human body plus human soul, rightly configured. Although that could be disputed, I will settle for this view for now. (Readers who deny this are invited to make the relevant mental changes to the argument that follows.)

The upshot of this discussion of "person" and "nature" in Christology is that when we say that Christ is a divine person with a human nature, echoing the Christology of the Council of Chalcedon, we are saying that there is only one person "in" the greater composite Christ, the divine person of the Word. He assumes a human nature in the incarnation. This means he has metaphysical ownership over a concrete particular, in this case, the concrete particular of the human body and human soul of Jesus of Nazareth, that are normally united together in the human nature of Christ. So Christ comprises a complete human nature that is assumed by a divine person. Recall that, strictly speaking, the Word is a "part" of this whole. He is not identical to Christ. He is the divine person joined with a human nature; but he is not identical to that human nature. His human nature, like his divine nature, is a "part" of the composite whole that is Christ, a bit like the human soul and human body are both "parts" of the composite whole that is a human being.

Turner's objection

With these metaphysical distinctions in mind, we may turn to consider Turner's objection. Recall that Turner's objection has two parts. The first of these is that the Word cannot be possibly hypostatically united to just any human nature. The second of these is that human natures cannot be configured such that they may be assumed by a divine person, given a metaphysics of human persons that, as he puts it, "deploys an identity relation between a person and her concrete human nature or else some essential component of her concrete human nature."

How does he reach these conclusions? In the following manner.[7] First, and following a suggestion in an earlier paper on the same topic by Andrew Jaeger,[8] Turner assumes the following *Necessity of Identity principle* (NI):

(NI) if it is possible that x = y, then necessarily x = y.

This seems to be a fairly uncontroversial construal of a classical, Leibnizian way of thinking about necessity. To this he adds a careful construal of AHF, which I shall call the *Assumption Thesis* or AT.[9] This is:

(AT) In the Incarnation, it is possible that God could have united hypostatically to any concrete human nature, including the concrete human nature of an actually existing human person, provided that (1) the hypostatic union with the concrete human nature happens simultaneous with the nature's creation and (2) that the hypostatic union with the nature does not result in two persons.

I have two concerns with AT as it stands. First, I am not sure what Turner means by the suggestion that God could have hypostatically united himself to a concrete human nature of an *actually existing human person*, given the two caveats he registers in this working definition. For presumably, such a divine action would fail to meet condition (1), according to which "the hypostatic union with the concrete human nature happens simultaneous with the nature's creation." Of course, in principle, a divine person could unite himself to an existing human nature, but then, as Turner himself points out, we would not have a case of incarnation as such, but more like a case

---

[7]In order to give a fair hearing to Turner's objection, I shall rehearse it here trying to stick as close as possible to the form the argument takes in his paper.

[8]See Andrew Jaeger, "Hylemorphic Animalism and the Incarnational Problem of Identity," *Journal of Analytic Theology* 5 (2017): 145–62.

[9]Turner has an earlier version of the Assumption Thesis, borrowed from Jaeger, and labels this AT* to distinguish it from the earlier, more ambiguous, iteration. But that is a complication we can skip here. So I shall just refer to this as the Assumption Thesis, or AT.

of the adoption of an existing human person, or of divine possession. And, for the purposes of a theologically orthodox Christology, such an outcome is not desirable even if it is possible in principle.

Second, for my own purposes at least, the way in which Turner frames AT may be too restrictive: the claim I am interested in is that the Word in principle could have assumed any human nature, not that the Word could have assumed any human nature in the particular action of the incarnation. I do not want to commit myself to the claim that the Word could have assumed *any old* human nature in the particular act of the incarnation. (For one thing, I think that the human nature of Christ is specifically generated in order to perform that particular task and would not have existed without being generated for that particular task. There are, I think, no worlds at which the human nature of Christ exists without being assumed by a divine person.) So here, as far as Turner's AT principle goes, I am only interested in the more general claim that in principle the Word could have assumed any human nature because human natures are configured such that they may be assumed by a divine person, which I take to be an important consideration when thinking about human participation in the divine life, because it is an eschatological goal for a full-orbed account of Christology.[10] We might say that I am interested in the question of whether the Word could be united to any given human nature in principle, not whether the Word could have united himself to any given human nature for the purposes of the particular redemptive act of incarnation. (I also think that divine persons are the proper referents for the action of assuming human flesh, not God *simpliciter*, as Turner stipulates here. But that is a minor point, easily changed.)

In order to avoid these confusions, I shall revise Turner's version of AT (call it AT2) like this:

(AT2) It is in principle possible that a divine person could have hypostatically united himself to any concrete human nature, becoming incarnate by means of that human nature, provided that (1) the hypostatic union with the concrete human nature happens simultaneous with the nature's creation and (2) that the hypostatic union with the nature does not result in two persons.

---

[10] As I make clear in Crisp, *The Word Enfleshed*.

Next, Turner adds what he calls the "identity view" of the metaphysics of human persons (IV), according to which:

(IV) Either a person who is a human person is identical to her concrete human nature or she is identical to an essential component of her concrete human nature.

Given NI, AT, and IV, Turner proceeds to reason that if it is possible that the Word is identical with some human nature or human organism, then necessarily he is identical with that human nature or human organism. He does this via two arguments. The first of these is the *Argument from Identity with the Nature*:

1. If it's possible that Christ's human nature (or CHN) is identical with a particular human person's concrete human nature, necessarily CHN is identical with that human person's concrete human nature.

(An aside: Turner clarifies that (1) means that Christ's human nature could have been the human nature that, in fact, became the human nature of some other human being—which I have already indicated is something that I think is a mistake.[11])

2. If it's possible that a particular human person is identical with her concrete human nature, necessarily that human person is identical with her concrete human nature.

3. It's possible that CHN is identical with a particular human person's concrete human nature and it's possible that this particular human person is identical with her concrete human nature.

4. Necessarily, CHN is identical with the particular human person in question.

The second is the *Argument from Identity with a Part of the Nature*:

1. If it's possible that CHN is identical with a particular human person's concrete human nature, necessarily CHN

---

[11]Turner, "Identity, Incarnation, and the *Imago Dei*," 9.

is identical with that particular human person's concrete human nature.

2. If it's possible that the particular human person in question is identical with an essential component of her concrete human nature (e.g., her soul), necessarily this human person is identical with an essential component of her concrete human nature.

3. It's possible that CHN is identical with the particular human person's concrete human nature and it's possible that this particular human person is identical with an essential component of her concrete human nature (e.g., her soul).

4. Necessarily, CHN is identical to the particular human person's concrete human nature, an essential component of which is that particular human person (who is identical to her soul).

From these two arguments Turner thinks it follows that either AT (or, in my case, AT2) or SV is false. That is, he thinks it cannot be the case that the Word could have assumed any old human nature. As I've already made clear, I think that some version of AT, that is AT2, is right. Turner presumes that I also think that SV is right, which would generate a problem for my position. As he puts it,

> The idea [for Crisp] is that, for any given individual human person, an important part of what it is for her to be made in the image of God is to be such that her concrete human nature has a latent potential such that it—the individual human nature— could have, in principle, been united hypostatically to the Logos. A major worry for this view, though, is that conceiving of the imago Dei in this way presupposes (AT*) [that is, AT, above]. It's a worry because, given §I, it looks like either (SV) or (AT*) [i.e., AT] is false. And, if so, then Crisp's theory is undermined, *if* he affirms (SV). It's not the case that individual concrete human natures have this latent potency. Thus, if the *imago Dei* is a feature of all human beings, and if (SV) is true, then it follows that a latent potency to be united hypostatically to the Logos is not part of what it is to be made in the image of God.[12]

---

[12]Ibid., 11.

Rebutting Turner's objection

What are we to say in response to Turner's objection? I have already explained that I am happy to embrace a revised version of AT, namely, AT2. So, let us focus our attention on the other substantive claim he thinks I hold, namely, IV, and the principle of necessity that underpins his reasoning, that is, NI. We will consider each of these two principles in this order, beginning with IV.

According to the central metaphysical claim of IV, human natures other than the human nature of Christ cannot be configured such that they may be assumed by a divine person:

(IV) Either a person who is a human person is identical to her concrete human nature or she is identical to an essential component of her concrete human nature.

But why think that? In setting out some central issues in the metaphysics of the incarnation in the first section of this paper, I said that "being a human person" is not an essential property of human concrete particulars, but one that a given entity possesses just in case it is not assumed by a divine person at the moment the human nature in question is created. Nor, for the same reason, is a human person identical to an essential component of her human nature, such as a soul. For in the case of the soul—which I take to be an essential component of human nature on the view sketch in the first section of the paper—it may, on certain views of the composition of human natures, form a human person. But, such a state of affairs obtains just in case the soul in question is not assumed by a divine person at the moment the soul in question is created. So whether the human person is a body-plus-soul composite or merely the soul, or some other putative essential component of human nature, in each case human personhood is a nonessential property of the substance in question. So it is not something that can be identical with the human person in the way Turner presumes.

To be fair to Turner, he is clear in his presentation of the issues that the worries he discusses depend on the acceptance of IV. He says at one point that his concern "generalizes to *any* metaphysics of human persons that suggests that a person is identical to her concrete human nature or is identical to an essential component of her concrete human nature."[13] And, as we saw in the excerpt from his paper cited in the previous section of this chapter, he is careful to couch his objection to my views in a conditional, "Crisp's theory is undermined, *if* he affirms (IV)." And, perhaps unsurprisingly, he thinks that there are good metaphysical reasons for accepting IV. For the denial of IV has the odd consequence that, as he puts it, "person" is not in the category of "substance."[14] However, for those committed to a different metaphysical picture of human persons and human natures, one that does not entail that a human person is either *identical* to her concrete human nature or *identical* to an essential component of her concrete human nature, this holds little terror.

With this in mind, we may now turn to consideration of the stipulated principle of necessity, NI, which underpins Turner's reasoning. This was,

(NI): If it is possible that x = y, then necessarily x = y.

The importance of this principle, as far as Turner is concerned, is that it delivers the claim that the Word cannot be possibly hypostatically united to just any human nature. For if it is possible that the Word is identical with some particular human nature, say yours or mine, then necessarily he is identical with that human nature.

However, once it is clear that there is no good reason to embrace IV, this aspect of Turner's objection also begins to dissipate. Note, *I am not denying NI.* I am merely pointing out that NI may be true and IV false. For NI is a general metaphysical claim about identity, and IV is a more specific metaphysical claim about the metaphysics of human persons. I take it that a more general claim about identity may be true, but the particular way in which we understand the metaphysics of human persons may allow for that without causing any problems for someone who, like me, favors a version of AT (namely, AT2). For recall that on the version of the model S account of compositional Christology I adumbrated in the first section of the chapter, humans are only *contingently* fundamental substances. So, given the Boethian account of persons with which we began, they are only contingently persons. The natural endowment of a human

---

[13]Ibid., 6.
[14]Ibid., 10. Here he is discussing the fact that both Tim Pawl and Thomas Flint have declared in their publications on the incarnation that they do not hold to IV.

person (the human body plus soul, rightly configured) becomes a human person provided a divine person does not "upload" himself into the human nature in question, so to speak, thereby assuming it. But this is perfectly consistent with NI.

Thus, on this way of construing model S, the Word may in principle assume any human nature (which is the theological claim with which I began). If the assumption obtains at the moment the human nature is created, then incarnation results and the AHF results in hypostatic union. In this case, no human person is formed because the independent existence of the human nature in question is blocked by the act of assumption. If the assumption happens temporally downstream from the first moment at which the human nature begins to exist, then (as we have already noted) things are more complicated. In such cases it looks like some form of adoptionism obtains. In such a case, the act of assumption involves the acquisition of an existing human person. So the result would not be *incarnation*, strictly speaking, but the adoption of an existing person. This may result in Nestorianism (two persons coexisting in one human nature). Alternatively, it might be a case of divine possession (where the human person is "submerged" by the divine person who acts as a kind of dominant partner in the union between the two persons).

Thus, I am happy to adopt a version of AT, namely, AT2, and deny IV. Now, if something like model S is right, then NI does not have any damaging consequences for the incarnation. Nor does it apply to the assumption of any other human being given a model S-style account of the assumption relation that informs the doctrine of the incarnation. For in none of these cases is the human being in question identical with the human person. So the inference from possibly x is identical to y to necessarily x is identical to y is not salient in the particular instance of the metaphysics of the assumption of human flesh by a divine person. For (on this way of thinking) human persons are not identical to human beings, nor are human beings identical to human persons.

Conclusion

We began with two substantive claims for which Turner seeks to argue. The first of these was that the Word cannot be possibly hypostatically united to just any human nature. The second of these was that human natures cannot be configured such that they may be assumed by a divine person, given a metaphysics of human persons that "deploys an identity relation between a person and her concrete human nature or else some essential component of her concrete human nature."[15] I called the conjunction of these two claims *Turner's objection*, and have sought to tackle both conjuncts.

Using the sort of three-part concrete compositional Christology I have defended elsewhere—what Thomas Flint calls the model S version of compositional Christology—I have argued that if we refuse to accept IV, then Turner's objection fails to damage the model S version of the three-part compositional account. Nor, for this reason, does it do any damage to my broader theological claims about the fact that a divine person could in principle assume any given human nature. For these broader claims depend on endorsing both some version of AT (in my case, AT2) *and* IV. Since I deny IV, the problem Turner has in view does not arise.

Similar reasoning is true, *mutatis mutandis*, of other compositional models of the incarnation that deny human personhood is an essential property of human beings, such as that offered by Tim Pawl and Thomas Flint (which Flint calls the model T, because it draws on the metaphysics of Thomas Aquinas). Deny IV and you can endorse a version of AT, understood according to a compositional metaphysics of the incarnation—or at least, understood according to two variants thereof, namely, model S and model T.

Nevertheless, even though Turner's objection does not defeat model S, it does help clarify one vital aspect of the sort of compositional Christology to be found in model S (and perhaps, *mutatis mutandis*, model T too). Careful elaboration of the metaphysics of the incarnation requires us to make difficult judgments about the assumption relation involved, and the implications that has for what we say about human personhood. Turner is right about this much: it is an odd consequence of the view I have defended that human personhood, unlike divine personhood, is not an essential property of human beings. But, of course, what is a metaphysical cost to one person may be a metaphysical advantage to another. Here is a potential advantage of this sort of view: it is one metaphysical indication of the manner in which human beings

---

[15]Turner, "Identity, Incarnation, and the *Imago Dei*," 2.

are dependent on God—in this case, dependent on God not acting in a particular way in assuming a given human nature in order that the human nature in question may form a fundamental substance independent of a divine person, and become a human person in its own right.

7

The Vicarious
Humanity of Christ

According to the Scottish Reformed theologian Thomas F. Torrance, although Christ "assumed our fallen and corrupt humanity when he became flesh," in this act of assumption "he sanctified it in himself, and all through his earthly life he overcame our sin through his purity, condemning sin in our flesh by sheer holiness of his life within it. That is why death could not hold him even when he entered into and submitted to it, for there was no sin in him."[1] This act of assuming what Torrance and others have called a "fallen" but not sinful human nature is part of the larger work of salvation, by means of which Christ reconciles fallen and sinful human beings to Godself. The idea is that God assumes human nature so as to act vicariously on behalf of fallen and sinful human beings. His assumption of a fallen but not sinful human nature is an important constituent of this view because, in assuming a fallen human nature, God the Son seeks to heal not just the particular human nature of Christ but also, through it, the whole of fallen and sinful humanity.

This is a grand theological claim. It is rooted in a Christology the seeds of which can be found in the works of Irenaeus and Athanasius, among others. Torrance's contribution to this topic, like that of Kathryn Tanner, another modern aficionado of this older Christology, is in many ways an attempt to retrieve some of the ancient theological motifs of early patristic Christology, refashioning

---

[1]Thomas F. Torrance, *Space, Time, and Resurrection* (Grand Rapids, MI: Eerdmans, 1976), 45.

them as concepts that can be deployed in contemporary dogmatics.[2] As such, this is a potentially fruitful theological endeavor. But can sense be made of it?

In earlier work addressing this question, I argued that God Incarnate could not have a fallen human nature if this means a human nature that bears original sin, because this would imply that a divine person is hypostatically united to something corrupt, which seems morally problematic.[3] For how can God be personally united to something that is corrupt given that his eyes are too pure to look upon evil (Hab. 1:13)? It would seem that such a view implies that God is capable of personal contact with moral corruption, which raises theological worries about divine purity and essential goodness. For surely the divine character cannot be besmirched by human wickedness. It also seems that, on such a view, Christ's human nature would be in need of salvation, rendering him incapable of acting as the mediator of salvation. For how can an entity that bears the moral corruption that he comes to undo be a fit agent for such an act of redemption if his own human nature stands in need of redemption? This seems to require an act of moral bootstrapping that is difficult to fathom—God assuming a nature that stands in need of salvation in order to bring about the salvation of such human natures, including the very nature he assumes in order to bring about this act of redemption!

Of course, one might argue that the sort of view Torrance has in mind does not commit him to the view that Christ bears a *sinful* human nature, only that he bears a *fallen* human nature. For, after all, the apostle Paul says that Christ's human nature was "in the *likeness* of sinful flesh" (Rom. 8:3), not that he assumed sinful flesh as such and without qualification. But what is a fallen human nature if it is not a human nature that bears the moral deformity of the Fall? A moral nature that is fallen is surely one that suffers from

---

[2] Tanner's views can be found in *Jesus, Humanity, and the Trinity*, and *Christ the Key* (Cambridge: Cambridge University Press, 2010). A sympathetic critique of Kathryn Tanner's Christology can be found in Crisp, *Revisioning Christology*, ch. 6. Other defenders of the notion that Christ had a fallen human nature include Edward Irving, Karl Barth, and (in more recent times) Thomas Weinandy.

[3] See Crisp, *Divinity and Humanity*, ch. 4.

the condition of original sin, otherwise what is meant by a "fallen" human nature? We will return to this question presently.

What is more, it would seem that possession of original sin is sufficient to render the human nature in question morally corrupt and plausibly an unfit object of hypostatic union with a divine person. By contrast, being made in the likeness of sinful flesh could mean something much milder than this—something like the Augustinian notion that Christ's human nature bears the effects of the Fall but not the disease of original sin. (I suggested in my earlier work on the notion of Christ's "fallen" human nature that this could be like a person who bears the symptoms of the measles without actually having the measles.) Christ's human nature feels the effects of the Fall in the limitations of fatigue, pain, physical suffering, hunger, and so forth. These, so we might think, are effects of the Fall, at least from an Augustinian point of view. But the fact that Christ's human nature bears these physical effects of sin does not imply that he bears original sin as well. For, he is traditionally thought to be impeccable—that is, constitutionally incapable of sinning.

That, or something very like it, was the core of my previous argument against the fallenness view. I still think that there are conceptual problems with the "fallenness" view of theologians like Torrance. However, in light of subsequent published work in this area,[4] I now think that there is a near-relative of this sort of view that can do the work that the "fallenness" view attempts to do, yet

---

[4]Particularly (in order of publication), Michael Allen, "Calvin's Christ: A Dogmatic Matrix for Discussion of Christ's Human Nature," *International Journal of Systematic Theology* 9.4 (2007): 382–97; Ian A. McFarland, "Fallen or Unfallen? Christ's Human Nature and the Ontology of Human Sinfulness," *International Journal of Systematic Theology* 10.4 (2008): 399–415; Ho-Jin Ahn, "The Humanity of Christ: John Calvin's Understanding of Christ's Vicarious Humanity," *International Journal of Systematic Theology* 65.2 (2012): 145–58; Darren O. Sumner, "Fallenness and Anhypostasis: A Way Forward in the Debate over Christ's Humanity," *Scottish Journal of Theology* 67.2 (2014): 195–212; and Rolfe King, "Assumption, Union and Sanctification: Some Clarifying Distinctions," *International Journal of Systematic Theology* 19.1 (2017): 53–72. Of these, the works of McFarland, King, and especially Sumner have been formative as will become apparent as we proceed. I owe the impetus for this return to the question of Christ's fallen human nature to pointed questions raised by Michael Rea in conversation.

without the problematic consequences of the position of Torrance, Barth, and others who defend the "fallenness" position.

In this chapter I will outline this alternative view. Although I do not endorse it, I think it is an alternative to my own position that is theologically defensible. I shall call it *the vicarious humanity of Christ view* or just "the vicarious humanity" view for short. Often the "fallenness" view of Christ's human nature and the vicarious humanity view are conflated.[5] The argument I give here distinguishes them. In a nutshell, I will show that, given a particular account of the metaphysics of the incarnation, the Word of God may assume a human nature that would be constitutionally fallen in abstraction from the act of assumption, so to speak, but that is "healed" of its fallen state—including the removal of original sin—through the very act of assumption by means of which the Word hypostatically unites himself to his human nature. Thus, the product of the act of assumption by the Word in the incarnation is that the human nature he unites himself with is rendered a fit vessel for his habitation. It is made constitutionally sinless (i.e., without sin, though peccable) and, through union with the Word, rendered impeccable (i.e., incapable of sinning). This state of affairs obtains by means of the Word's act of assumption, which is also an act of cleansing.

If this vicarious humanity view is right, then it is not the case that the Word assumes a human nature that is generated in a constitutionally sinless state. Rather, it is generated in a fallen state and then immediately rendered constitutionally sinless in the act of assumption, making it a fit vessel for the Word. This vicarious humanity view is, I think, a kind of theological olive branch— that is, a way of construing the notion of assumption such that it grants to the defenders of the fallenness view what they regard as essential for Christ to act on our behalf, healing our human natures. Yet it also preserves what I think is nonnegotiable from a more Augustinian perspective, namely, that the human nature possessed by the Word is sinless from the moment he assumes it. In other words, it is a kind of theological via media. Perhaps it may provide a dogmatic resolution to a rather vexed Christological matter.

---

[5]See, for example, J. B. Torrance, "The Vicarious Humanity of Christ," in *The Incarnation*, ed. T. F. Torrance (Edinburgh: Handsel Press, 1981).

The argument of the chapter proceeds as follows. In the first section, I outline the vicarious humanity view in dialogue and disagreement with three recent accounts of the fallenness of Christ's humanity. These are the views of Ian McFarland, Darren Sumner, and Rolfe King. This position generates some interesting theological puzzles, which I shall tackle in the second section. Then, in a concluding section, I offer some reflections on the potential theological benefits of this position.

The vicarious humanity of Christ

In a recent article on the subject of Christ's fallen humanity, Darren Sumner states that "The basic question in the dispute, then, is whether the notion of 'fallenness' is coherent, or has any useful content, if it does not entail sinfulness by necessity."[6] This is indeed the heart of the matter. The notion that Christ has a fallen but not sinful human nature requires some distinction between "being fallen" and "being sinful." There must be some theological space, so to speak, between these two notions if the distinction is to stand, and to be of use. The problem is that all existing attempts to give some account of this distinction are unable to make good on this requirement. In the current literature, defenses of the fallen humanity view usually fall into two camps. The first ends up with a doctrine according to which "being fallen" is equivalent to "being sinful." But then, God the Son assumes a fallen *and sinful* human nature, which generates significant theological problems. For how can a sinful entity provide a means of salvation from sin without some act of metaphysical bootstrapping of monumental proportions? A second way of dealing with the issue is to say that "being fallen" is equivalent to the much milder condition of suffering some limiting effects as a consequence of the Fall. One can call this a fallen human nature in the same way that such "fallenness" is applied to the whole of creation after the primal sin of our aboriginal parents (Rom. 8:20-21). In all other human beings, being fallen also includes some moral state that requires salvation. Yet on this way of thinking Christ's fallen human nature is not like that; it is fallen without any

---

[6]Sumner, "Fallenness and *Anhypostasis*," 196.

culpability or implication of the stain of sin, rather like the created order may said to be fallen and yet not sinful.

But perhaps this is the wrong way to approach the issue. Rather than attempt to find some way of differentiating between a fallen and sinful human nature, it might be simpler, and more satisfactory, to adopt a position that does not have that conceptual cost, and yet provides the theological benefits that are sought by those trying to make such a distinction. This is where the vicarious humanity view comes in.

To begin with, let us outline the view as clearly as possible. In an aside in his recent article on the topic of Christ's fallen human nature, Darren Sumner notes that what one thinks about the metaphysics of Christ's human nature has an important bearing on the issue of the moral status of the nature Christ assumes. Some hold that Christ's "human nature is 'concrete': it is the particular body, soul and spirit assumed by the Word of God." He goes on, "My suspicion is that advocates of the fallenness view will invariably opt for an abstract definition of a nature, as a conceptual list of attributes (or, in Barth's case, as the reality of a lived event)."[7] I think he is right to suggest that advocates of the fallenness view often seem to have in mind the idea that Christ's human nature is fundamentally a property of the Word, not a concrete particular, though I don't want to say that adoption of one entails the other. I also think he is right to suggest that one's position on the metaphysics of the incarnation makes an important difference in how one conceives of the question of the moral status of Christ's human nature—indeed, this is the point from which I wish to begin.[8]

I presume that Christ's human nature is a concrete particular. That is, it is a human body and soul, appropriately related.[9]

---

[7]Ibid., 199, n. 9.

[8]This matter is taken up at greater length in Christopher Woznicki, "The One and the Many: The Metaphysics of Human Nature in T. F. Torrance's Doctrine of Atonement," *Journal of Reformed Theology* 12 (2018): 103–26.

[9]If one is a physicalist, and denies that human beings have substantive souls, then Christ's human nature is a human body plus mind rightly configured, or a human animal, or whatever. The point is that whatever the concrete particular that is a human nature happens to be, that is, whatever the right view of the metaphysics of human beings turns out to be, Christ possesses such a nature. For a defense of the conjunction of physicalism about human beings and orthodox Christology, see

Suppose, for the sake of argument, that is right. Then, in assuming human nature, the Word is hypostatically united to a concrete thing, the body plus soul of Christ.[10] In several recent treatments of the fallenness view, it has been suggested that "fallenness" is a property of the human nature of Christ, not the hypostasis, whereas sin is a property of the hypostasis, not the nature.[11] In which case, the Word assumes a fallen human nature but does not make the property of this human nature his own. He possesses a fallen human nature without being morally corrupt or culpable in his *person*. This, it is said, is one way in which the distinction between fallenness and sinfulness can be made.[12]

However, it is not clear to me what the benefits of this view amount to if the human nature of Christ is a property. Perhaps the idea is that the human nature assumed by the Word is a rich property that includes as a conjunct the property of fallenness, but not the property of sinfulness. (Here I am supposing, for present purposes, that we can distinguish between "being fallen" and "being sinful.") But then it looks like the Word is related to the fallenness of his human nature in a potentially problematic way. For it is the *person* of the Word that exemplifies the property of having a human nature, and,

---

Crisp, *God Incarnate: Explorations in Christology* (London: T&T Clark, 2009), ch. 7, and Trenton Merricks, "The Word Made Flesh: Dualism, Physicalism, and Incarnation," in *Persons: Human and Divine*, eds. Peter van Inwagen and Dean Zimmerman (Oxford: Oxford University Press, 2007), ch. 12. For a recent collection of essays that take issue with such views, see R. Keith Loftin and Joshua R. Farris, eds. *Christian Physicalism? Philosophical Theological Criticisms* (London: Lexington Books, 2018).

[10]Physicalists about human beings are invited to make the relevant mental adjustment when the concrete human nature of Christ is referred to in what follows.

[11]Thus McFarland, "fallenness is a property of nature and sin of hypostasis (or person)." McFarland, "Fallen or Unfallen?" 412. Sumner agrees with McFarland that "The condition of fallenness is attributable only to the nature, not to the acting person." Sumner, "Fallenness and *Anhypostasis*," 212.

[12]For instance, Sumner at one point says that "the proper object of the predication of fallenness is Jesus' human nature, not his theandric person." ("Fallenness and *Anhypostasis*," 202.) That is an odd thing to say given his earlier claim that advocates of a fallenness view usually think of Christ's human nature as a property. How can one predicate fallenness of a *property*? Perhaps he means to say that fallenness is a conjunct of the rich property that is human nature—or something like that. Then fallenness is one conjunct of the property of human nature, not a property of the person of the Word *simpliciter*, and in abstraction, as it were, from the incarnation.

in virtue of exemplifying human nature, also exemplifies fallenness (but not sinfulness). This is like saying the Word exemplifies the property of thinking in virtue of which he exemplifies the property of being conscious. The person who is thinking, and is conscious, is the Word. Similarly, the person who is human and is fallen is the Word. In both cases, the Word exemplifies a property in virtue of which he also exemplifies another property that supervenes on the first, by which it is entailed. In the case of his humanity, he is said to exemplify the property of fallenness in virtue of exemplifying human nature. But if the human nature of Christ is an abstract thing like a property, then this seems tantamount to saying the Word begins to exemplify the property of human nature at the first moment of incarnation, and in so doing, exemplifies the property of fallenness as well (assuming fallenness is a property-conjunct of the human nature of Christ). For fallenness supervenes on, or is entailed by, human nature. But then it is difficult to see how the claim that fallenness is a property-conjunct of a human nature that a person exemplifies doesn't entail the conclusion that the person concerned exemplifies fallenness simply by exemplifying human nature. For in the case of the abstract nature view, according to which the human nature of Christ is an abstract thing, like a property, the Word is said to be the person who bears the properties in question. *He* is said to exemplify fallenness in virtue of exemplifying human nature. But that takes us back to our original quandary: Christ is said to bear the property of fallenness in virtue of exemplifying human nature. Yet somehow, in exemplifying fallenness, he does not also exemplify sinfulness. Rather than explaining how Christ can exemplify fallenness and yet not exemplify sinfulness, this way of thinking actually ends up simply posing the question once again, and in a more pointed way.[13]

---

[13]Here I am avoiding the complication this view raises regarding whether fallenness is an essential property of human nature. The defender of the sort of view McFarland and Sumner opt for on this question of fallenness as a property of human nature could simply say that fallenness is not an essential part of human nature as such. Rather, it is a contingent property of all human natures post-Fall introduced to all human natures as a result of the Fall. This is no different from saying as a consequence of some genetic mutation in a particular species all members of the species born from a particular sub-group thereafter all bear the mutation of their parents, though the mutation is not an essential part of the species as such.

McFarland seems to disagree. He says that

> careful analysis of the question of Christ's human nature allows
> a clear distinction to be drawn between *fallenness* and *sinfulness*
> as predicates in relation to the Chalcedonian categories of *nature*
> and *hypostasis*, respectively. Quite simply, fallenness is a property
> of nature and sin of hypostasis (or person). Even as nature and
> hypostasis are ontologically incommensurable categories, so are
> sinfulness and fallenness. A nature can be damaged (and thus
> fallen); but a nature cannot sin, because sin is ascribed to agents,
> and thus is a matter of the hypostasis.[14]

But, setting to one side the odd claim that sinfulness and fallenness
are in ontologically incommensurate categories (are they not both
properties?), this only underlines the point made in the previous
paragraph. If human nature is a property of the Word, and the human
nature of Christ includes as a property-conjunct "fallenness," then
it seems strange to say that the human nature assumed by the Word
is "damaged." It would be better to say that the property of human
nature includes fallenness, and that in beginning to exemplify human
nature, the Word begins to exemplify fallenness, whatever this
state is supposed to be. Whether or not (*per impossibile*) the Word
goes on to commit sin, he already possesses a human nature with
the property-conjunct of fallenness. So, presumably, assumption
of human nature on this way of thinking includes a potentially
significant moral cost to the Word, for it includes acquiring the
moral property of human fallenness.

   Things are rather different if Christ's human nature is said to
be a concrete particular. For then it is possible to see how Christ
could have a human nature (a property-bearer) that has certain
properties (like fallenness).[15] If this concrete particular is assumed

---

[14]McFarland, "Fallen or Unfallen?" 412–13.

[15]It is not clear (to me, at least) which view, if any, of the metaphysics of the incarnation
McFarland adopts. So if he adopts a concrete-nature view, then possibly the Word
adopts a concrete particular, his human nature, that bears the property of fallenness
but not sinfulness. Still, both fallenness and sinfulness seem to be properties on this
way of thinking (and so, the same sort of thing, ontologically speaking), and this still
does not explain how fallenness, a property of the human nature, is distinct from
sinfulness, a property of the person.

by a divine person, then he comes to be personally united to a particular concrete thing, which has certain properties. Although this doesn't explain how the Word can be hypostatically united to a fallen human nature without coming into close personal contact with a concrete thing that is morally compromised in some manner, it does provide us with the conceptual framework for making sense of the vicarious humanity view. The reason for this is that the assumption of a concrete particular means assuming a property-bearer. And this provides a metaphysical picture of the incarnation that has built into it some "wiggle room" between the Word, and the human nature he assumes. Although he makes the human nature of Christ his own from the first moment of incarnation onwards, it is a concrete particular that is distinct from the Word, a property-bearer with which he is only contingently, not essentially, united.

Although he eschews discussion of the metaphysics of Christ's human nature, Darren Sumner makes a distinction that is helpful in this regard. At the heart of his constructive proposal is the claim that Christ's human nature was anhypostatically fallen but enhypostatically sanctified, a view that, he says, represents a "broad spectrum of the Christian tradition."[16] This draws on the scholastic notion of the *communicatio gratiarum* (roughly, the communication of grace to the human nature of Christ fitting it for habitation by a divine person). I think this makes a lot of sense on the concrete-nature view of Christ's humanity. To see why, consider the following outline of a concrete-nature version of a vicarious humanity view:

1. At the first moment at which the human nature of Christ begins to exist, it is assumed by the Word.

2. This complete human nature comprises a concrete particular, that is, a human body plus soul rightly configured.

3. The generation of Christ's human nature in utero, and the assumption of that human nature by the Word are logically distinct events, even if they are chronologically simultaneous.

---

[16]Sumner, "Fallenness and *Anhypostasis*," 211. For discussion of the distinction, see Crisp, *Divinity and Humanity*, ch. 3.

The point in (3) is to distinguish the generation of Christ's human nature and its assumption. It might be thought that the human nature of Christ is not fully formed from the moment of conception, but at some later time in the process of development in utero.[17] If that is right, then the moment at which the human nature of Christ is generated in utero, and the moment at which the human nature of Christ is assumed by the Word, would be chronologically and conceptually distinct. However, even if these events are chronologically simultaneous, as most historic, orthodox Christology presumes, they are still logically distinct events.

4. The human nature of the Word would have been formed with the property of fallenness in abstraction, as it were, from the act of assumption (i.e., in its anhypostatic state).

Notice that (4) is cast in the form of a counterfactual. However, given that the Word assumes the human nature of Christ at the first moment it begins to exist, in the act of generation, Christ's human nature is formed with the property "being fallen." It is in the very act of assumption that the Word cleanses his human nature of its fallen state. These are logically distinct events, though they may be chronologically simultaneous.[18] Thus,

5. In the very act by means of which the human nature of the Word is united to his person (i.e., made enhypostatic), its fallen state is healed.

6. By healing his own human nature, the Word is able to act on behalf of all other fallen human beings, in his salvific work of reconciliation.

---

[17]I dispute this in Crisp, *God Incarnate*, ch. 6, where the view that Christ's human nature is assumed at some time later than its generation is labeled "temporary Apollinarianism." But, of course, the preceding argument does not commit its defender to such a view. That is the purpose of phrasing (3) such that the two events are logically distinct even if it turns out they are not chronologically distinct.

[18]Similarly, the striking of the match and the combustion of the sulfur coating (or other, similar combustible material) on the match-head with the oxygen-rich atmosphere in which the match is struck are logically distinct but chronologically simultaneous (or near-simultaneous) events that are causes of the lighting of the match.

This, in outline, is the vicarious humanity view. An important motivation in much of the literature in favor of the fallenness view is that Christ must assume a fallen human nature in order to heal fallen human natures.[19] On the vicarious humanity view just outlined, the Word *does* assume a fallen human nature, which he heals in the very act of assumption. It is, to use traditional theological categories, anhypostatically fallen, and yet made enhypostatically sinless through the very act of incarnation. This needs a little unpacking.[20]

The idea is that, in healing the assumed human nature of its constitutional fallenness, the Word renders it sinless—that is, he makes it like the putative prelapsarian human natures of our first parents, which were in principle peccable (i.e., capable of sinning) and yet without sin. But because in the act of assumption, his human nature is brought into hypostatic union with the Word, the healed sinless human nature of Christ is rendered impeccable for all practical purposes. That is, personal union with the Word ensures that the human nature of Christ never sins, though in abstraction from the hypostatic union (i.e., understood anhypostatically), the human nature of Christ once healed of its fallen condition is constitutionally sinless.[21] Although it is not impeccable without the presence of the Word, because the human nature of Christ is assumed by a divine person it is rendered impeccable. We might say that, once healed of fallenness in the act of assumption, it is constitutionally sinless yet impeccable via hypostatic union with the Word. Thus, on this vicarious humanity view, the assumption of human nature by the Word is also an act or communication of grace (*communicatio gratium*) by means of which the human nature of Christ is made a recipient of moral cleansing and fortification

---

[19]McFarland points out that it is difficult to provide reasons for why the Word must assume a fallen human nature (on the assumption, culled from Gregory Nazianzus, that the "unassumed is the unhealed," found in his *Epistle 101*). However, it may be that one could invoke criteria of fittingness that may provide reasons for thinking this an appropriate divine act of condescension. See McFarland, "Fallen or Unfallen?" 406–7.

[20]One reason for doing so is that the distinction between these things is sometimes misunderstood. See, for example, Sumner's treatment of my way of construing this in "Fallenness and *Anhypostasis*," 200.

[21]This reasoning follows my discussion in Crisp, *God Incarnate*, ch. 6.

through union with the Word. This grace is twofold: it heals the human nature of fallenness in the act of assumption, making it sinless; and it renders the sinless human nature to all intents and purposes practically impeccable through hypostatic union. For this reason, there is no possibility that the Word might sin by means of the human nature he assumes. There are no worlds at which God Incarnate succumbs to temptation, on this view. Nevertheless, he assumes a human nature capable of real temptation.[22] Like an invincible pugilist, God Incarnate is able to undergo real struggle with opposition in his human nature in the form of temptations, although the final outcome is secure. As with the invincible pugilist, so with God Incarnate: he must finally overcome moral obstacles placed before him, remaining impeccable—or in the case of the pugilist, remaining invincible.[23]

At this juncture it is worth turning to another recent entry into this discussion, an article by Rolfe King. In support of Sumner and against the sort of vicarious humanity view just outlined, King writes that "Any position which holds that a nature has a capacity to sin, yet that it is impossible that it could sin, is contradictory. And given that the possibility of sinning only applies to the hypostasis, it is impossible that Jesus, being the Son of God, could sin."[24] He goes on to say,

> Rather than claiming that Christ's human nature had the capacity to sin, anhypostatically considered (that is, that it was anhypostatically fallen), one might claim that Christ's human nature had the capacity for fallenness if united to an unfallen human hypostasis. Perhaps this is what advocates of the fallenness view are aiming for. However, this would not entail that Christ was *posse peccare*, or that the assumption was of a fallen, or anhypostatically fallen, nature.[25]

---

[22]See also Crisp, *God Incarnate*, ch. 6.
[23]For a more detailed discussion of these issues see Crisp, *God Incarnate*, ch. 6.
[24]Rolfe King, "Assumption, Union, and Sanctification: Some Clarifying Distinctions," *International Journal of Systematic Theology* 19.1 (2017): 62–63.
[25]King, "Assumption, Union, and Sanctification," 63.

There are several things to be said by way of response to this. First, there is nothing contradictory in claiming that the human nature of Christ has a capacity to sin, yet that it is impossible that it could sin—provided we mean by this that Christ's human nature is capable of sinning *unless it is hypostatically united to the Word*. An example will help make the point. Suppose we consider the case of a masked vigilante who dons a bulletproof suit in order to fight crime in the fictional city of Gotham. Without the suit, the vigilante is vulnerable to all sorts of attack, including being shot by a gun. We might say he is constitutionally vulnerable to bullet wounds as a normal human being. However, when he is encased in the suit he is rendered invulnerable to bullet wounds. He remains constitutionally capable of being wounded by a gunshot (because he remains human while wearing the suit, and humans are constitutionally vulnerable to bullet wounds). Yet being "united" with his suit renders him incapable of such wounding. Indeed, provided he is wearing the suit, he will remain invulnerable to such attack.

Clearly, in this example, the vigilante in the suit is bulletproof and provided he continues to wear the suit there are no circumstances in which he will be susceptible to gunshot wounds, though he is constitutionally capable of receiving such wounds without the suit. Something similar obtains with respect to the incarnation on the vicarious humanity view. Once it has been cleansed of fallenness in the act of assumption, the human nature of Christ is sinless but peccable in abstraction, as it were, from the incarnation.[26] That is, it is rendered *constitutionally* sinless—anhypostatically sinless, if you will. But hypostatic union renders it impeccable. The human nature of Christ does not don a special suit, of course. But the principle is the same: by being united with something invulnerable to the particular weakness in question (in the case of Christ, the weakness of peccability), the human nature of Christ is made invulnerable to it. And given that there are no circumstances in which the human

---

[26]Not all defenders of a fallenness view of Christ's human nature seem to see this. For instance, Trevor Hart defends the view that Christ is merely sinless and not impeccable. See Trevor Hart, "Sinlessness and Moral Responsibility: A Problem in Christology," *Scottish Journal of Theology* 48.1 (1995): 37–54. The problem with this view is that it entails that there are circumstances, and possible worlds, in which God Incarnate sins. But it is impossible for God to sin. So it is impossible for God Incarnate to sin. In which case, such reasoning fails to get off the ground, so to speak.

nature of Christ does exist without being hypostatically united to the Word, there are no circumstances in which his human nature sins, because there are no circumstances in which *he* (i.e., the Word) sins. For God is impeccable. So union with a human nature renders the acquired human nature impeccable for all practical purposes for as long as it is hypostatically united to a divine person. There is nothing contradictory in that.

Second, King claims that the possibility of sinning only applies to the hypostasis, not to the assumed human nature of Christ. Yet, strictly speaking, on the vicarious humanity view the possibility of sinning *does* apply to the human nature of Christ in abstraction from the incarnation, so to speak. For, given the metaphysics of the incarnation favored here, like any human nature, the human nature of Christ is a concrete particular that would form a fundamental substance or human person without the act of assumption. However, since the human nature of Christ is formed specifically for incarnation by the miraculous work of the Holy Spirit, there are no circumstances in which the human nature of Christ exists without assumption by the Word. This is because the human nature of Christ is formed for the specific task of incarnation—it is a bespoke human nature generated for the Word; he has metaphysical ownership of it; it is *his* human nature. As has already been pointed out, the human nature of Christ, as a concrete particular, is a property-bearer. It is, in a sense, a substance or substance-like thing. But it is not a *fundamental* substance that exists independent of a divine person as a human person (what the medievals called a *supposit*[27]). Instead, it is the human nature of a divine person. If, *per impossibile*, it had existed without the incarnation, then it would have formed a mere human person with a fallen human nature, which would (presumably) have sinned. However, the act of assumption by the Word renders this impossible, making the assumed human nature constitutionally sinless, and practically impeccable through the hypostatic union.

---

[27]Compare Tim Pawl (following Thomas Aquinas modified by William Ockham), "*X* is a supposit (hypostasis) if and only if *x* is a complete being, incommunicable by identity, not apt to inhere in anything, and not sustained by anything." Pawl, *In Defense of Conciliar Christology*, 32. Pawl takes this to be the standard medieval view of a supposit or fundamental substance.

Once this much is clear, the mistake in King's reasoning also becomes clear. Recall that he thinks, "one might claim that Christ's human nature had the capacity for fallenness if united to an unfallen human hypostasis." This seems metaphysically confused: usually one would think that mere humans are identical with their human natures, not merely *united* to their human natures.[28] In any case, that is not the claim being made here, and is no part of the vicarious humanity view we have outlined. For, as I have expounded the metaphysics of the incarnation according to the vicarious humanity view, the idea is that the Word heals his human nature of its fallenness in the very act of assumption, rendering it constitutionally sinless, and via the hypostatic union, impeccable. Thus, King is wrong to think that there is no possibility on this view that "Christ was *posse peccare*, or that the assumption was of a fallen, or anhypostatically fallen, nature." Christ's human nature is able to sin in abstraction from the incarnation (because it is fallen, anhypostatically speaking); and it is made sinless (but still peccable) through assumption by the Word. Its hypostatic impeccability—if we may speak of it as such—is nothing to do with any natural property of the human nature assumed by the Word. Rather, it is a consequence of the hypostatic union, and the communication of divine grace that this entails (i.e., an aspect of the *communicatio gratium*).

Theological consequences of the vicarious humanity view

This completes the constructive portion of the chapter. We now turn to some of the theological consequences of the vicarious humanity view I have expounded.

---

[28]James T. Turner reminds me that this would not be true of constitution theorists about the metaphysics of human beings, like the late Lynne Rudder Baker. But assuming King is not a defender of such a view, his claim here seems confused. For an exposition of Baker's view, see Lynne Rudder Baker, *Persons and Bodies: A Constitution View*. Cambridge Studies in Philosophy (Cambridge: Cambridge University Press, 2000).

The first of these is that it bucks the traditional Reformed doctrine of the immediate sanctification of Christ's human nature by the work of the Holy Spirit in the miracle of the virginal conception.[29] According to this traditional Reformed teaching, in generating the human nature of Christ in the womb of the Virgin, the Holy Spirit is the divine person upon whom terminates the work of ensuring that the human nature formed is without sin, and is, as a consequence, unfallen. Yet on the vicarious humanity view, the action performed by the Holy Spirit in the generation of the human nature of Christ does not include ensuring that the human nature is sinless. Rather, the Holy Spirit generates the human nature of Christ in a fallen (and potentially sinful) state, like any other mere human nature post-Fall. It is the Second Person of the Trinity whose action of assumption sanctifies his human nature. The net result is similar: in both cases the human nature of Christ is sanctified, rendered sinless through an act of divine grace, and made impeccable through hypostatic union. But the act of sanctifying the human nature terminates on different divine persons of the Godhead in distinct actions, depending on which view one takes.

This raises a related point about the doctrine of the inseparable operations.[30] Traditionally, one of the important ways in which the Holy Spirit is said to be active in the incarnation is by means of his miraculous action in the virginal conception of Christ's human nature. The vicarious humanity view does not deny this role to the Third Person of the Trinity, although it does understand it differently in important respects. The Holy Spirit is still involved in the miracle of virginal conception, being the divine person upon whom terminates the act of providing the missing genetic material necessary for the production of a human male zygote. But his work ends there, so to speak. The act of sanctifying the human nature of

---

[29]For discussion of this point, see Heinrich Heppe, *Reformed Dogmatics*, trans. G. T. Thompson (London: Collins, 1950), 424–27.

[30]That is, the inseparable operations of the Trinity in creation. This depends on the ancient Catholic theological maxim that all the external works of the Trinity are inseparable (*opera trinitatis ad extra sunt indivisa*)—carried out by all three divine persons, though particular actions may terminate upon particular divine persons as with the incarnation. For a recent treatment of these issues with respect to the incarnation, see Adonis Vidu, "Trinitarian Inseparable Operations and the Incarnation," *Journal of Analytic Theology* 4 (2016): 106–27.

Christ is given over to the Second Person of the Trinity. This does mean that on the vicarious humanity view the Spirit's work in the incarnation is circumscribed somewhat, which some may regard as a theological cost.[31] Nevertheless, it does not appear to undermine the doctrine of inseparable operations, though it does redistribute particular aspects of the work of incarnation to different divine persons than is traditional (at least in the Reformed tradition).

A third issue the vicarious humanity view raises has to do with the distinction between the conceptual and chronological aspects of the assumption of Christ's human nature, on which the view turns. Earlier I said that there is a logical or conceptual distinction to be made between the generation of a fallen human nature by the Third Person of the Trinity, and its assumption by the Second Person of the Trinity even if there is no temporal lapse between the two actions. This, I said, is like the act of striking a match and the resulting combustion of the sulfur coating on the match-head given the presence of an oxygen-rich atmosphere in which the match is struck. These two things, namely the presence of the sulfur coating on the match-head and the fact that it is located in an oxygen-rich atmosphere at the moment it is struck, are logically distinct but chronologically simultaneous conditions for the lighting of the match. The sulfur coating and the oxygen-rich atmosphere must both be present at the moment the match is struck for it to ignite. Suppose something similar applies to the act of assumption in the incarnation. Then, God the Son assumes his human nature at the very moment in which it is generated. The human nature in question is miraculously formed in the womb of the Virgin by the agency of the Holy Spirit. The act of generating the human nature in question and the act of assuming that human nature are simultaneous, though conceptually distinct. Both these things are

---

[31]Of course one could adopt the vicarious humanity view and also adopt a version of Spirit Christology that would expand the role traditionally played by the Holy Spirit in sustaining the hypostatic union as per John Owen, Jonathan Edwards, or, more recently Myk Habets or Ralph Del Colle. But that is a question distinct from the issue of whether Christ had a fallen human nature, and one to which defenders of the vicarious humanity view are not necessarily committed.

needed at the moment of incarnation. And both these things must happen simultaneously.[32]

I presume all orthodox theologians would agree with this much. The difficulty lies with my further claim that in generating the human nature in the womb of the Virgin, the Holy Spirit generates a fallen human nature that is simultaneously assumed by the Son who at the self-same moment of assumption cleanses the nature in question of fallenness in the very act of assuming it. The important thing to note here is that all these different things occur simultaneously on the vicarious human nature view. Like the striking of the match there are numerous simultaneous but conceptually distinct things going on at once. But given that orthodox theologians already agree that the act of generating the human nature of Christ that terminates on the Spirit and the act of assuming it that terminates on the Son are conceptually distinct though simultaneous, it is difficult to see why there should be an objection to the addition of the distinction between the generation of a fallen human nature and the cleansing of it in the act of assumption. For all that is added here is a further way in which these two simultaneous acts may be differentiated. We might think of this as a way of further bolstering an existing, commonplace, theological distinction concerning the Son's act of assuming human nature. This also seems to be no more objectionable than the venerable distinction between the anhypostatic and enhypostatic human nature of Christ, which helps make an important conceptual point regarding the incarnation. My thought is that by means of the distinction at the heart of the vicarious humanity view, we can make another helpful clarification of what it is that the act of assumption entails. This clarification (or amplification of an existing distinction) makes clearer how it is that the act of generating the human nature of Christ and the act of assuming it are conceptually distinct but simultaneous divine actions.

---

[32]Otherwise, the human nature of Christ is generated at one moment, and assumed at another. In which case there is a moment at which the human nature in question exists unassumed, which implies one or more unorthodox view such as Apollinarianism or Nestorianism, depending on how the metaphysics play out.

Conclusion

In dialogue and conversation with several recent essays on the fallenness of Christ's human nature, and in light of earlier discussion, especially that of Thomas F. Torrance, I have argued that there is a way of accounting for the central claims of the fallenness view, yet without the theological costs outlined in my earlier work on the topic. This alternative I have called the vicarious humanity view.

The benefits of this view should be obvious. It is able to make sense of the notion that Christ assumes and heals a fallen human nature, thereby underlining the fact that he is like us in every way, sin excepted (Heb. 4:15). He really is made in the likeness of sinful flesh (Rom. 8:3). But his human nature is not sinful. Though it is generated fallen, it is cleansed of this fallen state upon contact with the Word in the act of assumption. This communication of divine grace renders the human nature of Christ constitutionally sinless though peccable, and, through hypostatic union, impeccable for all practical purposes. (The assumption here is that it is the hypostatic union that prevents the human nature of Christ from ever sinning.) Thus, this view is able to meet the concerns of those, like the present author, for whom it is impossible for the Word to be personally united to a sinful, or even a fallen, human nature. This position is not without its drawbacks, however, and I have set out some of the most difficult. Nevertheless, it has real theological promise and represents an important dogmatic olive branch in what has become a significant recent theological debate about the moral status of Christ's human nature.

8

Edwards's Atonement Quandary

In the course of one of his "Miscellanies" notebook entries on the atonement, the great New England divine, Jonathan Edwards, asks, "how can it be a fit and becoming thing in Christ, thus to love and unite himself to those that are infinitely ill-deserving, and when justice requires that they be the objects of eternal hatred and indignation? Is not the [sic] thus taking their part and uniting himself to them a making himself guilty of their sin?"[1] His answer to this quandary is intriguing: "Christ does as it were hereby bring their guilt upon himself, but not in any blameable sense."[2] He goes on to elaborate on this point: "It was not esteemed a fit thing for Christ thus by love to unite himself to such guilty ones, unless he had manifested a readiness to bear their guilt himself and suffer their punishment."[3] That is, it is because Christ takes upon himself the guilt of sinners, acting as their penal substitute, that this

---

[1] "Miscellanies" entry, "No. 483. Righteousness and Satisfaction of Christ," in *The "Miscellanies": Nos. a-z, aa-zz, 1-500, The Works of Jonathan Edwards*, Vol. 13, ed. Thomas A. Schafer (New Haven, CT: Yale University Press, 1994), 526. As with previous chapters, all references are to the Yale edition of Edwards's Works, cited as "WJE" followed by volume number and page reference.
[2] Ibid.
[3] Ibid.

arrangement is a just and fitting one, rather than being unjust and inappropriate:

> It was but fair, and what justice required, that seeing Christ would so unite himself by love to sinners that had deserved wrath, that they might be partakers of the Father's love to him and so they be screened and sheltered, that he himself should receive the Father's wrath to them. That love of Christ which united him to sinners, assumed their guilt upon himself. So that Christ's death and sufferings were absolutely necessary, in order [to] our being delivered from destruction for the sake of Christ's worthiness and excellency, and through the love of God to him that loved us.[4]

However, there is a lacuna in Edwards's thinking here, one that, to my knowledge, he never adequately addresses. Even if Christ does take upon himself the work of a penal substitute for fallen human beings, such an arrangement in and of itself, and without further elaboration, does not explain *how* in uniting himself to those guilty of sin, he remains without guilt for sin, and is not besmirched or contaminated by that sin. To say, as Edwards does in this "Miscellanies" entry, that "Christ does as it were hereby bring their guilt upon himself, but not in any blameable sense" simply asserts without argument that atonement for human guilt doesn't compromise Christ's integrity. Let us call this apparently unresolved issue in Edwards's account of the atonement *the Edwardsian Quandary concerning the atonement*, or just *the Edwardsian Quandary* for short.

Edwards's doctrine of atonement is an interesting one, and the subject of ongoing scholarly discussion.[5] There are important

---

[4]Ibid. This "Miscellanies" No. 483 is discussed at greater length by Kyle Strobel in Oliver D. Crisp and Kyle Strobel, *Jonathan Edwards: An Introduction to His Thought*, ch. 5, and Oliver D. Crisp, *Jonathan Edwards and The Metaphysics of Sin* (New York: Routledge, 2016; originally published by Ashgate, 2005), *Appendix: The Imputation of Christ's Righteousness*.

[5]Recent examples include Brandon James Crawford, *Jonathan Edwards on the Atonement: Understanding the Legacy of America's Greatest Theologian* (Eugene, OR: Wipf and Stock, 2017); Oliver D. Crisp, *Jonathan Edwards Among the Theologians*, ch. 7; S. Mark Hamilton, "Jonathan Edwards on the

ways in which what he says about both salvation and atonement
resonate with broader themes in soteriology—having to do with
participation in the divine life by means of *theosis*—that I think
are important contributions to our understanding of Christ's
reconciling work.[6] However, rather than focusing on these wider
themes in Edwards's thought in particular, in this chapter I want
to use Edwards's question as a way of framing a more narrow
concern about whether Christ can be said to be guilty of the sin
of fallen human beings as their representative. For, the relationship
between culpability or blameworthiness, guilt, and punishment,
as well as notions of representation and substitution, are at the
heart of a number of traditional accounts of the atonement such
as that articulated by Edwards.[7] So getting a clearer picture of the
relationship between this cluster of concepts is a task that should
be of help to those for whom such notions are important load-
bearing structures in their doctrines of atonement—particularly
those sympathetic to a version of penal substitution, as Edwards
appears to have been.

Atonement," *International Journal of Systematic Theology* 15.4 (2013): 394–415;
S. Mark Hamilton, "Jonathan Edwards, Anselmic Satisfaction and God's Moral
Government," *International Journal of Systematic Theology* 17.1 (2015): 46–67;
S. Mark Hamilton, "Re-Thinking Atonement in Jonathan Edwards and New
England Theology," *Perichoresis* 15.1 (2017): 85–99; Peter Leithart, "New Science
of Sacrifice," in *The Ecumenical Edwards: Jonathan Edwards and the Theologians*,
ed. Kyle C. Strobel (New York: Routledge, 2016; originally published by Ashgate,
2015), 51–66; and Garry Williams, "Jonathan Edwards," in *T&T Clark Companion
to Atonement*, ed. Adam J. Johnson (London: Bloomsbury, 2017), 467–72.
[6]See, for example, the discussion in W. Ross Hastings, *Jonathan Edwards and the
Life of God: Toward an Evangelical Theology of Participation* (Minneapolis, MN:
Fortress, 2015); Michael J. McClymond, "Salvation as Divinization: Jonathan
Edwards, Gregory Palamas and the Theological Uses of Neoplatonism," in *Jonathan
Edwards: Philosophical Theologian*, eds. Paul Helm and Oliver D. Crisp (Aldershot:
Ashgate, 2003), 139–60; Kyle C. Strobel, "Jonathan Edwards and the Polemics of
Theosis," *Harvard Theological Review* 105.3 (2012): 259–79; Strobel, "Jonathan
Edwards's Reformed Doctrine of Theosis," *Harvard Theological Review* 109.3
(2016): 371–99; Crisp and Strobel, *Jonathan Edwards*, ch. 6; and Brandon G.
Withrow, *Becoming Divine: Jonathan Edwards's Incarnational Spirituality within
the Christian Tradition* (Eugene, OR: Wipf and Stock, 2011).
[7]This is true of versions of penal substitution. It is also true of closely related
doctrines like satisfaction, the governmental view of atonement, and John McLeod
Campbell's understanding of Christ's vicarious penitence.

Thus, this chapter is an attempt to address a kind of theological puzzle that is helpfully illustrated for us by Edwards, and one that he in particular doesn't seem to have resolved satisfactorily. Although the focus of attention is not on Edwards's theology per se, but upon the quandary that he raises, we shall circle back to Edwards at the end of the chapter to see whether our rumination may help to plug the lacuna in his thought. This, then, is a kind of exercise in Edwards*ian* theologizing—that is, theology done in the spirit (but not necessarily according to the letter) of Edwards himself.[8] We proceed as follows. The first section considers the question of human guilt for sin. In this connection, a key distinction with which Edwards would have been familiar is that between culpability and punishment in relation to guilt.[9] In the second section, I apply this discussion of guilt and culpability to the atonement. The third section deals with the complication of original sin in relation to guilt and atonement. In the final section I draw together the threads of the foregoing reasoning to make clear the theological upshot of this proposed solution to the Edwardsian Quandary.

Guilt and culpability

Normally, we tend to think that a person's guilt is inalienable. That is, it cannot be removed from the possessor of that guilt, and it cannot be transferred to another person innocent of the crime committed. An example will make the point.

Consider someone on trial for first-degree murder. Assume for the sake of simplicity that the evidence in favor of the defendant's guilt is overwhelming, and that the defendant has confessed to the crime. Now, normally we presume that where culpability can be shown beyond reasonable doubt, punishment should follow. Were we to prize these two things apart so that punishment did not necessarily follow on the heels of culpability, I suggest—other

---

[8]Hence, our focus is on the theological issues Edwards helpfully raises, not upon finding some solution to these issues from within Edwards's work (in part because Edwards doesn't appear to have addressed them himself).

[9]See, WJE3, IV. III.

things being equal[10]—that this would be thought of as a potentially serious problem with any judgment reached. For instance, suppose the judge in passing sentence upon the accused said, "Despite the overwhelming evidence of your culpability for this crime, it is the judgment of this court that your nominated penal substitute should take your place, so that you may not be punished; your substitute will take upon himself or herself the penal consequences for your actions." Normally, this would be thought a travesty of justice rather than an instance of it. The reason for this is that we think that under normal conditions there must be a fit between punishment and crime, one that has to do with this question of the moral link between culpability and desert.

I suggest that part of this matter of "fit" between crime and punishment has to do with a presumed deep moral connection between the crime itself (especially if it is a heinous crime, like a felony), and the blameworthiness of the person who committed the crime. This presumed moral connection is what pumps the intuition that punishment must be served upon the guilty party, rather than upon someone else. Other things being equal, it is normally the guilty party that is regarded as culpable. It would not normally be thought just for the punishment to be served upon some penal substitute innocent of the crime committed if it is a felony. (And, of course, this is an important traditional objection to theological accounts of penal substitution that goes back to the work of Faustus Socinus in the sixteenth century.[11]) This is the case for at least three reasons.

---

[10]This *ceteris paribus* clause stands in for various conditions that would bear upon strict culpability such as whether the defendant was compos mentis when committing the crime, whether it was committed under duress, and so on.

[11]For discussion of this matter see William Lane Craig, "Is Penal Substitution Incoherent? An Examination of Mark Murphy's Criticisms," *Religious Studies* 54.4 (2018): 509–46; Oliver D. Crisp, "The Logic of Penal Substitution Revisited," in *The Atonement Debate: Papers from the London Symposium on the Atonement*, eds. Derek Tidball, David Hilborn, and Justin Thacker (Grand Rapids, MI: Zondervan, 2008), 208–27; Stephen R. Holmes, "Penal Substitution," in *T&T Clark Companion to Atonement*, ed. Adam J. Johnson (London: Bloomsbury, 2017), 295–314; and David Lewis, "Do We Believe in Penal Substitution?" in *A Reader in Contemporary Philosophical Theology*, ed. Oliver D. Crisp (London: T&T Clark, 2009), 328–34.

First, the penal substitute is not the person who committed the crime. She or he is innocent. So (on this way of thinking) it would be improper to treat a penal substitute *as if* she or he were the guilty party, visiting harsh treatment upon him or her. This would involve a kind of moral fiction that is insupportable.

Second, and closely related to this, it seems to me that—strictly speaking—it is not possible to punish an innocent person. This is just a category mistake, like saying the number 2 is green. Punishment can only be meted out to one who is culpable for a crime. By definition the innocent person is not the culpable party, so it makes no moral sense to say that the penal substitute is "punished" in place of the guilty person. The penal substitute could take upon himself the harsh treatment that in the case of the guilty person would constitute punishment. However, if this harsh treatment were meted out to the innocent substitute, it would still be merely unmerited harsh treatment, rather than punishment (strictly speaking) precisely because it is an innocent person suffering, not one guilty of a crime.[12]

Third, and following on the heels of the previous two points, guilt seems to be an inalienable quality. That is, it seems that guilt is a property that in principle cannot be transferred from one person to another. The murderer is the one who committed the crime, not his brother or mother or daughter or anyone else—only him.[13] What is more, the murderer is the one *guilty* of having committed the crime, not his brother or mother or daughter or anyone else— only him. His guilt cannot be parceled out to another. It cannot be transferred like money from one bank account to another. It remains the property of the one who has committed the crime. Now, the punishable aspect of guilt can be met, so that the one guilty of the crime is no longer liable for punishment. If the murderer serves a life sentence in prison, say, then upon being released we would say

---

[12]I am not denying that innocent people are "punished" in modern legal systems. My point is just that when an innocent person is treated harshly in this way, it is not in fact a punishment, and cannot in fact be a punishment because the notion of punishment is inextricably linked to the notion of desert and culpability—neither of which pertains to someone innocent of the crime committed. For an attempt to show that the innocent cannot be punished, see A. M. Quinton, "On Punishment," *Analysis* 14.6 (1954): 133–42.

[13]Presuming he had no accomplice; and presuming no other parties were involved.

that although he is the one guilty of having committed the murder, he is no longer punishable for that crime because he has paid his debt to society. So what we might call the punishable aspect of guilt can be expunged through appropriate harsh treatment such as a custodial sentence. But the fact that this person committed the crime in question, that this person is the one culpable or blameworthy for having committed the crime—*that* fact cannot be removed by any form of punishment. In scholastic theology this difference was marked by the distinction between the *reatus culpae* (the culpability aspect of guilt) and the *reatus poenae* (the punishable aspect of guilt). The *reatus poenae* can be met through punishment, but the *reatus culpae* remains. I am simply reiterating substantially the same point here.[14]

With these three things made tolerably clear, we can see that the reason why it would not normally be thought just for some crime or sin to be served upon a penal substitute innocent of the crime committed has to do with the fact that morally suitable candidates for punishment must be blameworthy. Because they bear guilt they are culpable, and because they are culpable they are (in principle) punishable. Plausibly, guilt has a double-aspect. There is the punishable aspect of guilt as well as the culpability aspect that is inalienable. This is the lesson of the scholastic distinction between *reatus culpae* and the *reatus poenae*. The punishable aspect of guilt is not inalienable because it can be expunged through some suitable penalty. Nevertheless, the punishable aspect of guilt cannot be transferred to another because a substitute is innocent and as a consequence is not a suitable moral candidate for punishment. The perpetrator alone is the one who must bear punishment in order to deal with the punishable aspect of guilt. And this cannot be transferred to an innocent party. Even if it were in principle transferrable, it wouldn't be punishment in the case of the innocent

---

[14]At one point Stephen Holmes suggests that this distinction between the *reatus culpae* and *reatus poenae*, as it is taken up in the work of the nineteenth-century Princeton theologian Charles Hodge, is a puzzling one. He says, "This seems to me counterintuitive; Hodge's argument for it is essentially that in the atonement it happened, so it must be possible." Holmes, "Penal Substitution," 298. This is an odd thing to say. For Hodge is simply reiterating an older, scholastic distinction, one which seems to track with our moral intuitions about punishment, not about atonement.

party precisely because she or he is innocent and therefore not a morally appropriate candidate for punishment. So the link between culpability and punishability is lost in the case of standard accounts of penal substitution that think of Christ's work as a substitute punishment for human sin.

Much more would need to be said on this subject in order to provide an air-tight argument for the connection between culpability, guilt, and punishment, and there is a sophisticated literature in jurisprudence on this topic.[15] However, I suggest that this brief foray provides some reason for thinking that the culpability aspect of guilt is *normally* thought to be the inalienable property of the person who has committed the crime. ("Normally" here functions as a kind of *ceteris paribus* condition, that is, "other things being equal." The "other things" here include conditions like the person guilty of the crime being a morally responsible agent, being compos mentis when committing the crime or sin, and so on.) Moreover, although the punishment aspect of guilt may be met by the application of an appropriate penalty, it is *normally* met by the one guilty of having committed the crime, not by some penal substitute who is innocent of the crime and therefore ineligible for consideration as a suitable target-candidate for the harsh treatment of punishment.[16]

---

[15]For instance, see R. A. Duff and David Garland, eds. *Punishment: A Reader. Oxford Readings in Socio-Legal Studies* (Oxford: Oxford University Press, 1994); and Thomas A. Nadelhoffer, ed. *The Future of Punishment. Oxford Series in Neuroscience, Law, and Philosophy* (Oxford: Oxford University Press, 2013). An important rebuttal of the sort of intuitions I am trading on here can be found in David Boonin, *The Problem of Punishment* (Cambridge: Cambridge University Press, 2008).

[16]This is not true of fines, which may be paid by a party other than the guilty party. (This includes significant fines, such as obtain in convictions for serious fraud.) Fines incur what David Lewis calls a "debt of punishment." (See Lewis, "Do We Believe in Penal Substitution?") They are a special case where we do allow penal substitution of a sort. So, Lewis avers, we are all—religious and nonreligious alike—in two minds about penal substitution because we all allow it on at least some occasions (e.g., in the case of Christ for theologians like Edwards, and in the case of fines in society at large). Granted. Hence, the *ceteris paribus* usage of "normally" in the formulation above should be taken to mean something like, "normally, except in the case of fines …" I would imagine many Christian theologians, like Edwards, for whom human sin requires the death of Christ, would think of sin as being closer to a felony than a "debt of punishment" like a fine (*pace* Anselm). For an interesting recent theological

The transfer of guilt in atonement[17]

We turn to the question of the transfer of guilt from one person to another, and, more specifically, from fallen human beings to Christ who (according to the sort of penal substitutionary arrangement familiar to theologians like Edwards) takes upon himself the penalty due for sin. Recall that our target here is to provide some reason that may motivate Edwards's claim that "Christ does as it were hereby bring their guilt upon himself, *but not in any blameable sense.*"

In his recent essay on penal substitution, the British theologian Stephen Holmes offers three traditional ways in which the worry about transference of guilt has been addressed by defenders of penal substitution.[18] I will take them in the reverse order to which they appear in his essay. First, there is the notion of legal relaxation so that the strict demands of the law may be relaxed in order that a "vicarious equivalent punishment"[19] may be accepted in place of the one legally demanded. This is an odd arrangement, and one that Holmes finds insufficient because "it is not clear why Jesus had to suffer such humiliation and agony" if "there is not absolute legal requirement for the penalty of death to be inflicted."[20] However, the defender of this view can surely reply that the issue is not the relaxation of the penalty, but the relaxation of the question of who suffers the penalty. The full force of the penalty is still in place, for the wages of sin is death (Rom. 6:23).[21] But on this view Christ

---

discussion of some of these things see Joshua Farris and S. Mark Hamilton, "The Logic of Reparative Substitution: Contemporary Restitution Models of Atonement, Divine Justice, and Somatic Death," *Irish Theological Quarterly* 83.1 (2018): 62–77.

[17]This issue is also dealt with in Crisp, *The Word Enfleshed*; Crisp, "Scholastic Theology, Augustinian Realism and Original Guilt," *European Journal of Theology* 13.1 (2004): 17–28; and Crisp, "Federalism vs. Realism: Charles Hodge, Augustus Strong and William Shedd on The Imputation of Sin," *International Journal of Systematic Theology* 8 (2006): 1–17. The discussion here follows the shape of these other treatments of the topic.

[18]Holmes, "Penal Substitution," 297–99.

[19]Ibid., 299.

[20]Ibid.

[21]It could be argued that Christ's death is not a strict equivalent to the death pursuant to the wages of sin in Rom. 6:23 because the death in view in Romans is spiritual death that involves being cut off from God everlastingly. Christ is not cut off from God's presence everlastingly. So his death is not a strict equivalent to the wages

may act as a penal substitute taking upon himself the penalty if the requisite legal relaxation obtains.

Nevertheless, there is still a real problem with this view. The problem is this: the legal arrangement envisaged is a kind of fiction, where God allows an exception to a legal norm so that Christ may be treated as if he is the one guilty of the sin, and can suffer the penal consequences of that sin in place of the guilty sinner. Consequently, no guilt is really transferred to Christ on this view. Rather, God imputes our guilt to Christ, treating him as if he were guilty. But we have already seen that a standard objection to this line of reasoning is that it is not morally appropriate. Christ is not guilty of any sin and it is not morally acceptable to make an innocent person suffer the penalty of the guilty. Even if such an arrangement were tolerated, it would not be the right sort of moral arrangement for atonement to take place because Christ, as an innocent party, cannot in principle be punished. Since the retributive exercise of divine justice is usually in view in penal substitutionary doctrines of atonement, the fit between crime and punishment, and, more specifically, between culpability and guilt, is legally salient. But Christ is not culpable (he is not a sinner); he is not guilty (the legal relaxation arrangement presumes that he is not guilty, hence the need for relaxation of the demands of the law); and, therefore by definition he is not punishable.

The second way in which defenders of penal substitution have tried to provide some reason for thinking guilt is transferred from fallen human beings to Christ in atonement has to do with the distinction between the culpability and punishable aspects of guilt referred to earlier. Taking up Charles Hodge's way of construing these things, Holmes says that the distinction itself somehow provides a basis for distinguishing an aspect of guilt that is transferrable in principle because it is separable from culpability, namely, the punishable

---

of sin. I think this must be granted to the objector. In which case, Holmes's point may be rephrased as an objection about strict equivalence, and defenders of penal substitution may fall back on a weaker notion of suitable equivalence in order to bolster their argument. For discussion of this and other related matters to do with the value of the atonement see Oliver D. Crisp, "Salvation and Atonement: On the Value and Necessity of the Work of Jesus Christ," in *God of Salvation: Soteriology in Theological Perspective*, eds. Ivor J. Davidson and Murray A. Rae (Aldershot: Ashgate, 2011), ch. 7.

aspect of guilt.[22] But we have already noted that the distinction itself does no work in explaining how guilt can be transferred from one party to another. It merely helps us to see that there is an aspect of guilt that is inalienable (culpability), and another aspect that is not inalienable, and may be met by a penalty served (the punishable aspect). However, because an innocent person cannot in principle suffer punishment, and because it would be immoral to serve the harsh treatment for sin upon an innocent substitute like Christ, this does not explain how guilt can be transferred from fallen human beings to Christ.[23]

This brings us to the third way of making good on the transfer of guilt according to historic defenders of penal substitution. This depends on a strong doctrine of union with Christ that can be found in the work of some Reformed theologians such as John Calvin.[24] In his debate with Osiander, Calvin writes:

> Now, lest Osiander deceive the unlearned by his cavils, I confess that we are deprived of this utterly incomparable good [i.e., righteousness] until Christ is made ours. Therefore, that joining together of Head and members, that indwelling of Christ in our hearts—in short, that mystical union—are accorded by us the highest degree of importance, so that Christ, having been made ours, makes us sharers with him in the gifts with which he has been endowed. We do not, therefore, contemplate him outside ourselves from afar in order that his righteousness may be imputed to us but because we put on Christ and are engrafted

---

[22]Holmes, "Penal Substitution," 298.

[23]Holmes thinks this distinction "counterintuitive," but I do not understand why, and he doesn't really explain his thinking. Nor is it entirely clear to me that he has been as charitable to Hodge as he might have been. But I shall pass over that for now.

[24]Holmes also names William Ames in this regard, but the relevant section in his *Marrow of Theology* (trans. John Dykstra Eusden [Grand Rapids, MI: Baker, 1968 (1629)]) makes clear that although he is willing to talk of the mystical union of the Church with Christ (I.xxxi.15) his understanding of union with Christ in justification (I.xxvii.1) is to be construed in terms of "the pronouncing of a sentence," which "does not denote in the Holy Scriptures a real or physical change. There is rather a judicial or moral change which takes shape in the pronouncing of the sentence and in the reckoning." (I.xxvii.7, p. 161 Eusden trans.)

into his body—in short because he deigns to make us one with him.[25]

Commenting on Calvin's position in particular, Holmes writes, "The union of the believer with Christ results in 'Christ-and-the-church' being a single moral agent" so that there "is not transference of guilt . . . the head being held responsible for the sins of the body."[26] Calvin does use such concrete, Pauline imagery in his account of union with Christ, although it is not clear to me that he thinks of Christ-and-the-church as one moral agent. But, in any case, to my way of thinking this sort of approach to the question of the transfer of guilt is by far the most promising way forward. Holmes thinks it is "difficult to hold . . . in the face of conceptions of personhood as unassailable interiority that arose at the beginning of the nineteenth century."[27] But that seems an odd judgment to make.[28] Notions of participation in the divine and of some strong doctrine of union with Christ, are familiar enough in Reformed theology, with analogous doctrines to be found in other branches of the Christian tradition as well going back to the patristic period.[29] Such doctrines are not merely of historical interest, but are invoked in contemporary constructive theological discussion of the topic as well.[30]

---

[25]Calvin, *Institutes*, 3. 11. 10.

[26]Holmes, "Penal Substitution," 297.

[27]Ibid., 298.

[28]For an account of the atonement that draws on such a notion of union with Christ, see Crisp, *The Word Enfleshed*, ch. 7.

[29]The literature on this topic is large. A good place to begin in Reformed thought is Canlis, *Calvin's Ladder*. Also of note are Billings, *Calvin, Participation, and the Gift*, and Evans, *Imputation and Impartation*.

[30]See Crisp, *The Word Enfleshed*, Tanner, *Christ the Key*, Thomas Torrance, *The Mediation of Christ* (Grand Rapids, MI: Eerdmans, 1984), and, among New Testament scholars, Michael J. Gorman, *The Death of the Messiah and the Birth of the New Covenant: A (Not So) New Model of the Atonement* (Eugene, OR: Wipf and Stock, 2014); and Grant Macaskill, *Union with Christ in the New Testament* (Oxford: Oxford University Press, 2013). There are other recent "participation" accounts of the atonement in the recent literature, including works by philosophers Tim Bayne and Greg Restall, "A Participatory Model of the Atonement," in *New Waves in Philosophy of Religion*, eds. Yujin Nagasawa and Eric I. Wielenberg (London: Palgrave Macmillan, 2009), 150–66. If Holmes's point is that modern notions of personhood make "union" accounts of atonement difficult to motivate,

But perhaps Holmes's claim is that modern notions of personhood require some idea of essential interiority. Then his question might be, How can a person, understood as unassailable interiority, participate in or be united to another person? Why wouldn't they just be two unassailable interiorities? That is a better way of reasoning, but it is not at all clear to me that there is some monolithic notion of personhood common to all moderns that requires such an unassailable interiority, such that it would present a significant obstacle to the claim Calvin makes.[31]

Nevertheless, providing some plausible metaphysical story according to which Christ-and-the-church may somehow constitute one entity so that God may "transfer" the sin of fallen humanity to Christ as "head" of the body is a tall order, but perhaps not insuperable. Let us sketch out one such scenario. First, let us distinguish substitution, representation, and participation. In substitution, one thing stands in for another, taking the place of the first thing. Thus, if Christ is a substitute for fallen human beings in his act of atonement, then he stands in the place of fallen human beings, substituting for them in some way (as he does in penal substitution—taking upon himself the punishment, or penal consequences, of human sin). In representation, one entity stands in for another as a member of the *same group*.[32] Christ may be our representative provided he is like us in relevant ways—he is a member of the same group (humanity) as those whose interests he represents in atonement. Participation connotes the sharing of something held in common between two parties, as when two people participate together in an act of worship. Both people are included in the expression of the liturgy; they participate together. If one of those people is the minister and the other a member of the congregation, then the minister may be said to inaugurate and undertake the liturgy as the celebrant, though the member of the congregation also participates in the liturgy enacted by the celebrant. In a similar manner, Christ brings about atonement and

---

these recent works should at least demonstrate that such a judgment is not a foregone conclusion.

[31] I owe this concern to Steven Nemes.

[32] This point is made by Simon Gathercole in *Defending Substitution: An Essay on Atonement in Paul* (Grand Rapids, MI: Baker Academic, 2015), 20.

(on this way of thinking) fallen human beings may participate in the benefits that act brings about by means of union with Christ secured through the secret interior working of the Holy Spirit. As the New Testament scholar Morna Hooker puts it in commenting on Paul's theology of union with Christ in atonement:

> If Christ shares our death, it is in order that we might share his resurrection life. Paul's understanding of the process [of reconciliation with God via atonement] is therefore one of participation, not of substitution; it is a sharing of experience, not an exchange. Christ is identified with us in order that—in him—we might share in what he is.[33]

Hooker seems to think that this aspect of Paul's theology is aptly summed up by the Irenaean (and Athanasian) adage, "Christ became what we are in order that we might become what he is."[34] Similar sentiments have been expressed in several recent philosophical accounts of the atonement, which draw on New Testament Pauline scholarship like that of Hooker. In an essay that is indebted to the work of Douglas Campbell in particular, philosophers Tim Bayne and Greg Restall argue that Paul's use of the "Second Adam" motif (e.g., Rom. 5:12-19) "is code for Paul's conception of Christ's death as inaugurating a new human nature (Rom. 8:19-22; Col. 1:15-20). In Paul's eyes there is a deep sense in which we really are new creatures (Gal. 2:20). This new identity, grounded in the Christian's participation in the death and resurrection of Christ is symbolized—and perhaps constituted—by the rites of baptism and the Eucharist"[35] which are also participatory acts, in an institution (the church) that is itself said to be the "body of Christ" in Pauline theology.[36]

That said, *how* such participation language should be spelled out, metaphysically speaking, is somewhat less clear in Hooker's

---

[33]Morna D. Hooker, *From Adam to Christ: Essays on Paul* (Cambridge: Cambridge University Press, 1990), 26–27.

[34]Hooker, *From Adam to Christ*, 26. Compare Athanasius, "He, indeed, assumed humanity that we might become God." *On the Incarnation* §54.

[35]Bayne and Restall, "A Participatory Model of the Atonement," 160.

[36]Ibid.

work, as well as in Bayne and Restall's essay. Bayne and Restall
even admit that their view may be thought to be just a poor gloss
on a jumble of biblical metaphors that are not supposed to be taken
with metaphysical seriousness.[37] Their response to this worry is to
claim that there are two ways in which participation language in
the Pauline understanding of atonement has real bite. The first is the
moral change involved in becoming united to Christ. To be in Christ
is to have a moral center in Christ—to be morally reoriented so that
one's moral identity is now located in Christ, and in participation
in Christ's life, not in life apart from Christ. "To be in Christ is for
one's identity as a moral agent—as a moral self—to be centred on
Christ."[38] Second, this involves a change from an "old" state to a
"new" one, which "Paul regards . . . as a work in progress."[39] They
link this change to moral identity, which is not always determinate.
"One and the same person can be caught between two or more
moral identities, as they endorse and affirm different sets of
relations, values and commitments."[40]

The idea seems to be that the moral change to the individual
believer brought about via union with Christ and participation in
the benefits of his reconciling work is a real change that takes time,
and that remains incomplete in the individual believer this side of
the grave. Yet there is a real sense in which this redemptive action
involves the believer in being identified with Christ, participation
in his benefits, and moral change that this brings about. Christ
represents us, becoming one of us as a human being, and identifying
with us, in order that we might become what he is. This is not an
exchange, but an act of representation. The language of participation
expresses the mysterious way in which, by the secret working of
the Holy Spirit, the believer is united to Christ and his benefits—
benefits that have tangible results in moral transformation, even if
this transformation is incomplete in this life.

Let us summarize thus far. I have said that the fact of guilt is
nontransferable and inalienable, though its punishable aspect can
be remitted. Biblical and Reformed theological language about

---

[37]Ibid., 161–62.
[38]Ibid., 163.
[39]Ibid.
[40]Ibid.

Christ's participation in our humanity in order to redeem us in atonement has (I think) much to commend it, and has been taken up in several recent treatments of this topic. But if Christ somehow participates in our humanity in order to redeem us from sin, does that implicate him in our guilt as well? Is that what Edwards means when he says that "Christ does as it were hereby bring their guilt upon himself, but not in any blameable sense"? I think he means that Christ somehow takes upon himself the punishable aspect of guilt. But given that this is tied up with a doctrine of original sin we must turn next to consideration of that matter before circling back to pronounce judgment upon Edwards.

Original sin, guilt, and atonement

In much of the Reformed tradition, original sin is said to be a moral corruption that affects human beings post-Fall, and that includes the notion of original guilt. This is the idea that I am not merely the bearer of the moral corruption of sin bequeathed to me by the first ancestral pair. I am also said to be guilty of the sin of the first ancestral pair. Both the primal sin committed by Adam and Eve and the guilt of that sin are somehow transmitted or imputed to all subsequent human beings. But original guilt is subject to the same sort of worries about the transfer of guilt as we saw obtain in the case of the atonement. That is, if guilt is not a transferable property, then it is not clear how I can be said to be guilty of Adam's sin.

It could be argued that original guilt is a distinct and separable part of the doctrine of original sin.[41] Perhaps human beings do bear the corruption of original sin, but do not also bear original guilt. This is consistent with a strand of early Reformed thought, exemplified by the theology of Huldrych Zwingli. It also reflects the teaching of several important early confessions in the Reformed tradition. So

---

[41]I have argued for this in Oliver D. Crisp, "On Original Sin," *International Journal of Systematic Theology* 17.3 (2015): 252–66; Oliver D. Crisp, "Sin," in *Christian Dogmatics: Reformed Theology for the Church Catholic*, eds. Michael Allen and Scott R. Swain (Grand Rapids, MI: Baker Academic, 2016), 194–215. See also Chapter 5 of this volume.

there is some support for this view in the Reformed tradition, even if later Reformed theology tended to include a doctrine of original guilt as well.

Suppose this view is right. Then, the guilt that Smith bears for her sin is not original guilt, as such, but the guilt accruing to the actual sins she performs because she bears the corruption of original sin. The condition of original sin will yield actual sin if a person lives long enough to commit actual sin (and is a moral agent capable of sinning). That is true of Smith, let us say. Nevertheless, this does not mean that Smith has no guilt. It only means that Smith does not bear the guilt all humans bear in virtue of being born with original sin (i.e., original guilt) *plus* the guilt for her own actual sins. Instead, she merely bears the guilt incurred for her own (actual) sins. This guilt for actual sins committed by Smith still requires atonement, of course, and that is one of the things that Christ's reconciling work seeks to address. Nevertheless, it is important to note that the issue of guilt here is rather different if we construe it in terms of actual guilt for actual sins committed by fallen individuals and not also in term of a doctrine of original guilt.

How then can the actual guilt for actual sins that Smith has committed be dealt with by Christ on this way of thinking? Well, if we take the option of conceiving of the transference of guilt in terms of some strong doctrine of union with Christ, coupled with our scholastic distinction between the culpability aspect of guilt and its punishable aspect, then we have a scenario in which Christ's atonement deals with the punishable aspect of Smith's actual guilt for her actual sin. (It does more than this, of course. For instance, Christ's atonement heals Smith of the corruption of original sin, and it brings her into renewed relationship with God by the power of the Holy Spirit who unites her to Christ, and it begins her on a trajectory "into" the divine life, so to speak, in the process of *theosis*—but we do not need to complicate matters by considering all these additional details here.) But this only makes our original question more pressing. How can Christ's reconciling work deal with the punishable aspect of Smith's guilt when Christ is innocent of Smith's sin and is an agent distinct from Smith? In other words, even if original guilt is removed from our account of original sin, there is still a problem concerning the transfer of the punishable aspect of Smith's guilt (i.e., the guilt for Smith's actual sin) from Smith to Christ.

At this juncture the defender of penal substitution runs into real difficulties if she wants to continue to maintain that Christ is *punished* in the place of fallen human beings. One way to meet this worry is to deny that Christ is, in fact, punished for fallen human beings, opting instead for the view that Christ suffers the *penal consequences* of human sin. In this connection, the penal consequences of human sin is the harsh treatment that in the case of mere human beings would be punishment, but in the case of Christ is not. Opting for the idea that Christ's atonement involves him suffering the penal consequences of human sin but not punishment for human sin is a weaker version of the doctrine of penal substitution.[42] But it may be a more defensible version of the doctrine as well. For it does mean that Christ can be said to represent fallen human beings without having to incorporate the idea that the punishable aspect of Smith's guilt for her actual sin is transferred to Christ in the act of atonement. Instead, Christ may be said to suffer the penal consequences of human sin, including the penal consequences for the guilt of Smith's actual sin, without thereby being made guilty of Smith's sin, or being treated as if he were guilty of Smith's sin, and so on.

Taking stock

We are now in a position to take stock. To this end, I will set out a series of numbered statements that synthesize the foregoing reasoning into one constructive account:

1. Original sin renders human beings incapable of being united to Christ without some act of atonement. This original sin comprises a moral corruption that means all human beings born in the state of sin will in due course commit actual sins for which they are guilty. Though fallen human beings are not guilty for being born with the moral stain of original

---

[42]For a recent discussion of this version of penal substitution, see Christopher Woznicki, "Do We Believe in Consequences? Revisiting the 'Incoherence Objection' to Penal Substitution," in *Neue Zeitschrift für Systematische Theologie und Religionsphilosophie* 60.2 (2018): 208–28.

sin, they are culpable for the actual sins they commit on the basis of this moral corruption.

2. Guilt for sin normally renders human beings culpable. There is the inalienable aspect of guilt (*reatus culpae*) that is the property of the person who has committed the actual sin. It is not transferrable to another. The person who is the one guilty of a particular sin remains the one guilty of that particular sin irrespective of punishment. Then there is the punishable aspect of guilt (*reatus poenae*) that may be met by suitable harsh treatment of the sinner. In an act of legal relaxation, it is possible that some other person suffer the harsh treatment that would have been suffered by the guilty party without such an act of substitution. In that case, the harsh treatment undergone by a penal substitute is not punishment, strictly speaking, because the penal substitute is innocent of the sin committed. Instead, such harsh treatment visited upon a penal substitute is the suffering of the penal consequences that should be visited upon the sin of the guilty party without the interposition of an act of penal substitution on the basis of legal relaxation.

3. Christ is an appropriate candidate for such an act of penal substitution because he is God Incarnate. He has a complete and sinless human nature (so that he does not have sin or guilt himself, which would render him incapable of acting as a penal substitute because he would then be in a state of sin requiring salvation himself). And this human nature is united to a divine person such that the act of atonement is suitably equivalent to the sort of harsh treatment that would be visited upon fallen human beings in the absence of atonement.

4. In taking upon himself the penal consequences of human sin, Christ suffers the harsh treatment that would be visited upon fallen humans absent atonement. This is an appropriate substitutionary act because Christ is a suitable representative of fallen humanity (being fully human himself). So Christ can be treated as a representative standing in for fallen human beings.

5. This act of representation may be fictional. That is, it may be such that the act is morally and legally appropriate because God ordains that it is so (a view that finds some support in Edwards's work, for example[43]), treating Christ as a suitable representative and penal substitute. But it may be that God brings about a union between Christ and those he comes to reconcile such that Christ's action is predicated on a mystical union between himself and those he represents so that he is in some sense really united to them and really capable of representing their interests. (Compare a situation in which a person may really represent the interests of her spouse because she is united to her spouse in matrimony. There is a legal union between the two, but there is also a real union between the two. This twofold union is the reason why one spouse may represent the other. Were a friend to offer to represent one of the spouses it would not be appropriate precisely because the friend is not legally and really united like the two espoused partners in a marriage union. Such language is familiar to readers of the Pauline corpus in the New Testament.)[44]

6. Christ's atonement is an act of penal substitution on the basis of legal relaxation for the actual sin and guilt accrued by fallen human beings. It is also a means by which fallen human beings are restored to fellowship with God by removing the stain of original sin. This latter action is

---

[43]See WJE3, IV. III.

[44]An aside: as a matter of interest, Edwards thinks that the real union between Christ and his church is the basis of the legal union between them. He writes, "what is real in the union between Christ and his people, is the foundation of what is legal; that is, it is something really in them, and between them, uniting them, that is the ground of the suitableness of their being accounted as one by the Judge." WJE19, 158. For discussion of this point, see, for example, Brandon Withrow, *Becoming Divine*, 163–68. But the reverse might be the case as is true in a marriage: one partner is legally joined to another whereupon they may consummate their legal union in a real union of bodies. This is an important theological difference, but for our purposes we do not need to make a judgment about which of these is right. For on either way of thinking Christ represents those with whom he is united legally and really on the basis of which he is able to atone for human sin and reconcile fallen human beings to God.

brought about by the renewing work of the Holy Spirit in regeneration who brings moral order to the corrupt soul in the course of sanctification, and who unites the human soul to Christ.

The Edwardsian Quandary with which we began this chapter had to do with how in atoning for human sin "Christ does as it were hereby bring their guilt upon himself, but not in any blameable sense." This, as we saw, is not an issue Edwards himself finally resolves—it is a kind of lacuna in his thinking. I have argued that, strictly speaking, Christ does not bring upon himself the guilt of fallen humanity. Indeed, he cannot do so because he is innocent of sin. Nevertheless, in acting as a representative and a penal substitute, he may be said to take upon himself the penal consequences of the sin of fallen human beings. Although this is not a matter of taking on the guilt of fallen human beings, it is still a vicarious act of representation that involves suffering the penal consequences for human sin. So, if Edwards thought that Christ really does take upon himself human guilt in atonement, then it seems he was mistaken for the reasons we have given here. However, Edwards was a canny theologian who often used phrases like "as it were" in order to guard against the application of too strict a relation between one thing and another. He clearly saw the difference between the inalienable and punishable aspect of human guilt for sin. And he also thought that a real union with Christ is the foundation of the legal union with Christ in atonement. I have argued that the application of a doctrine of legal relaxation in penal substitution is able to deal with the problem of punishment that some versions of the doctrine yield. Applied to the Edwardsian Quandary, we may say this: though Christ did not suffer the punishment for human sin and guilt, he did suffer the penal consequences of that sin and guilt. Whether that representative act is fundamentally legal or real, this milder version of penal substitution does, I think, have promise as a way of addressing the worry that the Edwardsian Quandary raises for defenders of account of atonement that involves an act of representative substitution, such as the doctrine of penal substitution.

9

Character and True Virtue

Traditionally, Reformed theologians have had a rather gloomy view of human character. Theological anthropology in the Reformed tradition is usually associated with the notion of "total depravity." On this way of thinking, human beings are corrupt as a consequence of original sin, and morally vitiated. The idea is not that fallen humans are incapable of doing any good actions, or even that all the actions they do perform are *totally* depraved, but rather that all their moral actions are tainted by the effects of sin.[1]

Alongside this rather pessimistic view of the moral nature of fallen human beings, there is a suspicion (among some notable modern Reformed thinkers at least) of the virtue tradition in Christian ethics. As Kirk Nolan puts it, "While there have been periods in which Reformed conceptions of virtue were articulated, the impact of those periods goes largely unnoticed in today's Reformed churches." This is all the more notable "given the fact that an account of virtue may be found in the works of some of its most prominent thinkers."[2] Reformed moral thought is usually associated with the ethics of divine commands, situated in the context of covenantal theology, and law, rather than with the emphasis on the development of

---

[1] For recent discussion of this aspect of Reformed thought, see Crisp, "Sin," *Christian Dogmatics*.

[2] Kirk J. Nolan, *Reformed Virtue after Barth: Developing Moral Virtue Ethics in the Reformed Tradition*. Columbia Series in Reformed Theology (Louisville, KT: Westminster John Knox, 2014), 11. However, for a rather different account of the role and influence of virtue theory in Reformed thought, see Pieter Vos, "Calvinists among the Virtues: Reformed Theological Contributions to Contemporary Virtue Ethics," *Studies in Christian Ethics* 28.2 (2015): 201–12.

habit through practice characteristic of the virtue tradition.[3] In the *Nicomachean Ethics* Aristotle maintained that "the virtues, then, come neither by nature nor against nature, but nature gives the capacity for acquiring them, and this is developed by training."[4] To some Reformed thinkers this Aristotelian emphasis on habituation in order to develop the virtues undermines the claim that fallen human beings are incapable of pleasing God without divine grace, as well as the notion that the moral character of human beings must be renewed by means of divine grace in order to live the good life.[5]

These two issues, namely, the "pessimism" of Reformed theological anthropology and the (modern) Reformed suspicion of virtue ethics as a way of conceiving moral theology, have a direct bearing upon Reformed notions of character. Rather than trying to survey representative accounts of Reformed views on human character as a way of pursuing this line of inquiry further, in this chapter I propose to focus on what I take to be arguably the most sophisticated, and certainly one of the most influential, accounts of moral character in the Reformed tradition as a case study. This is the position developed by Jonathan Edwards.

Edwards is salient for two reasons, corresponding to the two issues with which we began. He wrote one of the most thorough and influential treatments of original sin in the Reformed tradition, which elaborates upon the doctrine of total depravity that can be found in the work of Magisterial Reformers like Calvin.[6] He was also a theologian enamored of a version of virtue theory in moral theology. In fact, his account of virtue presents an understanding

---

[3]Thus: "It is commonly held that Reformed ethics is basically accomplished as an ethics of divine commandments, creational orders and—to a lesser extent—(human) rights, whereas theological virtue ethics is in particular developed in the Roman Catholic tradition." Vos, "Calvinists among the Virtues," 201. For an interesting attempt at rapprochement between Reformed divine command theory and post-MacIntyrian narrative and virtue ethics, see Richard J. Mouw, *The God Who Commands* (Notre Dame: University of Notre Dame Press, 1991).

[4]Aristotle, *Nicomachean Ethics*, trans. F. H. Peters (New York: Barnes and Noble, 2004 [1893]), Bk II. 1, 1103a. (p. 23.)

[5]See Vos, "Calvinists among the Virtues," 203–4 and Nolan, *Reformed Virtue after Barth*, ch. 2, which tackles Karl Barth's objections to virtue theory.

[6]Jonathan Edwards, WJE3.

of human character that reflects important elements of Reformed thought while innovating within the tradition. He is therefore an important test case of how Reformed theologians might engage with notions of virtue and character today.

His Reformed theological sensibilities are also evident in his characteristically doctrinal approach to ethics. In contemporary treatments of Edwards's moral thought he is sometimes presented as if he is merely another eighteenth-century moral sense theorist like Francis Hutcheson. But, as Stephen Wilson observes, although he was "certainly influenced by moral sense theory," he was "far from the more or less Anglican position attributed to him by some ethicists."[7] In fact, by Edwards's own estimation doctrinal theology funds moral rumination. "Duties are founded on doctrines," he writes, "and the revelation we now have of the Trinity, of the love of God, of the love of Christ to sinners, of his humiliation" and of other Christian doctrines "make a vast alteration with respect to the reason and obligations to many amiable and exalted duties, so that they are as it were new."[8] Attending to this doctrinal foundation makes an important difference to how we understand Edwards's views on the related issues of virtue and character, as we shall see.[9]

We proceed as follows. First, I shall give an overview of some of the main doctrinal themes that bear upon Edwards's moral thought. Then, in the second section, I address some problems that these themes raise for his account of virtue and character. The closing section offers some reflections on the prospects for retrieving a broadly Edwardsian approach to virtue and character as a resource for contemporary Reformed moral theology.

---

[7]Stephen A. Wilson, *Virtue Reformed: Rereading Jonathan Edwards's Ethics*. Brill Studies in Intellectual History (Leiden: E. J. Brill, 2005), xxv.
[8]WJE13: 416.
[9]This cuts against the views of those who, like Philip L. Quinn, regard the first chapter of *True Virtue* as an argument that can (and, perhaps, should) be extracted from its theological context for its philosophical claims alone. See Quinn, "Honoring Jonathan Edwards" *Journal of Religion Ethics* 31.2 (2003): 299–321, and Quinn, "The Master Argument of *The Nature of True Virtue*," in *Jonathan Edwards: Philosophical Theologian*, eds. Paul Helm and Oliver D. Crisp (Farnham: Ashgate, 2003), ch. 6.

Doctrinal themes in Edwards's moral theology

After a period in which the study of Edwards's moral theology languished, there have been a number of treatments of this aspect of his writings.[10] His most important work in this regard is his dissertation on *The Nature of True Virtue*. However, as recent studies of his thought have emphasized, it is a mistake to attempt to treat this work, or his moral theology more generally, in isolation from his wider corpus. His understanding of human beings and their relationship to God as creator and sustainer, and as the divine Trinity, has an important bearing on the shape of his ethics.[11] With that in mind, in what follows we shall focus on four key theological themes in Edwards's moral thought: his view of God's relation to creation; his understanding of human beings in a state of sin; his account of infused habits; and his situating of his account of true

---

[10]See, for example, the symposium on Edwards's ethics in *Journal of Religious Ethics* 31.2 (2003), with contributions from Jean Porter, Stephen A. Wilson, Gerald R. McDermott, William C. Spohn, Roland A. Delattre, and Philip L. Quinn. The two most substantial recent treatments of Edwards's moral thought can be found in Wilson, *Virtue Reformed*, and Elizabeth Agnew Cochran, *Receptive Human Virtues: A New Reading of Jonathan Edwards's Ethics* (University Park: The Pennsylvania State University Press, 2011). Also of note is William J. Danaher Jr., *The Trinitarian Ethics of Jonathan Edwards*. Columbia Series in Reformed Theology (Louisville, KT: Westminster John Knox, 2004). Among older studies of Edwards's moral thought, Roland A. Delattre's *Beauty and Sensibility in the Thought of Jonathan Edwards: An Essay in Aesthetics and Theological Ethics* (New Haven, CT: Yale University Press, 1968), Norman Fiering's *Jonathan Edwards's Moral Thought and Its British Context* (Chapel Hill: University of North Carolina Press, 1981); Clyde A. Holbrook's work, *The Ethics of Jonathan Edwards: Morality and Aesthetics* (Ann Arbor: The University of Michigan Press, 1973), and the editorial introduction to WJE8 by Paul Ramsey, are worthy of mention. There is also useful material in Stephen R. Holmes, *God of Grace and God of Glory, An Account of the Theology of Jonathan Edwards* (Edinburgh: T&T Clark, 2000); Michael J. McClymond and Gerald R. McDermott, *The Theology of Jonathan Edwards* (New York: Oxford University Press, 2012), John E. Smith, *Jonathan Edwards, Puritan, Preacher, Philosopher* (London: Chapman, 1992), and Kyle C. Strobel, *Jonathan Edwards's Theology: A Reinterpretation* (London: Bloomsbury, 2013).
[11]Thus, for example, Cochran, *Receptive Human Virtues*, Danaher, *The Trinitarian Ethics of Jonathan Edwards*, Strobel, *Jonathan Edwards's Theology*.

virtue in the broader context of the participation of human beings in the life of God.

a. God and creation

Like many Reformed theologians, divine sovereignty played an organizing role in Edwards's thought. He believed that the creation is the emanation of the divine life.[12] God "communicates" himself in creation, as Edwards puts it, in the "overflow" of his own divine fullness. He is the one truly *excellent* being, the uncreated spirit upon whom all created spirits immediately depend for their continued existence moment-to-moment. Excellency, in this connection, is a semi-technical term that has to do with beauty and symmetry (an aesthetic dimension); agreement, consent, and equality between the parts of a thing and the whole thing (a relational component); and the being of a thing (an ontological component).[13] It is a quality that, on Edwards's reckoning, implies plurality, for, as he says in discussing excellency in his early philosophical notes, "one alone . . . cannot be excellent."[14] This divine excellency is expressed in God's triune life so that Edwards can say:

> As to God's Excellence, it is evident it consists in the *Love of himself* . . . he exerts himself towards himself, no other way, than in infinitely loving and delighting in himself; in the mutual love of the Father and the Son. This makes the Third, the Personal Holy Spirit, of the Holiness of God, which is his infinite Beauty; and this is God's Infinite Consent to Being in general. And his love to the creature is his excellence, of the communication of Himself, his complacency in them, according as they partake of more or less of Excellence and beauty, that is, of holiness (which consists in love); that is, according as he communicates more or less of his Holy Spirit.[15]

---

[12]See *The End for Which God Created the World* in WJE8.
[13]This, and the matter of excellency in the Trinity is analyzed in detail in Oliver D. Crisp, *Jonathan Edwards among the Theologians*, ch. 3.
[14]WJE6: 337.
[15]"The Mind," in WJE6: 364. Emphasis original.

The Holy Spirit is particularly associated in Edwards's thought with God's love, and with the communication of God's being in creation. What is more, "'Tis peculiar to God, that he has beauty *within himself*, consisting in Being's consenting with his own Being, or the love of himself, in his own Holy Spirit. Whereas the excellence of others is in loving others, in loving God, and in the communications of his Spirit."[16] The beauty or excellence of creatures, including the beauty or excellence of virtue communicated by God, is a reflection of this maximal divine beauty or excellency, and creatures instantiate these qualities as a reflection of the effulgence of the divine nature as the fountain or spring from which created "being" emanates.[17] Edwards also thinks that excellence or beauty is primarily a mental quality; "it is a beauty that has its original seat in the mind."[18] It is "the beauty of those qualities and acts of the mind that are of a *moral* nature,"[19] and therefore consistent with the ascription of praise and blame. Nevertheless, in order to "relish" this beauty (as Edwards puts it), the creature must be given the right temper[20]— and in fallen human beings that comes only through the regenerative work of the Holy Spirit. For it requires a "union of heart" with God[21] that is impossible without divine grace.

b. Human beings in a state of sin

Edwards affirms the common Reformed view of total depravity. Calvin defined original sin as "a hereditary corruption and depravity of our nature, extending to all the parts of the soul, which first makes us obnoxious to the wrath of God, and then produces

---

[16]WJE6: 365.

[17]WJE6: 591–92.

[18]*True Virtue* in WJE8: 539. Edwards was an idealist who believed the world comprises created minds and their ideas emanated or "communicated" by God. I have dealt with this at length in Crisp, *Jonathan Edwards on God and Creation*, and Crisp, "Jonathan Edwards, Idealism, and Christology," in *Idealism and Christian Theology, Idealism and Christianity*, Vol. 1, eds. Joshua R. Farris, S. Mark Hamilton, and James S. Spiegel (New York and London: Bloomsbury, 2016), ch. 8.

[19]WJE8: 539. Emphasis original.

[20]WJE8: 549.

[21]WJE8: 557, 571, 594.

in us works which in Scripture are termed works of the flesh."[22] Edwards's language is similar, "By original sin . . . is meant the innate sinful depravity of the heart," although he admits that in his own time it is "vulgarly understood" to include "not only the depravity of nature, but the imputation of Adam's first sin," thereby extending the definition to include the transmission of original sin as well.[23]

In his treatise *Original Sin*, he goes to great lengths to explain how fallen human beings can be responsible for the morally vitiated state of sin that is ascribed to them by God. He compresses much of the complexity of *Original Sin* in the seventh sermon in his *Charity and Its Fruits* series, which is an important source for his moral thought. There Edwards emphasizes the way in which the fall of humanity entailed the loss of the nobler principles organizing human moral nature, which were dependent on the immediate agency of the Holy Spirit. Without the presence of these higher principles, human beings became morally disordered, being governed by the "lower principles" stemming from self-interest. Thus, according to Edwards:

> The ruin which the Fall brought upon the soul of man consists very much in that he lost his nobler and more extensive principles, and fell wholly under the government of self-love. He is debased in his nature and become little and ignoble . . . as soon as he had transgressed, those nobler principles were immediately lost and all this excellent enlargedness of his soul was gone and he thenceforward shrunk into a little point, circumscribed and closely shut up within itself to the exclusion of others. God was forsaken and fellow creatures forsaken, and man retired within himself and became wholly governed by narrow, selfish principles. Self-love became absolute master of his soul, the more noble and spiritual principles having taken warning and fled.[24]

---

[22]*Institutes*, trans. Henry Beveridge (Edinburgh: T&T Clark, 1863 [1559]), 2. 1. 8, p. 217.

[23]WJE3: 107.

[24]Edwards, *Charity and Its Fruits* in WJE8: 252–53.

The moral disorder of human beings consequent upon the primal sin entailed a corruption of nature. Thereafter, human beings were bound to sin. This is the moral corruption of original sin. To it was added original guilt, that is, the guilt of our first parents transmitted to their progeny. Edwards spent some time trying to rebut objections to the notions of transmitted sin and guilt (which need not concern us here). He also attempted to give some account of the moral psychology of those in a state of sin (which does concern us). Like the Amryaldian theologians of the French Reformed Seminary at Saumur, he maintained that fallen human beings are naturally able to choose to love God, but have a "moral inability" to do so.[25] This moral inability he understands as equivalent to lacking a moral inclination to will to will the good with respect to pleasing God consequent upon original sin, though there is no natural impediment (no physical defect or obstacle) preventing fallen humans from willing the good.

The upshot of this is that human beings are quite incapable of pleasing God or displaying true virtue without some act of grace. According to Edwards, there are no circumstances in which a fallen human being would ever be able to will to will what is pleasing in the sight of God. Without the reparative work of the Holy Spirit indwelling the believer in regeneration and bringing about the reordering of human moral nature so that the inferior principles became organized once more by the superior principles of piety and holiness provided by the Holy Spirit—as it was prior to the Fall—human beings will never please God. Edwards is clear that moral bootstrapping from a state of sin into a state of grace, Pelagian-style, is theologically untenable.

c. Infused habits

An oft-repeated criticism of Edwards's understanding of infused grace is that it sounds more Catholic than Protestant.[26] For, as Paul Ramsey points out, Edwards clearly teaches "a doctrine of *infused*

---

[25]WJE1: 159, 362–63, and discussion of this in Crisp, *Jonathan Edwards among the Theologians*, ch. 6.

[26]Anri Morimoto makes this an important plank in his claim that Edwards's understanding of the order of salvation (*ordo salutis*) is influenced by Catholic as

righteousness," that is, of the infusion of Christ's righteousness via the Holy Spirit, "and not only a doctrine of Christ's righteousness *imputed* to us."[27] It was for this reason that Tryon Edwards edited out the language of infusion in his nineteenth edition of *Charity and Its Fruits*. However, Edwards's understanding of infused grace and infused habits are in fact variations on a Reformed theme.

Edwards maintained that in regeneration the human soul is *infused* with the Holy Spirit, the same Spirit that indwelt human beings before the Fall and had organized the lower principles of human nature before Adam's primal sin in a way that formed them according to the design plan of being able to participate in communion with God.[28] This infusion of divine grace in fallen human beings is not distinct from the divine nature; it is the infusion of the divine nature into the soul, the "communication" of the Holy Spirit to the regenerate. This is what Edwards calls the "new sense of things," and it is a radical reorientation of fallen human beings so that they may begin to please God and display true virtue.[29] In keeping with his Reformed forebears, Edwards believes that without the infusion of the grace that is the Holy Spirit, human beings cannot please God. Nor can they hope to display *true* virtue. The presence of the Holy Spirit in the soul enables fallen human beings to begin a journey "into" God, as it were, for in indwelling them he confers upon them his nature (but not his essence, in keeping with other traditional views about human participation in the divine life commensurate with *theosis*).[30] The Spirit provides

---

well as Reformation thought. See *Jonathan Edwards and the Catholic Vision of Salvation* (University Park: Pennsylvania State University Press, 1995).

[27]Paul Ramsey, WJE8: 739. Emphasis original. Ramsey shows that language of 'infusion' and 'infused grace' is found in the Reformed tradition prior to Edwards and is not eccentric.

[28]It seems that for Edwards the Holy Spirit must be present to organize the moral 'higher principles' of human nature rightly. Although there is 'natural conscience' and a moral sense that work after a fashion in fallen human beings, these cannot rise to the level of being truly virtuous without the action of the Holy Spirit. This seems to be the burden of *The Nature of True Virtue*, ch. V.

[29]*Religious Affections* in WJE2: 205–6.

[30]On Edwards's way of thinking, the infusion of the Holy Spirit in regeneration is commensurate with the declarative judgment of God in justification according to which human beings are declared to be just on account of the alien righteousness of Christ. It is just that imputed righteousness depends upon the real change brought

human beings with the "spiritual image of God." As a corollary to this, Edwards reasons that one cannot attain true virtue merely by habituation. He writes, "To say that a man who has no true virtue and no true grace can acquire it by frequent exercises of [it], is as much a contradiction as to say a man acts grace [*sic*] when he has no grace, or that he has it [when] he has it not."[31] Virtue and the habits of true virtue are, as Elizabeth Cochran has recently pointed out, *received* from God on Edwards's view. "Yet our reception is not passive," she writes. "For Edwards we actively participate in the virtue we receive; this participation makes our moral agency authentic."[32]

Philip Quinn criticizes Edwards on this very point. He thinks that "it does not seem impossible for us to have a loving attitude toward all existing things without a special gift of regenerating grace." He goes on to ask, "why should we think that anything more than . . . a mechanism of natural affinity built into human psychology is needed in order to account of the virtuous love of virtue?"[33] But for a Reformed theologian like Edwards, original sin poses an insuperable obstacle to a truly virtuous love of virtue, absent divine grace. The moral inability of which Edwards speaks in *Freedom of the Will*[34] renders human beings disordered and incapable of acting in a manner pleasing to God. But the infusion of grace enables regenerate humans to exemplify true virtue, from a virtuous disposition brought about through the direct work of the Spirit upon the soul in moral revivification.

We might put it like this. For Edwards, true virtue requires a love of God such that without this love no virtuous disposition may be formed. Yet such a disposition is entirely lacking in fallen human

---

about in the human heart by the infusion of the Holy Spirit. For this reason, in his sermon "Justification by Faith," Edwards can say "What is real in the union between Christ and his people, is the foundation of what is legal; that is, it is something really in them, and between them, uniting them, that is the ground of the suitableness of their being accounted as one by the Judge." (WJE19: 158.) For discussion of this point, see Withrow, *Becoming Divine*, ch. 5.

[31]'Miscellanies' 73 in WJE13: 242. The grammatically incorrect sentence is in the original.

[32]Cochran, *Receptive Human Virtues*, 20.

[33]Quinn, "Honoring Jonathan Edwards," 302.

[34]WJE1, Part III, §4.

beings. Thus, in *The Nature of True Virtue*, Edwards can write, "no affection whatsoever to any creature, or any system of created beings, which is not dependent on, nor subordinate to a propensity or union of the heart to God, the Supreme and Infinite Being, can be of the nature of true virtue."[35] Earlier remarks in his "Miscellanies" notebook underline the point:

> the habit of grace . . . is always begun with an act of grace that shall imply faith in it, because a habit can be of no manner of use till there is occasion to exert it; and all habits being only a law that God has fixed, that such actions upon such occasions should be exerted, the first new thing that there can be in the creature must be some actual alteration.[36]

So the habit of grace requires a prior act of grace by means of which the human soul is regenerated, whereupon virtuous habits, understood as moral laws that God has "fixed," may be instantiated and developed.[37]

d. The end for which God created human beings

It has sometimes been asserted that the rejection of a broadly Aristotelian scheme of moral theory in the wake of the Protestant Reformation has led to the evisceration of teleology or, as Alasdair MacIntyre puts it, "man-as-he-could-be-if-he-realized-his-*telos*."[38] In its theological guise the worry can be put like this: the voluntarism

---

[35] WJE8: 556–57.
[36] WJE13: 358.
[37] The notion of moral and natural laws here and elsewhere in Edwards's work has been the subject of much debate. It seems to me that law-like language in Edwards's thought should not be taken with full metaphysical seriousness, given his account of continuous creation: nothing persists long enough for laws of any kind to persist other than as divine "stable ideas" that God continues to apply to different world-stages at different times. For discussion of this point, see Crisp in *Jonathan Edwards on God and Creation*.
[38] Alasdair MacIntyre, *After Virtue: A Study of Moral Theory.* Third Edition (Notre Dame: University of Notre Dame Press, 2007 [1981]), 54.

underpinning divine commands tends to deprive moral theology of any sense of a goal or moral end beyond that of obedience to the divine will. According to MacIntyre's understanding of early modern moral thought, "the moral scheme which forms the historical background . . . had . . . a structure which requires three elements: untutored human nature, man-as-he-could-be-if-he-realized-his-*telos* and the moral precepts which enable him to pass from one state to the other."[39] Eighteenth-century moral philosophers excised the teleological element of moral inquiry, which left untutored human nature and moral precepts to hold human nature in check— precepts that recognized no essential human nature that has a purpose or goal achieved through habituating the virtues. The moral goal present in Aristotle's virtue ethics, appropriated by his Christian heirs, was reduced in post-Reformation moral theology to the need to adhere to divine commands.[40]

But recent work on the notion of union with Christ and participation in the divine life in Reformed theology has shown that this MacIntyrian narrative regarding Reformation theology, and of Reformed theology in particular, is wide of the mark. To take just one example, in the very opening passage of the *Institutes* where Calvin sets out his understanding of human corruption, he also makes clear that we should find virtue in God:

> So long as we do not look beyond the earth, we are quite pleased with our own righteousness, wisdom, and virtue; we address ourselves in the most flattering terms, and seem only less than demigods. But should we once begin to raise our thoughts to God, and reflect what kind of Being he is, and how absolute the perfection of that righteousness, and wisdom, and virtue, to which, as a standard, we are bound to be conformed, what formerly delighted us by its false show of righteousness will become polluted with the greatest iniquity; what strangely imposed upon us under the name of wisdom will disgust by its extreme folly; and what presented the appearance of virtuous energy will be condemned as the most miserable impotence.

---

[39]Ibid.
[40]This is charted by Vos in "Calvinists among the Virtues," 208–9.

So far are those qualities in us, which seem most perfect, from corresponding to the divine purity.[41]

In this passage the goal of human moral development is not made entirely clear. Recognition that God's virtue infinitely outstrips the dim reflection of this in human virtue provides no tangible account of what it is that fallen human beings should be aiming at, or whither they are bound. This Calvin provides elsewhere, explaining that participation on the divine life is the goal at which we should aim.[42] For example:

> This is the wonderful exchange which, out of his measureless benevolence, he has made with us; that, becoming Son of man with us, he has made us sons of God with him; that, by his descent to earth, he has prepared an ascent to heaven for us; that, by taking on our mortality, he has conferred his immortality upon us; that, by accepting our weakness, he has strengthened us by his power; that, receiving our poverty into himself, he has transferred his wealth to us; that, taking the weight of our iniquity upon himself (which oppressed us), he has clothed us with his righteousness.[43]

This is indicative of the way in which Calvin's theology makes it plain that union with Christ and participation in the divine life are the goals of a transformed human life. Far from eviscerating moral teleology, he relocates it as a goal of the Christian life understood in terms of the language of union and participation.

Although Jonathan Edwards was at pains to distance himself from being called a "Calvinist" for anything more than convention's sake, and like many puritans claimed no dependence on the thought

---

[41] *Inst.* 1.1.2, 38–39.

[42] Recent work that has emphasized this aspect of Calvin's work includes J. Todd Billings, *Calvin, Participation, and the Gift*; Julie Canlis, *Calvin's Ladder*; William B. Evans, *Imputation and Impartation*; Mark A. Garcia, *Life in Christ: Union with Christ and Twofold Grace in Calvin's Theology*; and Carl Mosser, "The Greatest Possible Blessing: Calvin on Deification."

[43] Calvin, *Inst.* 4.17.2. (Ford Lewis Battles trans.)

of Calvin in particular,[44] it is notable that his moral theology shares several distinctive features that are characteristic of Calvin's thought as well—and that may fairly be called "Calvinistic." These include a doctrine of total depravity (which, we have noted, he parsed somewhat differently than Calvin), a concern for locating virtue in the Godhead, and only derivatively in human beings with whom he is united (Cochran's "receptive human virtues"), and, related to this, a clear teleological focus in his moral theology.

Perhaps even more than Calvin, Edwards regarded the goal of the moral life as being aimed at participation in the life of God. He certainly wrote about it with great enthusiasm and precision, especially in *The End for Which God Created the World*. The reason for being holy and developing a moral character is, in Edwards's estimation, in order to be united with God in "an infinite strictness," although there will never come a time at which "this infinitely valuable good [that is, complete union with God] has been actually bestowed."[45] Like a mathematical asymptote, the believer is on a journey toward God, so to speak, which goes on forevermore, but which never leads to the loss of the human individual in the divine, like a drop of water in the ocean. Their earthly pilgrimage is only the beginning of a life directed toward ever closer union with God that continues everlastingly. The development of true virtue is directed toward this end. Edwards is unabashed about this. What is more, and with a nod to *The End for Which God Created the World*, he writes in *True Virtue* of the way in which this goal of union is subordinate to the more ultimate goal of glorifying God. He writes, "though we are not able to give anything to God, which we have of our own, independently; yet we may be the instruments of promoting *his glory*, in which he takes a true and proper *delight*."[46] Rather than feeling any embarrassment about instrumentalizing human beings in the purposes of God, Edwards revels in it in good

---

[44]Edwards avers, "I should not take it at all amiss, to be called a Calvinist, for distinction's sake: though I utterly disclaim a dependence on Calvin, or believing the doctrines which I hold, because he believed and taught them; and cannot justly be charged with believing in everything just as he taught." WJE1:131.

[45]Edwards, *The End for which God Created the World* in WJE8: 534, and 536 respectively.

[46]WJE8: 552, emphasis original.

Reformed fashion: our end, or goal, is to glorify God and delight in him.

The beauty or excellency that is true virtue is, according to Edwards, benevolence to Being in general, a "consent, propensity, and union of heart with Being in general." In Edwards's nomenclature, benevolence to "being in general" has to do with all existing beings. This, he thinks, must go hand in hand with "a supreme love to God" as the "foundation and fountain of all being and all beauty."[47] In a similar manner, in the first sermon in the *Charity and Its Fruits* series, Edwards avers, "all that virtue which is saving, and distinguishing of true Christians from others, is summed up in Christian or divine love."[48] Like Augustine, Edwards regards love to God and to all existing beings as the heart of true virtue. In the twelfth sermon of the series he reasons that all the virtues are concatenated together and imply one another, because they are communicated together by the immediate action of the Holy Spirit in the human soul in the work of regeneration.[49]

The communal dimension to true virtue is spelled out in his final sermon in his *Charity and Its Fruits* series, where he lays out his conception of heaven as a world of love. He writes that the heavenly society

> shall all be united together in a very near relation. Love seeks a near relation to the object beloved. And in heaven all shall be nearly related. They shall be nearly allied to God, the supreme object of their love . . . all shall be nearly related to Christ; for he shall be the Head of the whole society, and husband of the whole church of saints. All together shall constitute his spouse, and they shall be related one to another as brethren. It will all be one society, yea, one family.[50]

The desire for union and participation in the divine life characteristic of Edwards's eschatology is here clearly evident. Beauty or excellency

---

[47]*True Virtue* in WJE8: 550, 551.
[48]*Charity and its Fruits*, Sermon One, WJE8: 131.
[49]WJE8: 332.
[50]WJE8: 380.

displayed in the creature is a reflection of the beauty and excellency of God and finds its apogee in union with the divine in the heavenly society, bringing together the love to being in general and to God in particular that Edwards maintains is at the heart of true virtue, in a society that is everlasting and progressive in its increasing intimacy and union.

If we compare Edwards's views in *The End for Which God Created the World*, we find him expounding this progressive eschatological state of union in more detail. He writes, "But if strictness of union to God be viewed as thus infinitely exalted; then the creature must be regarded as infinitely, nearly and closely united to God."[51] What is more,

> If by reason of the strictness of the union of a man and his family, their interest may be looked upon as one, how much more one is the interest of Christ and his church (whose first union in heaven is unspeakably more perfect and exalted, than that of an earthly father and his family), if they be considered with regard to their eternal and increasing union![52]

Against the objection that the progressive state of increasing union between the believer and God here conceived will never yield complete union, Edwards remarks,

> I suppose it will not be denied by any that God, in glorifying the saints in heaven with eternal felicity, aims to satisfy his infinite grace or benevolence, by the bestowment of a good infinitely valuable, because eternal: and yet there never will come the moment, when it can be said, that now this infinitely valuable good has been actually bestowed.[53]

Asymptotic indeed!

---

[51]WJE8: 535.
[52]Ibid.
[53]WJE8: 536.

Some problems for Edwards's
moral theology

We come to objections to the Reformed theological cast of Edwards's ethics. Perhaps the most serious problems have to do with questions of creaturely moral agency. Let us focus on four of the most significant.

a. The problem of occasionalism

The first two problems, though metaphysical in nature, have a direct bearing upon his moral thought. They are also closely related and sometimes conflated in the literature dealing with Edwards's thought. Occasionalism is the doctrine according to which God is the sole cause of all that comes to pass. Creatures are merely the "occasions" of divine action. So, if Jones chooses to raise her arm her volition, her intentional action and the visible physical act of raising her arm are all caused by God on this view. Her volition and intentional act, as well as the physical movement of her arm, are not actions she causes; she is merely the occasion of God causing them.

Edwards clearly endorses the doctrine of occasionalism in his writings.[54] But this has an immediate moral implication: how can the formation of any virtuous disposition, or intention, or volition be truly that of the creaturely agent if God is the cause of all that comes to pass? I have written on this matter at length elsewhere.[55] For present purposes I shall say this. Edwards's doctrine of occasionalism does not necessarily undermine the claim that I am the one who forms the intention and wills a particular thing to obtain. I don't cause these things, that much is true on his view. But I am the entity doing the action, and I am the entity that identifies with these actions as mine; God does not. For at least some action

---

[54]For references, see Crisp, *Jonathan Edwards on God and Creation*, 24–26.
[55]See Crisp, *Jonathan Edwards on God and Creation*, and Crisp, "Jonathan Edwards and Occasionalism," in *Abraham's Dice: Chance and Providence in the Monotheistic Traditions*, ed. Karl W. Giberson (New York: Oxford University Press, 2016), ch. 10.

theorists this may be sufficient for agency, even if it is a very thin account of agency.[56] Nor is it inconsistent with his claims about true virtue, because virtues are received as a divine gift in the indwelling of the Holy Spirit and cultivated in conjunction with the Spirit's internal work of sanctification. Odd though it may look to modern eyes, Edwards's position in this respect is consistent.[57]

b. The problem of continuous creation

The second and related problem has to do with Edwards's doctrine of continuous creation. According to Edwards, in considering the metaphysics of creation much depends on the degree to which "created identity or oneness with past existence, in general, depends on the sovereign constitution and law of the Supreme Author and Disposer of the universe."[58] He thinks that "the communication or continuance of the same consciousness and memory to any subject, through successive parts of duration, depends wholly on a divine establishment."[59] Moreover, "the existence of created substances, in each successive moment, must be the effect of the immediate agency, will, and power of God."[60] In fact, "God's upholding created substance, or causing its existence in each successive moment, is altogether equivalent to an *immediate production out of nothing*, at each moment."[61] There has been some discussion of Edwards's doctrine of continuous creation in the recent philosophical-theological literature.[62] The moral problem this raises is that on

---

[56]Compare Harry Frankfurt (not an occasionalist): "If I'm in the condition where I'm doing what I want to do and I really want to do it, i.e. I decisively identity with my action, then I think I'm responsible for it. It makes no difference how it came about that that is the case. If it *is* the case then it follows that I am fully responsible." Ortwin de Graef, "Discussion with Harry Frankfurt," *Ethical Perspectives* 5.1 (1998): 32. Emphasis original.

[57]Although occasionalism is very much a minority sport, it is not without notable advocates in recent times among Christian philosophers. These include Jonathan Kvanvig, Hugh McCann, and Alvin Plantinga.

[58]*Original Sin* in WJE3: 397.

[59]WJE3: 398.

[60]WJE3: 401.

[61]WJE3: 402. Emphasis original.

[62]Examples include Oliver D. Crisp, *Jonathan Edwards and the Metaphysics of Sin*, and Michael C. Rea, "The Metaphysics of Original Sin," in *Persons: Divine and*

Edwards's way of thinking no created thing persists for more than a moment. But if creatures do not persist through time, then it is natural to ask how it is that creatures can be the appropriate subject of moral properties, let alone habits and dispositions. It could be argued that things persist through time in virtue of having temporal counterparts or in virtue of being extended four-dimensional entities, and this is indeed Edwards's view. However, it is still strange to think that numerically distinct entities are treated as one by Providence for the purposes of identity across time and moral responsibility, praise and blame. Yet this too is a consequence of Edwards's position.

c. The problem of theological voluntarism

This raises a third related issue, to do with theological voluntarism. In *Original Sin* Edwards avers that

> there is no identity or oneness in the case, but what depends on the arbitrary constitution of the Creator; who by his wise sovereign establishment so unites these successive new effects, that he treats them as one, by communicating to them like properties, relations, and circumstances; and so, leads us to regard and treat them as one. When I call this an arbitrary constitution, I mean, that it is a constitution which depends on nothing but the divine will; which divine will depends on nothing but the divine wisdom. In this sense, the whole course of nature, with all that belongs to it, all its laws and methods, and constancy and regularity, continuance and proceeding, is an arbitrary constitution.[63]

He goes on to say, "a *divine constitution* is the thing which *makes truth*, in affairs of this nature."[64] "'Tis this," he observes,

> that must account for the continuance of any such thing, anywhere, as consciousness of acts that are past; and for the continuance

---

Human, eds. Dean Zimmerman and Peter van Inwagen (Oxford: Oxford University Press, 2007), ch. 14.

[63]WJE3: 403–4.

[64]WJE3: 404. Emphasis original.

of all *habits*, either good or bad: and on this depends everything
that can belong to personal identity. And all communications,
derivations, or continuation of qualities, properties, or relations,
natural or moral, from what is past, as if the subject were one,
depends on no other foundation.[65]

On the face of it, this seems to be straightforwardly voluntarist:
God makes truth in continuous creation; the constitution of things
depends on God's will and wisdom, and nothing else. But if that
is the case, then it looks like the way things are constituted is
whimsical or capricious—and what does that say about the divine
character?

A rather different account of Edwards's views at this juncture is
given by Elizabeth Cochran. She maintains that Edwards presents
"a theologically coherent understanding of true virtue without
resorting to . . . voluntarist arguments" of the sort that require that
"the moral order was established by an arbitrary divine fiat, so that
God's will is the source of morality."[66] But as we have just seen,
this is just what Edwards does affirm in his treatise on *Original
Sin*. Cochran wishes to be charitable to Edwards. As she reads him,
"salvation, and the enabling of true virtue, are products of God's
will, but the activities of God's will are formed and dictated by
love and goodness."[67] There are reasons for thinking this when
reading, say, *The Nature of True Virtue*, or *Charity and Its Fruits*,
where love is clearly the supreme virtue into which all others can
be resolved, and which reflects something essential in the divine
nature. Nevertheless, Edwards says something quite different
in *Original Sin*. At the very least there seems to be a tension in
Edwards's thought here, and one that requires his interpreters to
make some difficult decisions with respect to the moral implications
of his views.

---

[65]WJE3: 405. Emphasis original.
[66]Cochran, *Receptive Human Virtues*, 25 and 23 respectively.
[67]Ibid., 31.

d. The problem of received human virtues, character formation, and moral responsibility

This brings us to the matter of received human virtues. Edwards believes that true virtue, as opposed to instincts of nature or natural conscience (which are not of the essence of true virtue, though they can resemble true virtue), is God-given in regeneration. But if true virtue is a gift, then it is difficult to see why Edwards thinks those with true virtue are responsible for their own moral formation. Truly virtuous habits and dispositions are the fruit of the indwelling of the Holy Spirit in the believer. They are the product of a reorganized moral nature that has been reset to factory standards, as it were, by being united to the Spirit of God as a consequence of the work of Christ. (Edwards believed that Christ's atonement *purchases* the Holy Spirit for the elect.) Add to this his theological voluntarism and his doctrines of continuous creation and occasionalism, and it really does begin to look like true virtue is just the consequence of an arbitrary (in Edwards's sense of a work of the divine will or *arbitrium*) work of God. Certain persons are chosen to exemplify true virtue and are given the gift of the Holy Spirit as a result.

Nevertheless, Edwards could reply that his account is simply trying to make sense of a biblical picture of virtue. The fact that God elects certain individuals to exemplify true virtue does not necessarily exonerate these individuals from moral responsibility for their actions. Nor does it mean those not chosen to receive this gift are without praise or blame for their actions. Consider the case of someone chosen by lottery to receive a large payout. They did not deserve this outcome. But how is that morally relevant to questions of how the person acts once elevated to the plutocracy? Or suppose that someone is reduced to penury through economic factors beyond their control. Though the person in question has not chosen this state of affairs, she is still a moral agent deserving praise or blame attaching to her actions upon finding herself in straitened circumstances.

Much more would need to be said if we were attempting to shore up Edwards's position against these objections. Here I have only been able to offer a brief sketch of how an Edwardsian might respond to some of the most pressing problems his Reformed doctrine bequeaths to his moral theology.

Toward an Edwardsian moral theology?

We have seen that Edwards is a canonical Reformed theologian whose moral thought is a counterexample to McIntyre's claim about the trajectory of Enlightenment (and, by extension, Protestant) ethics after the Reformation. Yet he does not fit within the typical typology of recent Christian theological appropriations of virtue either. He is not a Thomist/Aristotelian, like MacIntyre, and his focus is not that of a Stanley Hauerwas.[68] That is, he doesn't think of the virtues as a cluster of interconnected moral dispositions that are actualized through habituation in accordance with a particular tradition. Instead, and like Augustine, he thinks that virtue is unified in benevolence, though his particular construal of benevolence is rather different than the bishop of Hippo.[69] Nor does he think that virtue is primarily a matter of developing a community of character within the church characteristic of Hauerwas's thought. Instead, he thinks of virtue in primarily aesthetic-theological terms, as some sort of beauty or excellency (to use his term) that can only be perceived if God grants the new sense of the heart that is a prerequisite for true virtue.[70] His views are not without moral-theological cost, and there do seem to be internal tensions in the underlying metaethical claims he makes about God's motivation in creating the world. But this is hardly unusual for a thinker involved in a system-building project, like Edwards. Despite these problems, for theologians in the Reformed tradition Edwards presents an interesting case for thinking *theologically* about the moral life as the development of habits of virtue consequent upon the regenerative action of a sovereign God. Such a position strikes me as a worthy candidate for moral-theological retrieval if it involves repairing as well as recovering aspects of Edwards's moral-theological project.

---

[68]Here I follow the helpful characterization of Jean Porter and Stephen Wilson in their coauthored "Focus Introduction: Taking the Measure of Jonathan Edwards for Contemporary Religious Ethics," *Journal of Religious Ethics* 31.2 (2003): 185–86.

[69]According to some Thomists, Aquinas is not an Aristotelian either. See, for example, Eleonore Stump, "The Non-Aristotelian Character of Aquinas' Ethics," *Faith and Philosophy* 28.1 (2011): 29–43.

[70]Porter and Wilson comment, "for Edwards, true virtue is not shaped by the community; rather, it is bestowed by God, in accordance with God's inscrutable decrees." "Taking the Measure of Jonathan Edwards," 187. This seems right.

BIBLIOGRAPHY

Abraham, William J., *Canon and Criterion in Christian Theology: From the Fathers to Feminism* (Oxford: Oxford University Press, 1998).

Abraham, William J., Jason E. Vickers, and Natalie B. Van Kirk, eds. *Canonical Theism: A Proposal for Theology and the Church* (Grand Rapids: Eerdmans, 2008).

Adams, Marilyn McCord, *Christ and Horrors* (Cambridge: Cambridge University Press, 2006).

Ahn, Ho-Jin, "The Humanity of Christ: John Calvin's Understanding of Christ's Vicarious Humanity," *International Journal of Systematic Theology* 65.2 (2012): 145–58.

Allen, Michael, "Calvin's Christ: A Dogmatic Matrix for Discussion of Christ's Human Nature," *International Journal of Systematic Theology* 9.4 (2007): 382–97.

Ames, William, *The Marrow of Theology*, trans. John Dykstra Eusden (Grand Rapids: Baker, 1968 [1629]).

Anderson, James, *Paradox in Christian Theology: An Analysis of Its Presence, Character and Epistemic Status* (Milton Keynes: Paternoster Press and Eugene: Wipf and Stock, 2007).

Anselm of Canterbury, *Anselm: Basic Works*, trans. Thomas Williams (Indianapolis: Hackett, 2007).

Anselm of Canterbury, *S. Anselmi cantuariensis archiepiscopi opera omnia, volumen primum*, ed. Francis S. Schmitt (Edinburgh: Thomas Nelson & Sons, 1946 [1938]).

Aquinas, Thomas, *Summa Theologiae*, 5 Vols., trans. Fathers of the English Dominican Province (New York: Benzinger Brothers, 1911).

Arcadi, James M., "Kryptic or Cryptic? The Divine Preconscious Model of the Incarnation as a Concrete-nature Christology," *Neue Zeitschrift für Systematische Theologie und Religionsphilosophie* 58.2 (2016): 229–43.

Arcadi, James M., "Recent Developments in Analytic Christology," *Philosophy Compass* (2018): 1–12.

Aristotle, *Nicomachean Ethics*, trans. F. H. Peters (New York: Barnes and Noble, 2004 [1893]).

Armstrong, D. M., *A World of States of Affairs* (Cambridge: Cambridge University Press, 1997).

Asselt, Willem Van, J. Martin Bac, and Roelf T. te Velde, eds. *Reformed Thought on Freedom: The Concept of Free Choice in Early Modern Reformed Theology* (Grand Rapids: Baker Academic, 2010).

Augustine, *Confessions*, trans. R. S. Pine-Coffin (Harmondsworth: Penguin Classics, 1961).

Baker, Lynne Rudder, *Persons and Bodies: A Constitution View. Cambridge Studies in Philosophy* (Cambridge: Cambridge University Press, 2000).

Balserak, Jon, *John Calvin as Sixteenth Century Prophet* (Oxford: Oxford University Press, 2014).

Barth, Karl, *Church Dogmatics*, 4 Vols in 13 Parts, eds. G. W. Bromiley and T. F. Torrance (Edinburgh: T&T Clark, 1957–1975).

Bayne, Tim and Greg Restall, "A Participatory Model of the Atonement," in Yujin Nagasawa and Eric I. Wielenberg, eds. *New Waves in Philosophy of Religion* (London: Palgrave Macmillan, 2009), 150–66.

Beck, A. J. and Antonie Vos, "Conceptual Patterns Related to Reformed Scholasticism," *Nederlands Theologisch Tijdschrift* 57 (2003): 223–33.

The Belgic Confession, located at the website of the Christian Reformed Church, http://www.crcna.org/sites/default/files/BelgicConfession_2.pdf.

Billings, J. Todd, *Calvin, Participation, and the Gift: The Activity of Believers in Union with Christ*. Changing Paradigms in Historical and Systematic Theology (Oxford: Oxford University Press, 2007).

Billings, J. Todd and I. John Hesselink, eds. *Calvin's Theology and Its Reception: Disputes, Developments and New Possibilities* (Louisville: Westminster John Knox, 2012).

Blackburn, George A., ed. *Life Work of John L. Girardeau, D.D. LL.D.* (Columbia: The State Company, 1916).

Bolliger, Daniel, *Infiniti contemplatio: Grundzüge der Scotus und Scotismusrezeption im Werk Huldrych Zwinglis* (Leiden: E. J. Brill, 2003).

Boonin, David, *The Problem of Punishment* (Cambridge: Cambridge University Press, 2008).

Boulton, Matthew Myer, *Life in God: John Calvin, Practical Formation, and the Future of Protestant Theology* (Grand Rapids: Eerdmans, 2011).

Brierley, Michael W., "The Potential of Panentheism for Dialogue Between Science and Religion," in Philip Clayton, ed. *The Oxford Handbook of Religion and Science* (Oxford: Oxford University Press, 2006), ch. 37.

Buschart, W. David and Kent D. Eilers, *Theology as Retrieval: Receiving the Past, Renewing the Church* (Downers Grove: IVP Academic, 2015).

Calvin, John, *Concerning The Eternal Predestination of God*, trans. J. K. S. Reid (London: James Clarke, 1961).

Calvin, John, *Institutes*, trans. Henry Beveridge (Edinburgh: T&T Clark, 1863 [1559]).

Calvin, John, *Institutes of the Christian Religion, 2 Vols*, ed. John T. McNeill, trans. Ford Lewis Battles (Philadelphia: Westminster Press, 1960 [1559]).

Calvin, John, *New Testament Commentaries, Vol. 8: Romans and Thessalonians*, trans. Ross Mackenzie, eds. David W. Torrance and Thomas F. Torrance (Carlisle: Paternoster Press and Grand Rapids: Eerdmans, 1960).

Calvin, John, *New Testament Commentaries, Vol. 11: Commentaries on Galatians, Ephesians, Philippians and Colossians*, trans. T. H. L. Parker, eds. David W. Torrance and Thomas F. Torrance (Carlisle: Paternoster Press and Grand Rapids: Eerdmans, 1965).

Canlis, Julie, "Calvin, Osiander and Participation in God," *International Journal of Systematic Theology* 6.2 (2004): 169–84.

Canlis, Julie, *Calvin's Ladder: A Spiritual Theology of Ascent and Ascension* (Grand Rapids: Eerdmans, 2010).

Catechism of the Catholic Church (New York: Doubleday, 1995).

Choy, Kivin S. K. "Calvin's Defense and Reformulation of Luther's Early Reformation Doctrine of the Bondage of the Will," PhD dissertation, Calvin Theological Seminary, January 2010.

Clayton, Philip, "The Case for Christian Panentheism," *Dialogue* 37.3 (1998): 201–8.

Cline, Ernest, *Ready Player One* (New York: Random House, 2011).

Coakley, Sarah, *God, Sexuality, and the Self: An Essay "On the Trinity"* (Cambridge: Cambridge University Press, 2013).

Cochran, Elizabeth Agnew, *Receptive Human Virtues: A New Reading of Jonathan Edwards's Ethics* (University Park: The Pennsylvania State University Press, 2011).

Coleman, Andrew M., *A Dictionary of Psychology* (Oxford: Oxford University Press, 2001).

Congdon, David W., "Apokatastasis and Apostolicity: A Response to Oliver Crisp on the Question of Barth's Universalism," *Scottish Journal of Theology* 67.4 (2014): 464–80.

Cooper, John W. *Panentheism, The Other God of the Philosophers: From Plato to the Present* (Grand Rapids: Baker Academic, 2006).

Cortez, Marc, "The Human Person as Communicative Event: Jonathan Edwards on the Mind/Body Relationship," in Joshua R. Farris and Charles Taliaferro, eds. *The Ashgate Companion to Theological Anthropology* (Aldershot: Ashgate, 2015), 139–50.

Craig, William Lane, *God over All: Divine Aseity and the Challenge of Platonism* (Oxford: Oxford University Press, 2016).

Craig, William Lane, "Is Penal Substitution Incoherent? An Examination of Mark Murphy's Criticisms," *Religious Studies* 54.4 (2018): 509–46.

Crawford, Brandon James, *Jonathan Edwards on the Atonement: Understanding the Legacy of America's Greatest Theologian* (Eugene: Wipf and Stock, 2017).

Crawford, Brandon James, "Timeless Creation and God's Real Relation to the World," *Laval théologique et philosophique* 56.1 (2000): 93–112.

Crisp, Oliver D., "Analytic Theology as Systematic Theology," *Open Theology* 3 (2017): 156–66.

Crisp, Oliver D., *Analyzing Doctrine: Toward a Systematic Theology* (Waco: Baylor University Press, 2019).

Crisp, Oliver D., *An American Augustinian: Sin and Salvation in the Dogmatic Theology of William G. T. Shedd* (Milton Keynes and Eugene: Paternoster Press and Wipf and Stock, 2009).

Crisp, Oliver D., *Deviant Calvinism: Broadening Reformed Theology* (Minneapolis: Fortress Press, 2014).

Crisp, Oliver D., *Divinity and Humanity: The Incarnation Reconsidered* (Cambridge: Cambridge University Press, 2007).

Crisp, Oliver D., "Federalism vs. Realism: Charles Hodge, Augustus Strong and William Shedd on The Imputation of Sin," *International Journal of Systematic Theology* 8 (2006): 1–17.

Crisp, Oliver D., *Jonathan Edwards among the Theologians* (Grand Rapids: Eerdmans, 2015).

Crisp, Oliver D., "Jonathan Edwards and Occasionalism," in Karl W. Giberson, ed. *Abraham's Dice: Chance and Providence in the Monotheistic Traditions* (New York: Oxford University Press, 2016), ch. 10.

Crisp, Oliver D., *Jonathan Edwards and the Metaphysics of Sin* (Aldershot: Ashgate, 2005 and London: Routledge, 2016).

Crisp, Oliver D., "Jonathan Edwards, Idealism, and Christology," in Joshua R. Farris, S. Mark Hamilton, and James S. Spiegel, eds. *Idealism and Christian Theology, Idealism and Christianity Vol. 1* (New York and London: Bloomsbury, 2016), ch. 8.

Crisp, Oliver D., *Jonathan Edwards on God and Creation* (New York: Oxford University Press, 2012).

Crisp, Oliver D., "Jonathan Edwards on God's Relation to Creation," *Jonathan Edwards Studies* 8.1 (2018): 2–16.

Crisp, Oliver D., "On Original Sin," *International Journal of Systematic Theology* 17.3 (2015): 252–66.

Crisp, Oliver D., "On the Orthodoxy of Jonathan Edwards," *Scottish Journal of Theology* 67.3 (2014): 304–22.

Crisp, Oliver D., "Original Sin and Atonement," in Thomas P. Flint and Michael C. Rea, eds. *The Oxford Handbook of Philosophical Theology* (Oxford: Oxford University Press, 2009), ch. 19.

Crisp, Oliver D., *Revisioning Christology: Theology in the Reformed Tradition* (Aldershot: Ashgate, 2011).

Crisp, Oliver D., *Retrieving Doctrine: Essays in Reformed Theology* (Downers Grove: IVP Academic, 2011).

Crisp, Oliver D., "Retrieving Zwingli's Doctrine of Original Sin," *Journal of Reformed Theology* 10.4 (2016): 1–21.

Crisp, Oliver D., "Salvation and Atonement: On the Value and Necessity of the Work of Jesus Christ," in Ivor J. Davidson and Murray A. Rae, eds. *God of Salvation: Soteriology in Theological Perspective* (Aldershot: Ashgate, 2011), ch. 7.

Crisp, Oliver D., *Saving Calvinism: Expanding the Reformed Tradition* (Downers Grove: IVP Academic, 2016).

Crisp, Oliver D., "Scholastic Theology, Augustinian Realism and Original Guilt," *European Journal of Theology* 13.1 (2004): 17–28.

Crisp, Oliver D., "Sin," in Michael Allen and Scott R. Swain, eds. *Christian Dogmatics: Reformed Theology for the Church Catholic* (Grand Rapids: Baker Academic, 2016), 194–215.

Crisp, Oliver D., "The Logic of Penal Substitution Revisited," in Derek Tidball, David Hilborn, and Justin Thacker, eds. *The Atonement Debate: Papers from the London Symposium on the Atonement* (Grand Rapids: Zondervan, 2008), 208–27.

Crisp, Oliver D., *The Word Enfleshed: Exploring the Person and Work of Christ* (Grand Rapids: Baker Academic, 2016).

Crisp, Oliver D., Gavin D'Costa, Peter Hampson, and Mervyn Davies, eds. *Christianity and the Disciplines: The Transformation of The University* (London: T&T Clark, 2012).

Crisp, Oliver D. and Michael C. Rea, eds. *Analytic Theology: New Essays in the Philosophy of Theology* (Oxford: Oxford University Press, 2009).

Crisp, Oliver D. and Fred Sanders, eds. *Divine Action and Providence: Explorations in Constructive Theology* (Grand Rapids: Zondervan Academic, 2019).

Crisp, Oliver D. and Fred Sanders, eds. *The Task of Dogmatics: Explorations in Theological Method* (Grand Rapids: Zondervan Academic, 2017).

Crisp, Oliver D. and Kyle C. Strobel, *Jonathan Edwards: An Introduction to His Thought* (Grand Rapids: Eerdmans, 2018).

Cross, F. L. and E. A. Livingstone, eds. *The Oxford Dictionary of the Christian Church*, Third Edition (Oxford University Press, 1997).

Culp, John, "Panentheism," *Stanford Encyclopedia of Philosophy*, located at: https://plato.stanford.edu/entries/panentheism/, last retrieved 03/05/18.

Cuneo, Terence, *Ritualized Faith: Essays on the Philosophy of Liturgy.* Oxford Studies in Analytic Theology (Oxford: Oxford University Press, 2016).

Cunningham, William, *The Reformation and the Theology of the Reformers* (Edinburgh: T&T Clark, 1862).

Daeley, Justin J., "*Creatio Ex Nihilo*: A Solution to the Problem of the Necessity of Creation and Divine Aseity," *Philosophia Christi* 19.2 (2017): 291–313.

Danaher, William J. Jr., *The Trinitarian Ethics of Jonathan Edwards. Columbia Series in Reformed Theology* (Louisville: Westminster John Knox, 2004).

Daniel, Stephen H., "Edwards' Occasionalism," in Don Schweitzer, ed. *Jonathan Edward as Contemporary: Essays in Honor of Sang Hyun Lee* (New York: Peter Lang, 2010), 1–14.

Davies, Brian, *Introduction to the Philosophy of Religion*, Third Edition (Oxford: Oxford University Press, 2004 [1982]).

D'Costa, Gavin, *Theology in the Public Square: Church, Academy and Nation* (Oxford: Blackwell, 2005).

Delattre, Roland A., *Beauty and Sensibility in the Thought of Jonathan Edwards: An Essay in Aesthetics and Theological Ethics* (New Haven: Yale University Press, 1968).

Duff, R. A. and David Garland, eds. *Punishment: A Reader.* Oxford Readings in Socio-Legal Studies (Oxford: Oxford University Press, 1994).

Edwards, Jonathan, *Freedom of the Will, The Works of Jonathan Edwards, Vol. 1*, ed. Paul Ramsey (New Haven: Yale University Press, 1957).

Edwards, Jonathan, *Ethical Writings, The Works of Jonathan Edwards, Vol. 8*, ed. Paul Ramsey (New Haven: Yale University Press, 1989).

Edwards, Jonathan, *Letters and Personal Writings, The Works of Jonathan Edwards Vol. 16*, ed. George S. Claghorn (New Haven: Yale University Press, 1998).

Edwards, Jonathan, *The "Miscellanies": Nos. a-z, aa-zz, 1-500, The Works of Jonathan Edwards Vol. 13*, ed. Thomas A. Schafer (New Haven: Yale University Press, 1994).

Edwards, Jonathan, *Original Sin, The Works of Jonathan Edwards Vol. 3*, ed. Clyde A. Holbrook (New Haven: Yale University Press, 1970 [1758]).

Edwards, Jonathan, *Sermons and Discourses, 1734–1738: The Works of Jonathan Edwards, Vol. 19*, ed. M. X. Lesser (New Haven: Yale University Press, 2001).

Endres, John B., O.P., "The Council of Trent and Original Sin," *Proceedings of the Catholic Theological Society of America* 22 (1967), 51–91.

Evans, William B., *Imputation and Impartation: Union with Christ in American Reformed Theology*. Studies in Christian History and Thought (Milton Keynes: Paternoster Press, 2007).

Farris, Joshua and S. Mark Hamilton, "The Logic of Reparative Substitution: Contemporary Restitution Models of Atonement, Divine Justice, and Somatic Death," *Irish Theological Quarterly* 83.1 (2018): 62–77.

Feuerbach, Ludwig, *The Essence of Christianity*, trans. George Eliot (New York: Prometheus Books, 1989 [1841]).

Fiering, Norman, *Jonathan Edwards's Moral Thought and Its British Context* (Chapel Hill: University of North Carolina Press, 1981).

Finger, Thomas, *A Contemporary Anabaptist Theology: Biblical, Historical, Constructive* (Downers Grove: IVP Academic, 2004).

Flint, Thomas P., "Should Concretists Part with Mereological Models of the Incarnation?" in Anna Marmadoro and Jonathan Hill, eds. *The Metaphysics of the Incarnation* (Oxford: Oxford University Press, 2011), ch. 4.

Flint, Thomas P. and Michael C. Rea, eds. *The Oxford Handbook of Philosophical Theology* (Oxford: Oxford University Press, 2009).

Frankfurt, Harry G., *On Bullshit* (Princeton: Princeton University Press, 2005).

Gäb, Sebastian, "The paradox of ineffability," *International Journal of Philosophy and Theology* 78.3 (2017): 289–300.

Gäbler, Ulrich, *Huldrych Zwingli: Leben und Werk* (Zürich: Theologischer Verlag, 2004 [1983]).

Garcia, Mark A., *Life in Christ: Union with Christ and Twofold Grace in Calvin's Theology*. Studies in Christian History and Thought (Milton Keynes: Paternoster and Eugene: Wipf & Stock, 2008).

Gathercole, Simon, *Defending Substitution: An Essay on Atonement in Paul* (Grand Rapids: Baker Academic, 2015).

Gerrish, B. A., *Christian Faith: Dogmatics in Outline* (Louisville: Westminster John Knox, 2015).

Gerrish, B. A., *Grace and Gratitude: The Eucharistic Theology of John Calvin* (Minneapolis: Augsburg Fortress, 1993).

Girardeau, John L., *Calvinism and Evangelical Arminianism* (Harrisburg: Sprinkle Publications, 1984 [1890]).

Girardeau, John L., *Philosophical Questions*, ed. George A. Blackburn (Richmond: The Presbyterian Committee of Publication, 1900).

Girardeau, John L., *The Will in Its Theological Relations* (Columbia: W. J. Duffie and New York: The Baker & Taylor Co., 1891).

Göcke, Benedikt Paul, "Panentheism and Classical Theism," *Sophia* 52 (2013): 61–75.

Gordon, Bruce, *Calvin* (New Haven: Yale University Press, 2011).

Gordon, Bruce, "Huldrych Zwingli," *Expository Times* 126.4 (January, 2015), 156–68.

Gordon, Bruce, *John Calvin's Institutes of the Christian Religion: A Biography*. Lives of Great Religious Books (Princeton: Princeton University Press, 2016).

Gorman, Michael J., *The Death of the Messiah and the Birth of the New Covenant: A (Not So) New Model of the Atonement* (Eugene: Wipf and Stock, 2014).

Graef, Ortwin de, "Discussion with Harry Frankfurt," *Ethical Perspectives* 5.1 (1998): 15–19.

Gregory of Nazianzus, *Letter to Cledonius the Priest against Apollinarius*, in Philip Schaff and Henry Wace, eds. Nicene and Post-Nicene Fathers, 2nd Series, Vol. 7.

Guelzo, Allen C., *Edwards on the Will: A Century of American Theological Debate* (Eugene: Wipf and Stock, 2008 [1989]).

Gunton, Colin E., *The Promise of Trinitarian Theology* (Edinburgh: T&T Clark, 1991).

Habets, Myk and Bobby Grow, eds. *Evangelical Calvinism: Essays Resourcing the Continuing Reformation of the Church* (Eugene: Wipf and Stock, 2012).

Hamilton, S. Mark, *A Treatise on Jonathan Edwards, Continuous Creation and Christology* (N.P.: Jonathan Edwards Society Press, 2017).

Hamilton, S. Mark, "Jonathan Edwards, Anselmic Satisfaction and God's Moral Government," *International Journal of Systematic Theology* 17.1 (2015): 46–67.

Hamilton, S. Mark, "Jonathan Edwards on the Atonement," *International Journal of Systematic Theology* 15.4 (2013): 394–415.

Hamilton, S. Mark, "Re-thinking Atonement in Jonathan Edwards and New England Theology," *Perichoresis* 15.1 (2017): 85–99.

Hanson, Colin, *Young, Restless, Reformed: A Journalist's Journey with the New Calvinists* (Wheaton: Crossway, 2008).

Hart, D. G., Sean Michael Lucas, and Stephen J. Nichols, eds. *The Legacy of Jonathan Edwards: American Religion and the Evangelical Tradition* (Grand Rapids: Baker Academic, 2003).

Hart, Trevor, *Regarding Karl Barth: Toward a Reading of His Theology* (Eugene: Wipf and Stock and Milton Keynes: Paternoster Press, 1999).

Hart, Trevor, "Sinlessness and Moral Responsibility: A Problem in Christology," *Scottish Journal of Theology* 48.1 (1995): 37–54.

Hastings, W. Ross, *Jonathan Edwards and the Life of God: Toward an Evangelical Theology of Participation* (Minneapolis: Fortres, 2015).

Hazony, Yorman, *The Philosophy of Hebrew Scripture* (Cambridge: Cambridge University Press, 2012).

Hector, Kevin, *Theology Without Metaphysics: God, Language and the Spirit of Recognition*. Current Issues in Theology, No. 8 (Cambridge: Cambridge University Press, 2011).

Helm, Paul, *Calvin at the Centre* (Oxford: Oxford University Press, 2010).

Helm, Paul, *Faith and Understanding* (Edinburgh: Edinburgh University Press, 1997).

Helm, Paul, *John Calvin's Ideas* (Oxford: Oxford University Press, 2005).

Helm, Paul, "Jonathan Edwards and the Parting of the Ways?" *Jonathan Edwards Studies* 4.1 (2014), 21–41.

Helm, Paul, "Reformed Thought on Freedom: Some Further Thoughts," *Journal of Reformed Theology* 4.3 (2010): 185–207.

Helm, Paul, "'Structural Indifference' and Compatibilism in Reformed Orthodoxy," *Journal of Reformed Theology* 5.2 (2011): 184–205.

Helm, Paul, "Synchronic Contingency Again," *Nederlands Theologisch Tijdschrift* 57 (2003): 234–38.

Helm, Paul, "Synchronic Contingency in Reformed Scholasticism: A Note of Caution," *Nederlands Theologisch Tijdschrift* 57 (2003): 207–22.

Heppe, Heinrich, *Reformed Dogmatics*, trans. G. T. Thompson (London: Collins, 1950).

Higton, Mike, *A Theology of Higher Education* (Oxford: Oxford University Press, 2012).

Hinlicky, Paul R., *Beloved Community: Critical Dogmatics after Christendom* (Grand Rapids: Eerdmans, 2015).

Holbrook, Clyde A., *The Ethics of Jonathan Edwards: Morality and Aesthetics* (Ann Arbor: The University of Michigan Press, 1973).

Holmes, Stephen R., *God of Grace and God of Glory, An Account of the Theology of Jonathan Edwards* (Edinburgh: T&T Clark, 2000).

Holmes, Stephen R., "Penal Substitution," in Adam J. Johnson, ed. *T&T Clark Companion to Atonement* (London: Bloomsbury, 2017), 295–314.

Hooker, Morna D., *From Adam to Christ: Essays on Paul* (Cambridge: Cambridge University Press, 1990).

Horton, Michael, "Calvin's Theology of Union with Christ and the Double Grace: Modern Reception and Contemporary Possibilities," in J. Todd Billings and I. John Hesselink, eds. *Calvin's Theology and its Reception: Disputes, Developments and New Possibilities* (Louisville: Westminster John Knox, 2012), ch. 4.

Husbands, Mark and Daniel J. Treier, eds. *Justification: What's at Stake in The Current Debates* (Downers Grove: IVP Academic, 2004).

Hutchings, Patrick, "Postlude: Panentheism," *Sophia* 49 (2010): 297–300.

Inman, Ross, "Omnipresence and the Location of the Immaterial," in Jonathan L. Kvanvig, ed. *Oxford Studies in Philosophy of Religion*, Vol. 8 (Oxford: Oxford University Press, 2017), ch. 8.

Jacobs, Jonathan D., "The Ineffable, Inconceivable, and Incomprehensible God: Fundamentality and Apophatic Theology," in Jonathan L. Kvanvig, ed. *Oxford Studies in Philosophy of Religion 6* (Oxford: Oxford University Press, 2015), ch. 7.

Jaeger, Andrew, "Hylemorphic Animalism and the Incarnational Problem of Identity," *Journal of Analytic Theology* 5 (2017): 145–62.

Jenson, Robert W., *Systematic Theology, 2 Vols* (New York: Oxford University Press, 1995, 1999).

Johnson, Dru, *Biblical Knowing: A Scriptural Epistemology of Error* (Eugene: Cascade Books, 2013).

Kärkkäinen, Veli-Matti, *A Constructive Christian Theology for the Pluralist World, 5 Vols* (Grand Rapids: Eerdmans, 2013–2017).

King, Rolfe, "Assumption, Union and Sanctification: Some Clarifying Distinctions," *International Journal of Systematic Theology* 19.1 (2017): 53–72.

LaCugna, Catherine Mowry, *God for Us: The Trinity and Christian Life* (New York: Harpercollins, 1991).

Leith, John, *Creeds of the Churches, A Reader in Christian Doctrine from the Bible to the Present*, Third Edition (Louisville: John Knox Press, 1982 [1963]).

Leithart, Peter, "New Science of Sacrifice," in Kyle C. Strobel, ed. *The Ecumenical Edwards: Jonathan Edwards and the Theologians* (New York: Routledge, 2016; originally published by Ashgate, 2015), 51–66.

Lewis, David, "Do We Believe in Penal Substitution?" in Oliver D. Crisp, ed. *A Reader in Contemporary Philosophical Theology* (London: T&T Clark, 2009), 328–34.

Lewis, David, *On the Plurality of Worlds* (Malden: Blackwell Publishing, 1986).

Locher, Gottfried W., *Zwingli's Thought: New Perspectives* (Leiden: E. J. Brill, 1981).

Lowe, E. J., *The Four-Category Ontology: A Metaphysical Foundation for Natural Science* (New York: Oxford University Press, 2006).

Littlejohn, W. Bradford, *The Mercersburg Theology and the Quest for Reformed Catholicity* (Eugene: Wipf and Stock, 2009).

Loftin, R. Keith and Joshua R. Farris, eds. *Christian Physicalism? Philosophical Theological Criticisms* (London: Lexington Books, 2018).

Loke, Andrew Ter Ern, *A Kryptic Model of the Incarnation*. Ashgate New Critical Thinking in Religion, Theology and Biblical Studies (Aldershot: Ashgate, 2014).

Loke, Andrew Ter Ern, "On the Divine Preconscious Model of the Incarnation and Concrete-nature Christology: A Reply to James Arcadi," *Neue Zeitschrift für Systematische Theologie und Religionsphilosophie* 59.1 (2017): 26–33.

Loke, Andrew Ter Ern, "Sanday's Christology Revisited," *Journal of Theological Studies* 63.1 (2012): 187–97.

Luther, Martin, *The Bondage of the Will*, trans. J. I. Packer and O. R. Johnston (London: James Clarke, 1957).

Macaskill, Grant, *Union with Christ in the New Testament* (Oxford: Oxford University Press, 2013).

MacDonald, Scott, "What Is Philosophical Theology?" in Kevin Timpe ed. *Arguing about Religion* (New York: Routledge, 2009), 24–5.

Macleod, Donald, "Original Sin in Reformed Theology," in Hans Madueme and Michael Reeves, eds. *Adam, the Fall, and Original Sin: Theological, Biblical, and Scientific Perspectives* (Grand Rapids: Baker Academic, 2014), 129–46.

MacIntyre, Alasdair, *After Virtue: A Study of Moral Theory*, Third Edition (Notre Dame: University of Notre Dame Press, 2007 [1981]).

Marion, Jean-Luc, "In the Name: How to Avoid Speaking of 'Negative Theology,'" in John D. Caputo and Michael Scanlon, eds. *God, The Gift, and Postmodernism* (Bloomington: Indiana University Press, 1999), ch. 1.

McCall, Thomas H., *Which Trinity? Whose Monotheism? Philosophical and Systematic Theologians on the Metaphysics of Trinitarian Theology* (Grand Rapids: Eerdmans, 2010).

McClymond, Michael J., "Salvation as Divinization: Jonathan Edwards, Gregory Palamas and the Theological Uses of Neoplatonism," in Paul Helm and Oliver D. Crisp, eds. *Jonathan Edwards: Philosophical Theologian* (Aldershot: Ashgate, 2003), 139–60.

McClymond, Michael J. and Gerald R. McDermott, *The Theology of Jonathan Edwards* (New York: Oxford University Press, 2012).

McDermott, Gerald R., *Jonathan Edwards Confronts the Gods: Christian Theology, Enlightenment Religion, and Non-Christian Faiths* (New York: Oxford University Press, 2000).

McFarland, Ian A., "Fallen or Unfallen? Christ's Human Nature and the Ontology of Human Sinfulness," *International Journal of Systematic Theology* 10.4 (2008): 399–415.

McFarland, Ian A., *In Adam's Fall, A Meditation on the Christian Doctrine of Original Sin* (Oxford: Wiley-Blackwell, 2010).

McGinn, Colin, *The Problem of Consciousness: Essays Toward a Resolution* (Oxford: Blackwell, 1991).

Moberly, R. W. L., *Old Testament Theology: Reading the Hebrew Bible as Christian Scripture* (Grand Rapids: Baker Academic, 2015).

Moberly, R. W. L., *The Theology of the Book of Genesis*. Old Testament Theology (Cambridge: Cambridge University Press, 2009).

Moltmann, Jürgen, *The Trinity and the Kingdom*, trans. Margaret Kohl (London: SCM Press, 1981).

Morimoto, Anri, *Jonathan Edwards and the Catholic Vision of Salvation* (University Park: Pennsylvania State University Press, 1995).

Morris, Thomas V. and Christopher Menzel, "Absolute Creation," *American Philosophical Quarterly* 23.4 (1986): 353–62.

Mosser, Carl, "The Greatest Possible Blessing: Calvin and deification" in *Scottish Journal of Theology* 55.1 (2002): 36–57.

Mouw, Richard J., *The God Who Commands* (Notre Dame: University of Notre Dame Press, 1991).

Muller, Earl, "Real Relations and the Divine," *Theological Studies* 56 (1995): 673–95.

Muller, Richard A., *After Calvin: Studies in the Development of a Theological Tradition*. Oxford Studies in Historical Theology (Oxford: Oxford University Press, 2003).

Muller, Richard A., *Divine Will and Human Choice: Freedom, Contingency, and Necessity in Early Modern Reformed Thought* (Grand Rapids: Baker Academic, 2017).

Muller, Richard A., "Jonathan Edwards and The Absence of Free Choice: A Parting of The Ways in the Reformed Tradition," *Jonathan Edwards Studies* 1.1 (2011), 3–22.

Muller, Richard A., *The Unaccommodated Calvin: Studies in the Foundation of a Theological Tradition*. Oxford Studies in Historical Theology (Oxford: Oxford University Press, 2001).

Mullins, R. T., "The Difficulty with Demarcating Panentheism," *Sophia* 55 (2016): 325–46.

Natural Theology, Comprising "Nature and Grace" by Professor Dr Emil Brunner and the reply "No!" By Dr Karl Barth, with an Introduction by John Baillie (Eugene: Wipf and Stock, 2002 [1946]).

Nadelhoffer, Thomas A., ed. *The Future of Punishment*. Oxford Series in Neuroscience, Law, and Philosophy (Oxford: Oxford University Press, 2013).

Nadler, Steven, *Occasionalism: Causation among the Cartesians* (Oxford: Oxford University Press, 2011).

Neele, Adrian, *Before Jonathan Edwards: Sources of New England Theology* (New York: Oxford University Press, 2019).

Nevin, John Williamson, *The Mystical Presence: And The Doctrine of the Reformed Church on the Lord's Supper*. The Mercersburg Theology Study Series, ed. Linden J. DeBie (Eugene: Wipf and Stock, 2012).

Nolan, Kirk J., *Reformed Virtue after Barth: Developing Moral Virtue Ethics in the Reformed Tradition*. Columbia Series in Reformed Theology (Louisville: Westminster John Knox, 2014).

Opitz, Peter, *Ulrich Zwingli: Prophet, Ketzer, Pionier des Protestantismus* (Zürich: TVZ-Verlag, 2015).

Opitz, Peter, "Ulrich Zwingli," *Religion Compass* 2.6 (2008): 949–60.

Ott, Ludwig, *Fundamentals of Catholic Dogma*, trans. James Bastible (Rockford: Tan Books, 1955).

Parker, T. H. L., *Calvin: An Introduction to His Thought* (London: Geoffrey Chapman, 1995).

Partee, Charles, *The Theology of John Calvin* (Louisville: Westminster John Knox, 2008).

Pawl, Tim, *In Defense of Conciliar Christology: A Philosophical Essay* (Oxford: Oxford University Press, 2016).

Pelikan, Jaroslav, *Development of Christian Doctrine, Some Historical Prolegomena* (New Haven: Yale University Press, 1969).

Peterson, Gregory, "Whither Panentheism?" *Zygon* 36.3 (2001): 395–405.

Plantinga, Alvin, *Knowledge and Christian Belief* (Grand Rapids: Eerdmans, 2015).

Plantinga, Alvin, *Warranted Christian Belief* (New York: Oxford University Press, 2000).

Plantinga, Alvin and Nicholas Wolterstorff, eds. *Faith and Rationality: Reason and Belief in God* (Notre Dame: University of Notre Dame Press, 1981).

Porter, Jean and Stephen Wilson, "Focus Introduction: Taking the Measure of Jonathan Edwards for Contemporary Religious Ethics," *Journal of Religious Ethics* 31.2 (2003): 185–86.

Potter, George R., *Zwingli* (Cambridge: Cambridge University Press, 1977).

Pruss, Alex R., "Omnipresence, Multilocation, the Real Presence and Time Travel," *Journal of Analytic Theology* 1.1 (2013): 60–73.

Quinn, Philip L., "Divine Conservation, Continuous Creation, and Human Action," in Alfred J. Freddoso, ed. *The Existence and Nature of God* (Notre Dame: University of Notre Dame Press, 1983), 55–80.

Quinn, Philip L., "Divine Conservation, Secondary Causes, and Occasionalism," in Thomas V. Morris, ed. *Divine and Human Action: Essay in the Metaphysics of Theism* (Ithaca: Cornell University Press, 1988), 50–73.

Quinn, Philip L., "Honoring Jonathan Edwards," *Journal of Religion Ethics* 31.2 (2003): 299–321.

Quinn, Philip L., "The Master Argument of The Nature of True Virtue," in Paul Helm and Oliver D. Crisp, eds. *Jonathan Edwards: Philosophical Theologian* (Farnham: Ashgate, 2003), ch. 6.

Quinton, A. M., "On Punishment," *Analysis* 14.6 (1954): 133–42.

Rea, Michael C., *The Hiddenness of God* (Oxford: Oxford University Press, 2018).

Rowe, William, *Can God Be Free?* (Oxford: Oxford University Press, 2004).

Sanday, William, *Christology and Personality* (New York: Oxford University Press, 1911).

Schaff, Phillip, *History of the Christian Church, Vol. VIII: Modern Christianity. The Swiss Reformation*, Third Edition (Grand Rapids: Eerdmans, 1976 [1910]).

Schultz, Walter J. and Lisanne D'Andrea-Winslow, "Divine Compositionalism as Occasionalism," in Nazif Muhtaroglu, ed. *Occasionalism Revisited: New Essays from the Islamic and Western Philosophical Tradition* (N.P.: Kalam Research and Media, 2017), 219–36.

Shedd, William G. T., *Dogmatic Theology*, Third Edition, ed. Alan Gomes (Phillipsburg: Presbyterian and Reformed, 2003 [1888–1894]).

Sider, Theodore, *Writing the Book of the World* (Oxford: Oxford University Press, 2011).

Smith, John E., *Jonathan Edwards, Puritan, Preacher, Philosopher* (London: Chapman, 1992).

Sonderegger, Katherine, *Systematic Theology: The Doctrine of God, Vol. 1* (Minneapolis: Fortress Press, 2015).

Steinmetz, David C., *Calvin in Context* (New York: Oxford University Press, 1995).

Stephens, W. P., *The Theology of Huldrych Zwingli* (Oxford: Oxford University Press, 1986).

Stephens, W. P., "The Theology of Zwingli," in David Bagchi and David C. Steinmetz, eds. *The Cambridge Companion to Reformation Theology* (Cambridge: Cambridge University Press, 2004), ch. 8.

Stephens, W. P., *Zwingli: An Introduction to His Thought* (Oxford: Oxford University Press, 1992).

Stephens, W. P., "Zwingli's Sacramental Views," in E. J. Furcha and H. Wayne Pipkin, eds. *Prophet, Pastor, Protestant: The Work of Huldrych Zwingli after Five Hundred Years* (Allison Park: Pickwick Publications, 1984), 155–70.

Strobel, Kyle C., "Jonathan Edwards and the Polemics of Theosis," *Harvard Theological Review* 105.3 (2012): 259–79.

Strobel, Kyle C., "Jonathan Edwards's Reformed Doctrine of Theosis," *Harvard Theological Review* 109.3 (2016): 371–99.

Strobel, Kyle C., *Jonathan Edwards's Theology: A Reinterpretation* (London: Bloomsbury, 2013).

Stump, Eleonore, *Atonement*. Oxford Studies in Analytic Theology (Oxford: Oxford University Press, 2018).

Stump, Eleonore, "The Non-Aristotelian Character of Aquinas' Ethics," *Faith and Philosophy* 28.1 (2011): 29–43.

Stump, Eleonore, *Wandering in Darkness: Narrative and the Problem of Suffering* (Oxford: Oxford University Press, 2012).

Sumner, Darren O., "Fallenness and Anhypostasis: A Way Forward in the Debate Over Christ's Humanity," *Scottish Journal of Theology* 67.2 (2014): 195–212.

Svensson, Manfred and David VanDrunen, eds. *Aquinas among the Protestants* (Oxford: Wiley-Blackwell, 2018).

Tanner, Kathryn, *Christ the Key* (Cambridge: Cambridge University Press, 2010).

Tanner, Kathryn, *Jesus, Humanity, and the Trinity: A Brief Systematic Theology* (Minneapolis: Fortress Press, 2001).

Thistleton, Anthony C., *Systematic Theology* (Grand Rapids: Eerdmans, 2015).

Timpe, Kevin, ed. *Arguing About Religion* (New York: Routledge, 2009).

Thomas, Owen C., "Problems in Panentheism," in Philip Clayton, ed. *The Oxford Handbook of Religion and Science* (Oxford University Press, 2008), ch. 38.

Torrance, Thomas F., *Space, Time, and Resurrection* (Grand Rapids: Eerdmans, 1976).

Torrance, Thomas F., *The Mediation of Christ* (Grand Rapids: Eerdmans, 1984).

Torrance, T. F., ed. *The Incarnation* (Edinburgh: Handsel Press, 1981).

Triglot Concordia: The Symbolical Books of the Evangelical Lutheran Church: German-Latin-English. Published as a memorial of the quadricentenary jubilee of the Reformation anno Domini 1917 by resolution of the Evangelical Lutheran Synod of Missouri, Ohio, and Other States (St. Louis: Concordia Publishing House, 1921).

Tuggy, Dale, "The Unfinished Business of Trinitarian Theorizing," *Religious Studies* 39 (2003): 175–76.

Tuggy, Dale, "Trinity" *Stanford Encyclopedia of Philosophy*, located at: http://plato.stanford.edu/entries/trinity/, first published Thu Jul 23, 2009; substantive revision Fri Sep 13, 2013.

Turner, James T. Jr., "Identity, Incarnation, and the *Imago Dei*," *International Journal of Philosophy and Theology* (2019), https://doi.org/10.1007/s11153-019-09716-z

Unger, Peter, *All the Power in the World* (New York: Oxford, 2006).

Vanhoozer, Kevin J., "Love Without Measure? John Webster's Unfinished Dogmatic Account of the Love of God, in Dialogue with Thomas Jay Oord's Interdisciplinary Theological Account," *International Journal of Systematic Theology* 19.4 (2017): 505–26.

van Inwagen, Peter, *Existence: Essays in Ontology* (Cambridge: Cambridge University Press, 2014).

van Inwagen, Peter and Dean Zimmerman, eds. *Persons: Human and Divine* (Oxford: Oxford University Press, 2007).

Velde, Dolf te, *The Doctrine of God in Reformed Orthodox, Karl Barth, and The Utrecht School: A Study in Method and Content* (Leiden: E. J. Briill, 2013).

Vidu, Adonis, "Trinitarian Inseparable Operations and the Incarnation," *Journal of Analytic Theology* 4 (2016): 106–27.

Visser, Sandra and Thomas Williams, *Anselm*. Great Medieval Thinkers (Oxford: Oxford University Press, 2009).

Vos, Pieter, "Calvinists among the Virtues: Reformed Theological Contributions to Contemporary Virtue Ethics," *Studies in Christian Ethics* 28.2 (2015): 201–12.

Wainwright, William J., "Jonathan Edwards, William Rowe, and the Necessity of Creation," in Jeff Jordan and Daniel Howard-Snyder, eds. *Faith, Freedom, and Rationality: Philosophy of Religion Today* (London: Rowman and Littlefield, 1996), 119–33.

Webster, John B., *God Without Measure: Working Papers in Christian Theology Vol. 1: God and the Works of God* (London: T&T Clark, 2016).

Williams, Garry, "Jonathan Edwards," in Adam J. Johnson, ed. *T&T Clark Companion to Atonement* (London: Bloomsbury, 2017), 467–72.

Wilson, Stephen A., *Virtue Reformed: Rereading Jonathan Edwards's Ethics*. Brill Studies in Intellectual History (Leiden: E. J. Brill, 2005).

Withrow, Brandon G., *Becoming Divine: Jonathan Edwards's Incarnational Spirituality within the Christian Tradition* (Eugene: Wipf and Stock, 2011).

Wolterstorff, Nicholas, *Acting Liturgically: Philosophical Reflections on Religious Practice* (Oxford: Oxford University Press, 2018).

Wolterstorff, Nicholas, *The God We Worship: An Exploration of Liturgical Theology*. Kantzer Lectures in Theology (Grand Rapids: Eerdmans, 2015).

Woznicki, Christopher, "Do We Believe in Consequences? Revisiting the 'Incoherence Objection' to Penal Substitution," *Neue Zeitschrift für Systematische Theologie und Religionsphilosophie* 60.2 (2018): 208–28.

Woznicki, Christopher, "The One and the Many: The Metaphysics of Human Nature in T. F. Torrance's Doctrine of Atonement," *Journal of Reformed Theology* 12 (2018): 103–26.

Yadav, Sameer, "Mystical Experience and the Apophatic Attitude," *Journal of Analytic Theology* 4 (2016): 18–43.

Zachman, Randall C., "John Calvin," in Paul T. Nimmo and David A. S. Fergusson, eds. *The Cambridge Companion to Reformed Theology* (Cambridge: Cambridge University Press, 2016), 132–47.

Zwingli, Huldrych, *Commentary on True and False Religion* ed. Samuel Macauley Jackson and Clarence Nevin Heller (Durham: Labyrinth Press, 1981 [1929]).

Zwingli, Huldrych, *Huldreich Zwinglis Sämtliche Werke, Corpus Reformatorum*, Vols. 88–101, ed. Emil Egli, Georg Finsler, et al. (Berlin: Schwetschke und Sohn, 1905–1963).

Zwingli, Huldrych, *On Providence and Other Essays*, ed. Samuel Macauley Jackson (Durham: The Labyrinth Press, 1983 [1922]).

Zwingli, Huldrych, *Zwingli and Bullinger. Library of Christian Classics, Vol. 24*, ed. and trans., Geoffrey W. Bromiley (Philadelphia: Westminster Press, 1953).

INDEX